Realist Ethics

Just war thinking and realism are commonly presumed to be in opposition. If realists are seen as war-mongering pragmatists, just war thinkers are seen as naïve at best and essentially pacifistic at worst. Just war thought is imagined as speaking truth to power – forcing realist decision makers to abide by moral limits governing the ends and means of the use of force.

Realist Ethics argues that this oversimplification is not only wrong, but dangerous. Casting just war thought as the alternative to realism makes just war thinking out to be what it is not – and cannot be: a mechanism for avoiding war. A careful examination of the evolution of just war thinking in the Christian, Islamic, and Hindu traditions shows that just war thought is no stranger to pragmatic politics. From its origins, just war thought has not aimed to curtail violence, but rather to shape the morally imaginable uses of force, deeming some of them necessary and even obligatory. This book proposes a radical recasting of the relationship between just war thinking and realism.

Valerie Morkevičius is Associate Professor of Political Science at Colgate University. Her work focuses on the intersection between power and ethics, and the applicability of traditional just war thinking to contemporary challenges. Her recent publications include "Power and Order: The Shared Logics of Realism and Just War Theory" featured in *International Studies Quarterly*. She has also written chapters on just war thinking in Islam, Hinduism, and Protestantism, contributing to *World Religions and Norms of War* (2009), *The Prism of Just War: Asian and Western Perspectives on the Legitimate Use of Military Force* (2010), and *Religion, War and Ethics: A Sourcebook of Textual Tradition* (2014).

Realist Ethics

Just War Traditions as Power Politics

VALERIE MORKEVIČIUS

Colgate University

CAMBRIDGE
UNIVERSITY PRESS

CAMBRIDGE
UNIVERSITY PRESS

University Printing House, Cambridge CB2 8BS, United Kingdom

One Liberty Plaza, 20th Floor, New York, NY 10006, USA

477 Williamstown Road, Port Melbourne, VIC 3207, Australia

314–321, 3rd Floor, Plot 3, Splendor Forum, Jasola District Centre,
New Delhi – 110025, India

79 Anson Road, #06–04/06, Singapore 079906

Cambridge University Press is part of the University of Cambridge.

It furthers the University's mission by disseminating knowledge in the pursuit of
education, learning, and research at the highest international levels of excellence.

www.cambridge.org
Information on this title: www.cambridge.org/9781108402477
DOI: 10.1017/9781108235396

© Valerie Morkevičius 2018

First published 2018

Printed in the United States of America by Sheridan Books, Inc.

A catalogue record for this publication is available from the British Library.

Library of Congress Cataloging-in-Publication Data
NAMES: Morkevičius, Valerie Ona, author.
TITLE: Realist ethics : just war traditions as power politics / Valerie Morkevičius,
Colgate University
DESCRIPTION: New York, NY, USA : Cambridge University Press, 2018. |
Based on author's thesis (doctoral - University of Chicago, Dept. of Political Science, 2008)
issued under title: Unholy alliance : just war traditions as power politics. |
Includes bibliographical references.
IDENTIFIERS: LCCN 2017025040 | ISBN 9781108415897 (Hardback : alk. paper) |
ISBN 9781108402477 (pbk. : alk. paper)
SUBJECTS: LCSH: Just war doctrine. | War–Religious aspects–Christianity. | War–Religious
aspects–Hinduism. | War (Islamic law)
CLASSIFICATION: LCC KZ6396 .M67 2018 | DDC 172/.42–dc23
LC record available at https://lccn.loc.gov/2017025040

ISBN 978-1-108-41589-7 Hardback
ISBN 978-1-108-40247-7 Paperback

Skirta mano brangiausiems vaikams: niekada nesustokite svajoti, įsivaizduoti ir kurti

Contents

Acknowledgments

This book bears only my name, but is really the work of many hands.

I owe debts of gratitude to my colleagues at Colgate University, especially Ralitsa Donkova, Ed Fogarty, Rob L'Arrivée, Danielle Lupton, Navine Murshid, Ilan Nam, and Greg Wolf, who read chapter drafts at our research workshop, and especially to Noah Dauber, who cheerfully suffered through multiple revised drafts. The wisdom of my senior colleagues, particularly Tim Byrnes, Fred Chernoff, and Michael Johnston, helped me see this through to completion.

I am grateful for the open doors of my dissertation advisors at the University of Chicago, Robert Pape and John Mearsheimer, who have morphed into my career and book advisors. I only wish that Jean Bethke Elshtain and Iris Marion Young could have seen what became of this project.

My ISA circle of just war friends heard multiple iterations of this story, and their pushback helped develop my argument. I am especially thankful to James Turner Johnson and John Kelsay – who mentored me through the first book marathon and selflessly gave of their time to read drafts – and to Tony Lang, whose thoughtful critiques inspired me to make a final push that (in my view anyway) really improved the book.

Robert Dreesen at Cambridge University Press deserves thanks for rounding up an excellent set of reviewers who helped me see what needed to be improved. Thanks are also due to my copyeditor, David Anderson, especially for his close attention to the citations.

Anything you find useful or insightful or witty in this book is thanks to the folks listed above. Anything you find wanting is entirely my fault.

You wouldn't be holding this book in your hands, though, if it weren't for my family and friends. My grandparents inspired me to become an academic, and I write partly as to not let them down. My aunts and uncles and cousins have always encouraged me, even if they don't always understand why I do it. My friends – from elementary school to grad school, with my Allen Hall buddies in between – have always listened to my ramblings on politics and my writing woes with nonjudgmental ears. Sarah Ibis, my friend for a whole quarter century, not only heard all about this book back in our Hyde Park days, but also offered frank critique on its first full draft. Thank you all for keeping me well-grounded.

My parents and in-laws and my husband, Matas, have picked up my slack and put up with me working through more holidays than I like to admit. My household runs and the kids are fed and happy thanks to them, and to the tireless Sally Isbell. My colleague and neighbor and friend Krista Ingram has kept me sane and cheered me up (and voluntarily taken my children off my hands). And my children – Emilija, Ingrida, Lukas, and Jonas – have been ridiculously good sports, putting up with a mother who is often there but not there. Their patience and flexibility and willingness to take care of each other has made all the difference.

PART I

I

The Dangers of Just War Thinking (or how I learned to love realists)

I began to study just war thought in the spring of 2000. Sitting at the back of a gothic classroom inside the University Chicago's Divinity School, at the peak of the post–Cold War unipolar moment with the spring sun shining, Jean Bethke Elshtain's course on just war theory was intellectually stimulating, but also somehow *academic*. It seemed to me the good guys would be held back from fighting for the good by ascribing to such principles, and the bad guys wouldn't consider them at all. I worried that just war principles would *restrain* the good, even when their action could accomplish much. (What naïve assumptions I had about good and evil then!)

My assumptions about just war thought passed through September 11th and its immediate aftermath unscathed. But the build-up to the 2003 Iraq War shook my beliefs to the core. In lectures taught by realists such as John Mearsheimer and Robert Pape, I heard the coming war decried as a bad idea, premised on faulty assumptions about the nature of Saddam Hussein's regime and its relationship to al Qaeda. In fact, in September 2002, thirty-three international security scholars – including prominent realists such as Mearsheimer, Robert Art, Thomas Schelling, and Kenneth Waltz – published a full-page advertisement in the *New York Times* warning that a war in Iraq was neither necessary nor in the best interest of the United States. Although Hussein was certainly a "murderous despot," they presciently cautioned that a war against Iraq would be a costly diversion from the fight against al Qaeda.[1]

---

[1] "War with Iraq Is Not in America's National Interest," *New York Times*, September 26, 2002.

Rather than risking precious blood and treasure on war, they urged the United States and the United Nations to "maintain vigilant containment of Iraq."[2] In the pages of *Foreign Policy*, Mearsheimer and Walt argued against the war, claiming that "deterrence has worked well against Saddam in the past, and there is no reason to think it cannot work equally well in the future."[3] Ultimately, they concluded that "a compelling strategic rationale" for such a war was absent.[4] Likewise, Pape warned that fighting a unilateral war of choice was "more likely to endanger American security than to enhance it."[5] Altogether, such realists argued convincingly against seeking war with Iraq.

At the same time, I heard the Bush administration invoke those familiar old just war principles to rally the nation to war.[6] Meanwhile, the three most prominent just war thinkers in the United States argued that the war could potentially be just. Jean Elshtain took the strongest stance, claiming that even a preventive war would be justified. In her view, Iraq had forfeited its right to sovereignty by committing aggression against its neighbors and its own people, and by providing support to others who wished to commit such harms.[7] She expressed skepticism in the effectiveness of deterrence and pointed to the danger of Iraq acquiring weapons of mass destruction.[8] Labeling the opposition isolationist, Elshtain claimed that justice demanded U.S. intervention to protect innocents and uphold international order.[9] James Turner Johnson argued that the United States had a just cause on humanitarian grounds, although he cautioned that the war might not be prudent.[10] Deeply troubled by the lack of international consensus, he nonetheless concluded "that there

---

[2] Ibid.

[3] John J. Mearsheimer and Stephen M. Walt, "An Unnecessary War," *Foreign Policy*, 134, January/February 2003, 51–59, 56. For a similar discussion, see John J. Mearsheimer, "Hans Morgenthau and the Iraq War: Realism versus Neo-conservatism," online at *Democracy News Analysis* (opendemocracy.net), 2005.

[4] Ibid., 59.

[5] Robert A. Pape, "The World Pushes Back," *Boston Globe*, March 23, 2003, H1.

[6] For descriptions of the just war rhetoric of the day, consult Anthony Burke, "Just War or Ethical Peace? Moral Discourses of Strategic Violence after 9/11," *International Affairs* 80(2), 2004, 329–353; and Kimber Charles Pearce and Dean Fadley, "George Bush's 'Just War' Rhetoric: Paradigm of Universal Morality," *Journal of Communication and Religion* 16(2), 1993, 139–152.

[7] Jean Bethke Elshtain, "A Just War," *Boston Globe*, October 6, 2002, www.boston.com/news/packages/iraq/globe_stories/100602_justwar.htm.

[8] Ibid.   [9] Ibid.

[10] James Turner Johnson, *The War to Oust Saddam Hussein: Just War and the New Face of Conflict* (Lanham, MD: Rowman and Littlefield, 2005), 159.

are times when doing the right thing means acting alone or with a limited number of friends."[11] Michael Walzer took up a position between the two. A war to enforce the inspection regime would be legitimate, he argued, but not one fought in the name of "regime change."[12] Once the war was a fait accompli, however, he maintained that the intervention did "not fit the moral meaning of aggression," although he still had some reservations.[13]

What happened? How could a set of principles that seemed aimed to *restrict* the use of force act as so little of a brake? This surprising role reversal suggests that the bright line between realism and just war thinking is not as clear as we usually assume, nor does it function in the predicted way.[14] This puzzle made me curious about just war thinking's evolution in Western discourse and its correlates in other world religions. As the U.S.-led war on terror expanded, I huddled in the stacks of the Regenstein Library, tracing out the evolution of just war thinking in Christianity, Islam, and Hinduism.

I had expected – in typical liberal fashion – to see a constant evolution of just war norms toward the good, reflecting the moral progress of mankind. What I found was a history of power. The Christian, Islamic, and Hindu just war traditions represent an evolving compromise between norms and power politics, due to theorists' unconscious reflection of the norms and realities of warfare of their time, and their simultaneous effort to keep just war thinking relevant. Each just war tradition came to reflect the interests of the dominant powers within its sphere of influence. As Walzer put it, "the theory of just war began in the service of the powers."[15] Thus, just war theories legitimize certain kinds of violence, even as they restrict others.[16]

---

[11] Ibid.
[12] Michael Walzer, "Drums of War, Calls for Peace: How Should the Left Respond to a U.S. War against Iraq?," *Dissent* 50(1), 2003, 5–17, 5.
[13] Michael Walzer, "The Crime of Aggressive War," *Washington University Global Studies Law Review* 6(3), 2007, 635–643.
[14] I am not attempting to make an empirical argument here about the frequency of this type of role reversal. Rather, the existence of even a single case of such an apparent contradiction reveals that the underlying assumptions are flawed, which warrants a reconsideration of them.
[15] Michael Walzer, *Arguing about War* (New Haven, CT: Yale University Press, 2004), 3.
[16] Valerie Morkevičius, "Just War: An Ethic of Restraint or the Defense of Order?" in Allan Eickelmann, Eric Nelson, and Tom Lansford, eds., *Justice and Violence: Political Violence, Pacifism and Cultural Transformation* (Burlington, VT: Ashgate Press, 2005), 3–20.

I came to realize that the way just war thought had been used in the run-up to the Iraq war had not only failed to keep the United States out of an unnecessary and immoral war, but it may have even encouraged it to fight. Certain contemporary approaches to just war thinking have indeed, as Nicholas Rennger has argued, become "progressively *less* restrictive," more prone to see "the ethics of force as predominantly about the pursuit of justice."[17] This trend reflects just war thinking's absorption of certain liberal institutionalist principles, particularly a commitment to individual human rights, and to the establishment of a more robust international society. These are certainly laudable values, but appeals to such broad principles sadly morph all too easily into a sort of liberal crusading that seeks to create peace by forcibly remaking the world in its own image.

In this book, I argue that, historically, just war thinking has had far more in common with realism than with liberalism. What follows is a philosophical essay, exploring the historical evolution of just war thinking in three religious traditions – Christianity, Islam, and Hinduism – with the hope of revealing something we ordinarily overlook in our thinking about just war. I argue that for just war thinking to serve as a more effective restraint it needs to become *more* realist, not less. A firmly realist just war approach can avoid two pitfalls into which liberal idealism can fall at its extremes – paralysis in the face of massive injustices and the tendency to crusade for the advancement of particular liberal aims.

To develop this argument, the book makes several moves. In Chapter 2, I establish the deep parallels between realism and just war thought. The realist and just war traditions – both internally diverse – overlap in at least three ways. Both are deeply concerned with conflict *between political groups*. Both recognize the international system as anarchic and war prone. Both traditions see the international arena as characterized by necessity. And, more controversially, both share a concern with the maintenance of some type of order. Precisely what this order might look like, and how one is meant to achieve it, differs from theorist to theorist – but the concept remains central.

Chapter 3 describes my methodology for analyzing the evolution of just war thinking in Christianity, Islam, and Hinduism. I explain the differences between my approach and more traditional approaches to the history of ideas, arguing that there are good reasons to think carefully about the historical and political context in which authors produce their

[17] Nicholas Rengger, *Just War and International Order: The Uncivil Condition in World Politics* (Cambridge: Cambridge University Press, 2013), 9.

texts. I also introduce three broad factors that frame my analysis of the evolution of each just war tradition over time. The degree of conflict in the relationship between political and religious authorities, the extent of religious fractionalization in the international system, and the relative power of the polity in which the author lives affect the kinds of just war arguments that get made. When there is more tension between political and religious authorities, *ad bellum* questions about when to go to war – and especially about who may wage war – dominate the debate, rather than *in bello* discussions of how to fight. When just war thinkers imagine war is likely to involve co-religionists, they tend to approach *in bello* questions with more sensitivity than when the opponent is imagined to be of a different religious community. Likewise, just war thinkers in more powerful polities tend to be more ambivalent about civilian protection than those in weaker ones.

Chapters 4 through 6 are the book's backbone, exploring the historical development of the Christian, Islamic, and Hindu just war traditions in turn. In these chapters, I provide evidence for my claim that just war thinking has a deeply realist bent. One result of this internal realism is that each tradition changes over time, responding to the unique historical and political situations in which each society finds itself. The structure of each chapter emphasizes the correlation between the kinds of just war claims made by particular authors and the type of international system, domestic political organization, and security threats faced by their polities at the time.

Chapter 7, by way of a conclusion, explores the liberal turn in contemporary Western just war thinking. The chapter begins with a brief history of Christian just war thinking's transformation into secular international law in the early modern period. International law, however, is premised on a set of assumptions that differ quite significantly from those held by realists. When just war thinking was revived in the twentieth century, intuitions from the legal tradition worked their way in, making contemporary just war thought more prone to liberal idealism.

Ultimately, I critique the dangers posed by this liberal approach to just war thinking. Adopting liberal institutionalist assumptions can push just war thinkers in two opposite directions – toward pacifism or toward liberal crusading. I argue that the older realist approach is worth reviving, and make the case for reincorporating realist logics and scholarship into contemporary just war analysis. Realism, it turns out, is not the problem with just war thinking. Instead, it offers a chance to reinvigorate just war as a critical tradition.

2

Sharing the Middle Passage

Parallels between Realism and Just War Thinking

Realism has dominated American academics imagination since the end of the Second World War.[1] Given the dominance of American scholars in international relations as a discipline, the realist paradigm has become central to the way we describe, analyze, and argue about international relations, particularly in the English-speaking world.[2] This is not to say that realists are necessarily and unambiguously right, nor that realists have a monopoly on interesting and important research today. But there is no denying that the realist paradigm shapes contemporary international relations scholarship. Even realism's opponents are forced to explain their questions, methods, and ultimately their theories in reference to its logics.[3]

---

[1] Jack Donnelly, *Themes in International Relations: Realism and International Relations* (Cambridge: Cambridge University Press, 2002), 1; John A. Vasquez, *The Power of Power Politics: From Classical Realism to Neotraditionalism* (Cambridge: Cambridge University Press, 1998), 32, 43; Barry Buzan, "The Timeless Wisdom of Realism?" in Steve Smith, Ken Booth, and Marysia Zalewski, eds., *International Theory: Positivism and Beyond* (Cambridge: Cambridge University Press, 1996, 47–65, 48.

[2] Stanley Hoffman, "An American Social Science: International Relations," *Daedalus* 106(3), 1977, 41–60; Kalevi Holsti, *The Dividing Discipline: Hegemony and Diversity in International Theory* (London: Allen & Unwin, 1985); Steve Smith, "The United States and the Discipline of International Relations: 'Hegemonic Country, Hegemonic Discipline,'" *International Studies Review* 4(2), 2002, 67–85; Stephen M. Walt, "Is IR Still 'an American Social Science'?" *Foreign Policy*, June 6, 2011.

[3] Consider, for example, the efforts of some prominent neoliberal institutionalists to redirect the foreign policy conversation during the waning years of the George W. Bush administration. See G. John Ikenberry and Charles A. Kupchan, "Liberal Realism: The Foundations of a Democratic Foreign Policy," *The National Interest*, Fall 2004, 38–49, and

The American public, too, has in many ways become "comfortable with realist uses of force," thanks to the prominent influence of the first generation of postwar realists, especially public intellectuals such as Hans Morgenthau, Reinhold Niebuhr, George Kennan, and Henry Kissinger.[4] Survey research "reveals a strong realist bent among the American mass public," leading Americans to see the world in primarily Hobbesian terms.[5] Americans don't tend to trust other nations.[6] Their rather pessimistic "folk realist" worldview means that they see war as usually unavoidable, due to countries' clashing interests and inherent aggressive tendencies.[7]

Both inside and outside academia, it seems that realism has generated the model "of how to think and speak" about international politics.[8] Surprisingly, the same American public that seems to intuitively adopt a realist worldview also overwhelmingly believes that "moral principles" should underpin U.S. foreign policy.[9] Indeed, just as realism flourished in the postwar years, spanning the academic-public divide, so too did just war thinking. The revival of just war thought in the United States was initially a response to the shock of nuclear weapons; the intense moral debates over Vietnam ensured that the tradition had returned to stay.[10] By the time of the Persian Gulf War in the early 1990s, pundits observed that the "public grappling with the moral criteria and political logic of the just war tradition" had become deep and sustained.[11]

Joseph S. Nye, Jr., "Toward a Liberal Realist Foreign Policy: A Memo for the Next President," *Harvard Magazine* 110(4), 2008, 36–38.

[4] Daniel Drezner, "The Realist Tradition in American Public Opinion," *Perspectives on Politics* 6(1), 2008, 51–70, 52.

[5] Ibid., 63.

[6] Paul R. Brewer, Kimberly Gross, Sean Aday, and Lars Willnat, "International Trust and Public Opinion About World Affairs," *American Journal of Political Science* 48(1), 2004, 93–109. See also Joshua D. Kertzer and Kathleen M. McGraw, "Folk Realism: Testing the Microfoundations of Realism in Ordinary Citizens," *International Studies Quarterly* 56, 2012, 245–258, 248.

[7] Kertzer and McGraw, "Folk Realism," 248.

[8] Robert Hariman and Francis A. Beer, "What Would Be Prudent? Forms of Reasoning in World Politics," *Rhetoric and Public Affairs* 1(3), 1998, 300.

[9] Lee Feinstein, James M. Lindsay, and Max Boot, "On Foreign Policy, Red and Blue Voters Are Worlds Apart," Council on Foreign Relations, August 2004, 39, cited in Drezner, "The Realist Tradition," 56.

[10] While many contemporary genealogies of the rebirth of just war thinking mark Michael Walzer's seminal *Just and Unjust Wars* (1979) as the moment the tradition returned to the center of political discourse, it is more accurate to point to Paul Ramsey's *War and the Christian Conscience* (Durham, NC: Duke University Press, 1961).

[11] George Weigel, "The Churches and War in the Gulf," *First Things*, March 11, 1991. See also Jean Bethke Elshtain, "Just War as Politics: What the Gulf War Told Us about

The American public's juxtaposition of realism and just war thinking is quite surprising from a theoretical point of view.[12] In the academy, just war thinking's opposition to realism is treated as axiomatic.[13] If realists argue that everything goes in war, just war thinkers caution restraint.[14] If realists claim that the usual rules of morality governing domestic life cannot apply in the rough and ready world of international politics, just war thinkers insist that ethics must be brought to bear on the international arena as well.[15] If realists see little possibility for meaningful and sustained cooperation among the powers, just war thinkers call for the development of stronger institutions and better laws.[16] Put simply, the conventional wisdom holds that realists and just war thinkers don't speak the same language. According to this overly simplistic view, realists push states into wars, while just war thinkers try (and usually fail) to hold them back.

And yet, as we saw on the eve of the 2003 Iraq War, this view may not only be simplistic, but also wrong. To understand why this is the case, we'll need to look more closely at the traditions of realism and just war thinking, both of which are incredibly diverse. Then we'll explore the points of overlap between these two traditions. Although just war thinking is often imagined as a middle path between the shoals of realism and the sirens of pacifism, I argue that the theoretical parallels between realism and just war thinking are so significant that we should see the two traditions as sharing the middle passage. Just war's foil, then, is not

Contemporary American Life," in David E. Decosse, ed., *But Was It Just? Reflections on the Morality of the Persian Gulf War* (New York: Doubleday, 1992), 47.

[12] President Obama's Nobel Prize acceptance speech in 2009 is a case in point. Ronald E. Osborn, "Obama's Niebuhrian Moment (Part I)," *First Things*, January 11, 2010; Stephen M. Walt, "Was Obama's Nobel Peace Prize Speech Really Realist," *Foreign Policy*, December 18, 2009; Robert E. Terrill, "An Uneasy Peace: Barack Obama's Nobel Prize Peace Lecture," *Rhetoric and Public Affairs* 14(4), 2011, 761–779. For a reminder that Obama was not alone in invoking both traditions, see Cian O'Driscoll, "Talking about Just War: Obama in Oslo, Bush at War," *Politics* 31(2), 2011, 82–90.

[13] This view owes much to Walzer's treatment of the subject in *Just and Unjust Wars*. See Mark D. King's critique in "Just War as Compromise: Rethinking Walzer's Position on Realism," *Soundings* 95(12), 2012, 1–23.

[14] Nicholas Rengger, "On the Just War Tradition in the Twenty-first Century," *International Affairs* 78(2), 2002, 353–363, 354.

[15] Jean Bethke Elshtain, "Just War and Humanitarian Intervention," *Proceedings of the Annual Meeting, American Society of International Law* 95, 2001, 1–12, 1–2. See also Laurie Calhoun, "Regarding War Realism," *International Journal on World Peace* 18(4), 2001, 37–61, 40, 42; and Neta C. Crawford, "Just War Theory and the U.S. Counterterror War," *Perspectives on Politics* 1(10), 2003, 5–25, 6.

[16] Elshtain. "Just War and Humanitarian Intervention." 2.

realism – which itself calls for restraint in the use of force – but rather various sorts of pacifisms and crusading ideologies. The chapter wraps up with a discussion of what realism and just war thinking's shared assumptions mean for just war thinkers and their critics.

APPLES AND ORANGES?

My argument is that just war thinking has historically been far more closely wedded to realism than pacifism. But before we go much further, there is a methodological matter to address. It could be argued that realism and just war thinking *can't* be compared, as the former is descriptive – concerned with explaining state behavior – while the latter is normative, worried about how states *should behave*. However, this dichotomy oversimplifies matters. Realism may be primarily a descriptive theory, but realists are not only interested in understanding the functioning of the international system for scientific reasons; they also hope to derive functional prescriptions for decision makers. Thus Morgenthau – sounding much like a just war thinker – imagined himself as having the "responsibility to seek truth" and to "speak this truth to power."[17]

Once realists enter the realm of policy advising, they enter the world of politics, and their recommendations come to have normative ramifications.[18] Consider for a moment that most realist of concepts, the balance of power. Realist theory suggests that when economic and military power is more or less equally distributed between great powers, they are unlikely to go to war with each other, all things considered, because neither state is confident of winning. The balance of power is a "good" of a sort – it generates stability, thus avoiding wars (which are costly and almost always risky). The just war thinker Michael Walzer put it this way: when nineteenth-century statesmen went to war "on behalf of the balance, they thought they were defending, not national interest alone, but an international order that made liberty possible throughout Europe."[19] The normative implications of the emphasis on the balance of power are most evident in the works of classical realists. Morgenthau, for example, argued that the persistence of the balance of power system reflected a

---

[17] Murielle Cozette, "Reclaiming the Critical Dimension of Realism: Hans J. Morgenthau on the Ethics of Scholarship," *Review of International Studies* 34(1), 2008, 5–27, 8.

[18] Valerie Morkevičius, "Power and Order: The Shared Logics of Realism and Just War Theory," *International Studies Quarterly* 59(1), 2015, 11–22, 12–13.

[19] Walzer, Just and Unjust Wars, 76.

"moral consensus" about the value of that system.[20] Contemporary realism's emphasis on the structure of the system, particularly its focus on states as the unit of analysis, at first appears to sideline all moral considerations. Yet even Kenneth Waltz, in describing the unconscious functioning of the balance of power, reports that "great powers do not act only for their own sakes. They also act for the world's common good."[21] Prescription doesn't follow as far behind description as we might imagine.

Similarly, just war thinkers base their normative claims about the justice of specific wars on assumptions about how wars arise and how they are fought. Just war thinkers across time and space have perceived the international system to be anarchic, making war inevitable. Like classical realists, just war thinkers tend to share a rather dim view of human nature, leading them to value the state not only for the protection it offers vis-à-vis other states, but also for its role in maintaining domestic order. As we shall see later in this chapter, just war thinkers' prescriptions for moral behavior are premised on descriptive assumptions about the nature of international relations that are quite similar to those held by realists.

WHAT IS REALISM?

Realism is not so much a single theory as a "general orientation" or a "disposition."[22] Establishing a typology for a tradition that traces its lineage back to Thucydides in ancient Greece is no simple task. One approach is to divide realist thinkers between those who take a structural approach, focusing on the consequences of anarchy, and those who adopt a biological logic, emphasizing the flaws in human nature.[23] Another tack similarly distinguishes minimalist thinkers – who start from the assumption of international anarchy – from fundamentalist ones, who investigate human psychology, and from structuralists, who draw on economic theories to revise minimalist assumptions.[24] Yet another draws the

---

[20] Hans Morgenthau, *Politics among Nations*, 7th ed. (New York: McGraw-Hill, 2006), 228–231.

[21] Kenneth Waltz, *Theory of International Politics* (New York: McGraw-Hill, 1979), 205.

[22] Donnelly, *Themes in International Relations*, 6; Reinhold Niebuhr, *Christian Realism and Political Problems* (New York: Charles Scribner's Sons, 1953), 119; Robert G. Gilpin, "The Richness of the Tradition of Political Realism," *International Organization* 38(2), 1984, 287–304, 290.

[23] Donnelly, *Themes in International Relations*, 11.

[24] Michael W. Doyle, "Thucydidean Realism," *Review of International Studies* 16(3), 1990, 223–237.

distinction more philosophically, between practical realists, who aim to create a consensual understanding of how history works, so as to learn from it, and technical realists, who aim to uncover universal laws.[25]

Following the terminology used by many contemporary realists, we can think about three broad families of realists: *structural* realists (sometimes called *neorealists*) on the one hand, and *classical* and *neoclassical* realists on the other. In what follows, I briefly lay out the central claims of each version of realism. I especially emphasize their differing ideas about the potential for order in the international system, as the concern with order is one point where the overlap between realists and just war thinkers is imperfect.

Structural realists claim that the anarchic structure of the system itself is the primary determinant of state behavior.[26] They tend to treat states in the abstract. The internal structures of states – their economic systems, cultures, and regime types – are not considered important. The only variable that really matters is state capacity, that is, the amount of power a state has available to defend itself and to advance its interests on the world stage. In this view, states are rational (if wary) actors who are inherently self-interested.

Structural realists can further be divided into *defensive* and *offensive* realists. Defensive realists believe that states seek security through balancing. From this perspective, conflict arises not because states are especially aggressive, but because states are afraid. When states attempt to ensure their survival against perceived threats by building up their own military forces or even attempting to redraw borders, their frightened peers respond in kind. Thus, the security dilemma leads to war. Anarchy, in this view, punishes aggression, rather than rewarding it.[27] After all, a potential hegemon who attempts to break away from the pack is likely to be checked by peer competitors who prefer the status quo. Defensive realists argue that "states ought to generally pursue moderate strategies as the best route to security," since attempts to gain more power through aggressive expansion will likely backfire.[28] States' individual attempts to

---

[25] Richard K. Ashley, "Political Realism and Human Interests," *International Studies Quarterly* 25(2), 1981, 204–236.

[26] Waltz, *Theory of International Relations*, 97.

[27] Jack Snyder, *Myths of Empire: Domestic Politics and International Ambition* (Ithaca, NY: Cornell University Press, 1991), 11.

[28] Jeffrey W. Taliaferro, "Security Seeking under Anarchy: Defensive Realism Revisited," *International Security* 25(3), 2000–2001, 128–161, 129, 138.

pursue security generate order – a tendency toward stability and the status quo – through balancing.[29]

Offensive realists, on the other hand, believe that states seek security through power. In a world plagued with uncertainty, states seek to maximize their power because they can never know just how much power is needed to be secure.[30] The international system, for offensive realists, is far less stable – security is scarce, making war more likely.[31] Because hegemony virtually guarantees survival, states have an incentive to launch aggressive wars whenever victory seems likely.[32] Like their defensive realist counterparts, offensive realists contend that order is a "by-product of the self-interested behavior of the system's great powers," an "unintended consequence" of their continuous competition for security.[33] States cannot cooperate to pursue a peaceful world order because they cannot be sure their efforts will succeed (and cannot afford to gamble their survival) and because they cannot agree on a single formula for achieving peace in the first place.[34]

Structural realism emerged as a response to *classical realism*, which is sometimes also called traditional realism. Although classical realism's pedigree is centuries old, it really emerged after World War II as a response to the liberal idealism that had dominated the newly minted international relations discipline during the interwar years.[35] Classical realists point to the long history of realist thinking as evidence of the timelessness of the struggle for power. After all, the tradition's roots reach back to Machiavelli, or Hobbes, or Augustine, or Thucydides, depending on whom you ask.[36] These early realists identified human

[29] It is important to note that order in this sense is *not* at all hierarchical.

[30] John J. Mearsheimer, *The Tragedy of Great Power Politics* (New York: W. W. Norton, 2001), 35.

[31] Sean M. Lynn-Jones and Steven E. Miller, eds., *Offensive, Defense, and War* (Cambridge, MA: MIT Press, 2004), xiii; Benjamin Frankel, "Restating the Realist Case: An Introduction," in Benjamin Frankel, ed., *Realism: Restatements and Renewal* (London: Frank Cass, 1996), xv.

[32] John J. Mearsheimer, "The False Promise of International Institutions," *International Security* 19(3), 1994/1995, 11–12.

[33] Mearsheimer, *The Tragedy of Great Power Politics*, 49.   [34] Ibid., 50–51.

[35] The first stand-alone international relations department was established at what is now Aberystwyth University, in Wales, in 1919.

[36] Thucydides, Hobbes, and Machiavelli are the most frequently noted. Michael Doyle notes that each of these thinkers had a different vision of realism (Doyle, "Thucydidean Realism"). Several authors note Augustine as the starting point for the realist tradition, including most famously Niebuhr, *Christian Realism and Political Problems*, 120, but also Michael Joseph Smith, *Realist Thought from Weber to Kissinger* (Baton Rouge:

nature as the primary cause of conflict, explaining everything from familial squabbles to interstate wars.[37]

Classical realists share this view. To the classical realist, the world looks as it does due to "forces inherent in human nature."[38] Power is manifest in all social relations.[39] Power can be used to pursue one's interests, of course, but it also matters in itself – prestige and honor have mesmerized humans forever. It is at this juncture that ideas infiltrate classical realist arguments. "Man cannot help sinning when he acts in relation to his fellow men," Morgenthau wrote, "for no social action can be completely free of the taint of egoism which, as selfishness, pride, or self-deception, seeks for the actor more than is his due."[40] States, like individuals, are proud and self-righteous, self-interested, and power-hungry.[41] Aggression, therefore, "is somehow related to the character of power itself, and the effect which power has upon its possessors."[42]

Classical realists share structural realists' belief in the anarchic nature of the international system. Within that anarchy, order can result from the balance of power.[43] States' natural tendency to resist other states' efforts to hoard power generates a balance of power, which has "an essential stabilizing factor in a society of sovereign nations."[44] Unlike structural realists, who have pared down their vision of the state and the international system such that ideas no longer matter, classical realists are concerned with the interaction between power and ideas.[45] Hence, a thinker like Morgenthau is able to conceive the balance of power both as a natural tendency toward equilibrium and as the result of a "common awareness" of the value of the balance of power system as a framework

Louisiana State University Press, 1986), 1. Just how closely classical realism reflects its historical predecessors is debated. See Peter J. Ahrensdorf, "Thucydides' Realistic Critique of Realism," *Polity* 30(2), 1997, 231–265.

[37] This is not to say that they do not recognize the anarchy of the international system as a problem for order. See Steven Forde, "International Realism and the Science of Politics: Thucydides, Machiavelli, and Neorealism," *International Studies Quarterly* 39(2), 1995, 141–160.

[38] Hans J. Morgenthau, *Dilemmas of Politics* (Chicago: University of Chicago Press, 1958), 55.

[39] Niebuhr, *Christian Realism and Political Problems*, 120.   [40] Ibid., 237.

[41] Ibid., 30, 119.

[42] Herbert Butterfield, "The Scientific Versus the Moralistic Approach in International Affairs," *International Affairs* 27(3), 1951, 411–422, 413.

[43] Ibid., 416–418.   [44] Morgenthau, *Politics among Nations*, 179.

[45] Michael C. Williams, "Why Ideas Matter in International Relations: Hans Morgenthau, Classical Realism, and the Moral Construction of Power Politics," *International Organization* 58(4), 2004, 633–665, 634.

for action.[46] For other classical realists, order emerges only from dominance. For Niebuhr, dominion is essential to community, because it is a "prerequisite of its order."[47] Domestically, order is created and enforced by the dominant classes.[48] In a like manner, a weaker form of order can exist internationally, enforced by powerful states. Whether domestic or international, order requires "both force and prestige."[49]

Classical realism's pushback against structural realism led to the creation of a third variant of realist thought, *neoclassical realism*. Combining structuralist assumptions about the importance of the system and classical concerns with human nature, neoclassical realists argue that actual foreign policy decisions are shaped not only by objective distributions of power, but also by *perceptions* of that distribution, as well as by domestic constraints on translating resources into power, and power into action.[50] Thus, cultural variables (such as the norms held by a particular polity) and regime type affect the menu of foreign policy choices available to policy makers.

Neoclassical realists assert that dominant powers can organize an order of sorts based on the "hierarchy of power and prestige."[51] Prestige, like authority (its domestic equivalent), permits states to carry out their will without resistance. In other words, weaker states follow the lead of stronger states because of prestige, which is established both by moral claims and material benefits.[52] A state with significant prestige can establish "an international order of its own design – an order that it governs and that reflects its interests and desires, institutional architecture, and idiosyncratic norms and rules."[53]

So What Do Realists Have in Common?

Clearly, realism is a house with many rooms. For the sake of drawing parallels between realism as a tradition and just war thinking, however,

---

[46] Morgenthau, *Politics among Nations*, 229–230.
[47] Reinhold Niebuhr, *The Structure of Nations and Empires* (New York: Charles Scribner's Sons, 1959), 33.
[48] Ibid.   [49] Niebuhr, *The Structure of Nations and Empires*, 34.
[50] Gideon Rose, "Neoclassical Realism and Theories of Foreign Policy," *World Politics* 51 (1), 1998, 144–172, 147.
[51] Robert Gilpin, *War and Change in World Politics* (Cambridge: Cambridge University Press, 1981), 29, 198.
[52] Ibid., 30.
[53] Randall L. Schweller and Xiaoyu Pu, "After Unipolarity: China's Visions of International Order in an Era of U.S. Decline," *International Security* 36(1), 2011, 41–72, 51.

we need to move up one level of abstraction. What is it that all realists have in common? Five general moves typify the realist approach:

1. Realists view human nature pessimistically.
2. Realists treat groups as the primary unit of analysis for thinking about politics.
3. Realists believe that groups are inherently competitive.
4. Realists assume that the international system is anarchic.
5. Realists see themselves as participating in a tradition of statecraft, aimed at managing the disorder of the international system.

The previous section has hopefully served to illustrate the first four points. Regarding the fifth, realism is a tradition of statecraft that aims at helping decision makers navigate a disorderly world. Although realists do not necessarily agree about how order comes about in the international system, concern with order permeates realists' work. "Our age is insistently, at times desperately, in pursuit of a concept of world order," writes Kissinger, seeing potential for chaos on every side.[54] As we have seen, order for realists is separable from justice. Order can build on normative foundations – but it doesn't have to. Classical realists recognize that moral principles can serve to legitimate state's actions, and hence have a certain power; likewise, the way in which we speak about states as if they were moral persons "has some effect in constraining the state."[55] Morgenthau, for example, asserts that it is in the "permanent interest of states to put their normal relations upon a stable basis by providing for predictable and enforceable conduct with respect to those relations."[56] Even structural realists admit that privileging security over other values does not mean that states have no other values at all.[57] What sets realists apart from other kinds of international relations thinkers is not that they have no interest in norms, but rather their deep skepticism about the independent power of ideas to order the system.

Instead, realists "tend to regard the quest for order as ancillary to the great power struggle for power, consisting of efforts to moderate it, cut its costs, limit and terminate particular wars, promote cooperation, and work

---

[54] Henry Kissinger, *World Order* (New York: Penguin Press, 2014), 2.
[55] Robert W. Cox, "Multilateralism and World Order," *Review of International Studies* 18 (2), 1992, 161–180, 168.
[56] Hans J. Morgenthau, "Positivism, Functionalism, and International Law," *American Journal of International Law* 34(2), 1940, 260–284, 279.
[57] Charles L. Glaser, "Structural Realism in a More Complex World," *Review of International Studies* 29(3), 2003, 403–414, 412.

toward greater peace and justice."[58] Kissinger doesn't try to window-dress realism's approach to order. Order requires "a set of commonly accepted rules that define the limits of permissible action," he writes, but it simultaneously demands "a balance of power that enforces restraint where rules break down."[59] The pursuit of order never abolishes the struggle for power, although it influences the flow of international politics.[60]

Realists' concern with managing order drives many modern realists to become public intellectuals, participating actively in foreign policy debates.[61] Take, for example, the most prominent classical realists of the Cold War years. Kennan, Kissinger, and Morgenthau served various presidential administrations, while Niebuhr was a well-known political commentator. Likewise, as a theory, structural realism may be "silent" on ethical questions, but many structural realist scholars have not been.[62] Mearsheimer, for example, criticizes many contemporary political scientists for engaging in too much "science" and too little politics, lacking "any sense of social responsibility."[63] Instead, he urges international relations scholars to "study problems that are of great public importance" and to share that information publicly in a clear and timely way.[64] Stephen Walt, too, argued that academics fulfill their "true social purpose" by contributing to public debates.[65]

As a tradition of statecraft, realism is essentially consequentialist.[66] Realists emphasize the "duties of leadership," pointing out that "with

[58] Paul W. Schroeder, "Not Even for the Seventeenth and Eighteenth Centuries: Power and Order in the Early Modern Era," in Ernest R. May, Richard Rosecrance, and Zara Teiner, eds., *History and Neorealism* (Cambridge: Cambridge University Press, 2010), 78–102, 82.

[59] Kissinger, *World Order*, 9.

[60] Schroeder, "Not Even for the Seventeenth and Eighteenth Centuries," 82. See Mearsheimer, *Tragedy of Great Power Politics*, 29–54. See also Rosemary Foot, "Introduction," in Rosemary Foot, John Lewis Gaddis, and Andrew Hurrell, eds., *Order and Justice in International Relations* (Oxford: Oxford University Press, 2003), 1.

[61] Michael C. Desch, "It Is Kind to Be Cruel: The Humanity of American Realism," *Review of International Studies* 29(3), 2003, 415–426, 420.

[62] Glaser, "Structural Realism," 414.

[63] Mearsheimer, "Through the Realist Lens: The United States and Realism," interview with Henry Kreisler, April 8, 2002, http://globetrotter.berkeley.edu/people2/Mearsheimer/mearsheimer-cono.html.

[64] Ibid.

[65] Stephen M. Walt, "International Affairs and the 'Public Sphere,'" *Foreign Policy*, July 22, 2011, http://foreignpolicy.com/2011/07/22/international-affairs-and-the-public-sphere. See also Stephen M. Walt, "Theory and Policy in International Relations: Some Personal Reflections," *Yale Journal of International Affairs*, 7, 2012, 33–43.

[66] Lea Brilmayer, "Realism Revisited: The Moral Priority of Means and Ends in Anarchy," *Nomos* 41, 1999, 192–215, 193.

leadership comes responsibility for others, and this means sometimes having to do things that would be abhorrent to a private party."[67] Morgenthau cautions that while altruism is laudable for individuals, asking "nation to embark upon altruistic policies oblivious to the national interest is to really ask something immoral ... morally speaking, national egotism is not the same as individual elitism because the functions of the international society are not identical with those of international society."[68] Similarly, the Christian realist Reinhold Niebuhr argued that it "is obvious that fewer risks can be taken with community interests."[69] Reinhold's "ethical realism," while warning of the risks of "undiluted Machiavellianism," simultaneously cautioned against the cynical abandonment of all normative guides.[70] Mearsheimer, as a structural realist, admits that many leaders would like to see their own strongly held moral principles practiced in international relations, yet warns that they must recognize that in international politics "rules are broken with little consequence."[71] Lying, like other less than ideal behaviors, may be no "great virtue," but it is nonetheless "sometimes a useful instrument of statecraft in a dangerous world."[72]

The justification for such behavior, he argues, is survival – a claim that also underlies the classical realist position on international ethics.[73] In essence, realism's consequentialism is itself an ethical strategy, aimed at "self-limitation."[74] Realists recognize that a state's actions do not take place in a vacuum. The political, strategic, and normative fallout of any choice can be far-reaching, and the realist takes responsibility for thinking about whether the resulting world would be better or worse as a result. More so than any theoretical overlap, the fact that realism and just war thinking share this practical aim offers hope for the possibility of greater cooperation between scholars working in these traditions in the future.

---

[67] Ibid., 212.

[68] Hans J. Morgenthau, *In Defense of the National Interest: A Critical Examination of American Foreign Policy* (New York: Alfred A. Kopf, 1951), 36.

[69] Reinhold Niebuhr, *Moral Man and Immoral Society: A Study in Ethics and Politics* (Louisville: Westminster John Knox Press, 1932), 267.

[70] John Bew, *Realpolitik: A History* (Oxford: Oxford University Press, 2016), 199, 201.

[71] John J. Mearsheimer, *Why Leaders Lie* (Oxford: Oxford University Press, 2011), 8.

[72] Ibid., 12.   [73] Ibid., 28.

[74] Michael C. Williams, *The Realist Tradition and the Limits of International Relations* (Cambridge: Cambridge University Press, 2005), 172, 174.

ON JUST WAR TRADITIONS

Rather unfortunately, just war thinking is sometimes described as a *theory*, evoking a legalistic collection of principles and rules that could be "used as a kind of moral slide-rule."[75] I've studiously avoided using the expression "just war theory" in this book. Instead, I use the term "just war tradition" to reflect the fact that for most of its history, just war thinking has been a tradition of practical reasoning, emphasizing the analysis of real cases more than the refinement of principles.[76] Just war thinking remains valuable today because the tradition is "a fund of practical moral wisdom, based not in abstract speculation or theorization, but in reflection on actual problems encountered in war as these have presented themselves in different historical circumstances."[77] As a tradition – a sort of common language – it "gathers together the learning of previous generations," to help us ask the right questions guide our decision-making in the present.[78]

But even the phrase "just war tradition," which is frequently invoked by those who take a more historical view of the Western tradition, is not quite suited to our purposes here.[79] For there is not one, but many just war traditions, of which three with roots in different world religions form the heart of this study. Furthermore, multiple traditions of just war thinking can flourish within a single religious tradition. While Catholic and Protestant just war thinking share enough that it is possible to speak of a "Christian" just war tradition – and likewise Sunni and Shi'a approaches to just war overlap enough that a discussion of an "Islamic" approach to just war is conceivable – the differences between these

---

[75] Rengger, "On the Just War Tradition," 360. See also Chris Brown, "Just War and Political Judgment," in Anthony Lang and Cian O'Driscoll, eds., *Just War: Authority, Tradition and Practice* (Washington, DC: Georgetown University Press, 2013), 35, 43. The term "theory" is also used by those who, like Michael Walzer, wish to develop a revised version of just war thinking – one that is not directly tied to the religious tradition that preceded it. For example, consider Walzer's use of "theory" and "doctrine" to describe just war thinking in "The Triumph of Just War Theory (and the Dangers of Success)," *Social Research* 69(4), 2002, 925–944.

[76] Rengger, "On the Just War Tradition," 360.

[77] James Turner Johnson, *Can Modern War Be Just?* (New Haven, CT: Yale University Press, 1984), 15.

[78] Cian O'Driscoll, "Divisions within the Ranks? The Just War Tradition and the Use and Abuse of History," *Ethics and International Affairs*, 27(1), 2013, 47–65, 50.

[79] For a defense of just war as a tradition, see James Turner Johnson, "Contemporary Just War Thinking: Which Is Worse, to Have Friends or Critics," *Ethics and International Affairs* 27(1), 2013, 25–45, 40.

sectarian accounts suggests that we must take care when engaging in such exercises of abstraction.[80]

The just war tradition in the West is an especially large tent. Western just war discourse, like realism, "is a gerrymandered edifice scarred by social transformation and moral crisis."[81] In addition to Christian ideas of just war, there are now at least three predominantly secular approaches to just war in the West: contemporary secular just war thinkers may be neoclassical thinkers, Walzerians, or revisionists.

A dwindling population of living just war thinkers can properly be called *neoclassical* just war thinkers. Such thinkers draw on the history of the Western just war tradition (and sometimes non-Western traditions) to think critically about how the classical just war principles can be interpreted and reinterpreted to analyze the moral problems of contemporary war. James Turner Johnson, for example, explains that his "overall task ... is to bring the moral tradition of just war to bear on contemporary war so as to identify its particular injustices and to advance an argument as to how to respond to them and seek to remedy them."[82] In Johnson's view, "contemporary just war thought would benefit from giving more attention to the historical tradition," as the "classical conception of just war was focused on problems of good governance," and not only individual morality.[83] Other thinkers in this vein include Jean Bethke Elshtain, Oliver O'Donovan, Cian O'Driscoll, and Paul Ramsey. The historical approach cautions us against presuming that the answers we reach today are definitive, instead emphasizing the "contextual quality of all moral rules."[84] Indeed, in this view our "conversation with past generations" can help us recognize our own parochialism, reminding us that our own situatedness can limit our imaginations.[85]

---

[80] Recent literature on comparative just war thinking has done just this, treating the broad Catholic/Protestant and Sunni/Shi'a cleavages as significant enough to warrant separate chapters. See, for example, Vesselin Popovski, Gregory Reichberg, and Nicholas Turner, eds., *World Religions and Norms of War* (New York: United Nations University Press, 2009), Howard Hensel, ed., *The Prism of Just War* (Ashgate, 2010), and Gregory Reichberg and Henrik Syse, eds., *Religion, War, and Ethics: A Sourcebook of Textual Traditions* (Cambridge: Cambridge University Press, 2014).

[81] Jean Bethke Elshtain, "Reflections on War and Political Discourse: Realism, Just War, and Feminism in a Nuclear Age," *Political Theory* 13(1), 1985, 39–57, 44.

[82] James Turner Johnson, *Morality and Contemporary Warfare* (New Haven, CT: Yale University Press, 1999), 7.

[83] Johnson, "Contemporary Just War Thinking: Which Is Worse, to Have Friends or Critics," 41. See Rengger, *Just War and International Order.* 93.

[84] O'Driscoll, "Divisions within the Ranks?" 51.   [85] Ibid., 52.

The *Walzerian* approach to just war is populated by those who follow in Michael Walzer's footsteps, referring broadly to the historical tradition, but fundamentally deriving their ethical conclusions from their moral intuitions. Johnson has called Walzer the first revisionist, and not without reason. Walzer's *Just and Unjust Wars* revitalized just war thinking in the West, melding the traditional Christian language of the just war criteria with secular legal and philosophical arguments. Like neoclassical just war thinkers, the Walzerian approach is collectivist, emphasizing groups rather than individuals.[86] Indeed, like structural realism, the Walzerian approach is decidedly statist.[87] Walzer's defining mark on the discipline is clear, as Walzerians abound. Among the more prominent are A. J. Bellamy, Daniel Brunstetter, Michael Gross, and Brian Orend.

A third set of just war thinkers – the *revisionists* or reductionists – approach just war thinking from a radically different perspective. Although they use the language of just war, revisionists have radically reimagined the logics of just war thinking by reasoning from the individual up. Such thinkers "practice a form of philosophical theorizing that values logical coherence and rigor ... [emphasizing] individual morality ahead of the requirements of good government, and [prescribing] the use of right reason to both extrapolate ethical rules from first principles and apply them to real world cases."[88] Revisionists have more in common with the careful analytical work and individualist approach of Kant than with the casuistical methods employed by neoclassical and Walzerian just war thinkers. Well known revisionists include Jeff McMahan and David Rodin, of course, but also Cécile Fabre, Helen Frowe, and James Pattison.

What Is Just War Thought?

The plethora of just war traditions means that an additional level of abstraction is needed to meaningfully compare the assumptions and logics of realism and just war. For this reason, when I am referring to the idea of just war – to the conviction that war may be morally permissible in a certain set of circumstances – I use an even broader term: *just war thinking*. The argument I make in this book relies on the idea that we

---

[86] James Pattison, "When Is It Right to Fight? Just War Theory and the Individual-Centric Approach," *Ethical Theory and Moral Practice* 16(1), 2013, 35–54.

[87] Morkevičius, "Power and Order." See also Endre Begby, Gregory M. Reichberg, and Henrik Syse, "The Ethics of War. Part II: Contemporary Authors and Issues," *Philosophy Compass* 7(5), 2012, 328–347, 331.

[88] O'Driscoll, "Divisions within the Ranks?" 49.

can speak meaningfully about the ethics of war across the boundaries of specific religious (and secular) traditions. I am not making the dangerous claim – already well-critiqued in the literature – that there is a single language of just war that "we" all share.[89] Instead, I follow John Kelsay's claim that despite the difficulties of translation across different languages of just war, "we do well to act on the faith that 'nothing human is foreign to us.'"[90]

By this, I mean that we can recognize just war thinking when we see it, even in traditions foreign to our own. We recognize just war thinking as a common habit of human thought across time and space *because it asks the same sorts of questions, even if the answers are different.* This is not unlike the way in which contemporary realists recognize the realist aspects of Thucydides and Kautilya (an Indian scholar from the fourth century BCE). By including non-Western traditions of just war thought in this analysis, I hope to show that the realist aspects of just war thinking are so essential to the logic of just war that they transcend time and space – even though the specific moral judgments do not.

So What Do Just War Thinkers Have in Common?

The diversity of just war traditions means that this question is much harder to answer than it was in the realist context. Traditional just war thinkers (whether in the Christian, Islamic, or Hindu tradition) as well as contemporary neoclassical and Walzerian just war thinkers share much with realists. Like their realist counterparts, such just war thinkers

1. ... view human nature pessimistically.
2. ... treat groups as the primary unit of analysis for thinking about politics.
3. ... believe that groups are inherently competitive.
4. ... assume that the international system is anarchic.

---

[89] Nigel Biggar, "Natural Flourishing as the Normative Ground of Just War," in Anthony F. Lang, Cian O'Driscoll, and John Williams, eds., *Just War: Authority, Tradition and Practice* (Washington, DC: Georgetown University Press, 2013), 49. See also Nicholas Rengger, "The Wager Lost by Winning: On the 'Triumph' of the Just War Tradition," in Lang and O'Driscoll, *Just War: Authority, Tradition and Practice*, 285. And, of course, Walzer, *Just and Unjust Wars*, 16, 44.

[90] John Kelsay, "The Triumph of Just War Theory and Imperial Overstretch," in Lang and O'Driscoll, *Just War: Authority, Tradition and Practice*, 270.

5. ... see themselves as participating in a tradition of statecraft, aimed at managing the disorder of the international system.

Revisionist just war thinking shares none of these assumptions, except, perhaps, the last. Focusing on individual rights and duties and the possibility of achieving a truly ideal set of principles for war fighting, revisionism has far more in common with liberal idealism than it does with realism. In what follows, then, we'll set revisionism aside for the time being. The dangers revisionism poses for just war thinking as a tradition of statecraft will be taken up in the final chapter.

A Pessimistic Account of Human Nature

In the West, just war's pessimism can be traced all the way back to Augustine. For Augustine, it was the fallen nature of mankind that made the use of force permissible – even necessary – in the earthly kingdom. As Augustine put it, human nature is such that "all men desire to be at peace with their own people, while wishing to impose their will upon those people's lives. For even when they wage war on others, their wish is to make those opponents their own people, if they can – to subject them, and to impose on them their own conditions of peace."[91] Islamic scholars were equally pessimistic about human nature. Although the Qur'an asserts that Allah forgave Adam and Eve, humanity's free will means that humans are continuously tested. Although *shari'a* has been provided to guide humans toward right action, human pride means humanity is more likely to obey than to submit. Thus, force – whether in the implementation of criminal punishments or in the international arena – is unfortunately necessary, as a form of punishment. Likewise, the Hindu tradition warns that humans would behave like beasts if it weren't for force justly used by princes on behalf of the vulnerable.[92]

Contemporary just war thinkers, too, see human nature pessimistically. This quite in contrast with the liberal tradition, which Elshtain argues denies "the reality of human nature altogether."[93] For both neoclassical just war thinkers and Walzerians, human nature remains fallible. Biggar, for example, argues that "not all human beings are well motivated

---

[91] Augustine of Hippo, *City of God*, XIX:12, 867.
[92] Maganlal A. Buch, *The Principles of Hindu Ethics* (Baroda, India: "Arya Sudharak" Printing Press, 1921), 353.
[93] Jean Bethke Elshtain, "Politics and Persons," *Journal of Religion* 86(3), 2006, 402–411, 402.

or well intentioned" – our rational selves are overthrown by passions that cause us to "lose the ability to constrain ourselves out of respect for justice towards others."[94] Being realistic about human nature requires recognizing that humans "are capable of becoming so wedded to evil that sweet reason, for all its patience, cannot detach them."[95] Walzer is even willing to countenance violating the just war convention when faced with "evil objectified in the world."[96]

Groups as the Unit of Analysis

Traditional just war thinkers highlight the role of groups – and sometimes even states, but this requires a bit more nuanced explication. The roots of the tradition precede the Westphalian system. Aquinas, for example, restricted the right to wage war to those with legitimate authority, but such authority could be held by a variety of political entities.[97] Just war thinkers' concern with separating public war from private war (i.e., dueling) pushed the nexus of legitimate authority upwards, to the individual at the top of the feudal pyramid who owed no higher allegiance (at least, no higher *political* allegiance) to anyone. By the time of Vitoria and Grotius, this role is clearly assigned to the heads of independently sovereign political communities – that is, to the newly emerging states.[98]

Contemporary just war thinking of the neoclassical and Walzerian types, for better or worse, tends to take this state-centrism for granted. For Ramsey, the state is the "'subject' of political action."[99] Walzer likewise argues that it is beside the point to ask whether states are the "products of ancient wars" or the legacy of "ignorant, drunken, or corrupt mapmakers."[100] Whatever their origins, borders take on lives of their own, demarcating separate and unique societies. Within these borders, a "common life" is established, and it is this life that is worth protecting by force, if necessary.[101] Even if the regime is oppressive,

---

[94] Nigel Biggar, *In Defense of War* (Oxford: Oxford University Press, 2013), 9.

[95] Ibid., 12.   [96] Walzer, *Just and Unjust Wars*, 253.

[97] Thomas Aquinas, *Political Writings*, ed. R. W. Dyson (Cambridge: Cambridge University Press, 2002), 240.

[98] Francisco Vitoria, *Vitoria: Political Writings* (Cambridge: Cambridge University Press, 1991), 301. See also Roland Bainton, *Chrsitian Attitudes Toward War and Peace: A Historical Survey and Critical Re-Evaluation* (New York: Abingdon Press, 1960), 87.

[99] Paul Ramsey, *The Just War: Force and Political Responsibility* (Lanham, MD: Rowman & Littlefield, 2002), 9.

[100] Walzer, *Just and Unjust Wars*, 57.   [101] Ibid., 54–55.

even if the borders are bad, states within which a meaningful common life exists possess the legitimate authority to defend themselves.[102] As one of Walzer's critics points out, "repeatedly it is the survival and well-being of the state that is his ultimate appeal, which means that reason of state begins to show itself in the guise of the just war theory."[103]

Groups as Inherently Competitive in Conditions of Anarchy

Historically, just war thinkers have seen war as an unavoidable part of existence in a fallen world. While just war thinkers have "never accepted that political communities can legitimately pursue their interests irrespective of what those interests are," just war thinking has also "never supposed that war can be abolished or overcome."[104] Like structural realists, most just war thinkers accept that the world of states is anarchic, in the sense that there is no single overarching power to keep the peace. This largely stems from the tradition's pessimistic evaluation of human nature after the fall. Humans cannot help but sin. Greed, power lust, and fundamental distrust generate perpetual conflict. As Augustine quipped, men don't fight because they don't want peace, but rather because they want it to be the kind of peace they wish for.[105] Human groups are likely to have different values, and these differences spark conflict. As we shall see in the following chapters, traditional just war thinkers in the Christian, Islamic, and Hindu just war traditions may occasionally paint a picture of what a completely peaceful world order would look like – but these are eschatological visions rather than roadmaps for policy.

Domestically, the ruler holds these competing social interests and centrifugal powers in check. Internationally, however, no such authority exists. Walzer makes the connection between anarchy and war explicit: because there is no universal authority, "every conflict threatens the whole structure with collapse."[106] As a result, although war is unfortunate, it is also sometimes necessary. Fundamentally, as Ramsey pointed out, just war thinkers recognize that "the use of power, and possibly the use of force, is of the *esse* of politics ... You never have politics without

[102] Ibid., 55.
[103] Robert L. Holmes, *On War and Morality* (Princeton: Princeton University Press, 1989), 170.
[104] Rengger, *Just War and International Order*, 48.
[105] Augustine of Hippo, *City of God* (London: Penguin Books, 1984), XIX.12.
[106] Walzer, *Just and Unjust Wars*, 59.

the use of power, possibly armed force."[107] In short, "just war thinkers and realists ... share a judgment about the nature of political power as essentially coercive and war as a necessary instrument of politics."[108]

Just War Thought as a Tradition of Statecraft

Historically, the Christian just war tradition directed itself at heads of state – Augustine, Aquinas, Vitoria, and others were quite consciously writing for an audience of kings. As we shall see Chapter 4, they were as busily engaged in correspondence with the monarchs and generals of their time about specific ethical dilemmas as they were in penning esoteric treatments of the subject. What's more, the canonical just war tradition made a clear distinction between killing carried out by an individual (which could be homicide, justifiable self-defense, or dueling) and killing carried out on behalf of a political entity (which is to say, war). Islamic scholars similarly relied on specific cases to develop their just war arguments, making it clear that their concern was as much with practice as theory. Many were judges, and some even served as court advisors. And in Chapter 6, several of the Hindu texts we will examine were written explicitly as advice for kings.

Just war thinking, far from being idealist or utopian, is a tradition of theorizing about *policy*. And policy itself "is the meeting-place of the world of power, and the world of morality, in which there takes place the concrete reconciliation of the duty of success that rests upon the statesman and the duty of justice that rests upon the civilized nation that he serves."[109] Ramsey takes just war thinking to provide "the moral *context* for policy decision," understanding it to be a "normative theory of and for practice."[110] Johnson argues for "a theory of statecraft rooted in just war tradition" that can respond both to needs for "a broader theoretical context for moral judgments and a deeper historical context for policy formulation."[111] Avoiding the pitfalls of pure "utopianism, moral outrage, [and] realism," this sort of just war thinking would

---

[107] Ramsey, *The Just War*, 5.

[108] Helmut David Baer and Joseph E. Capizzi, "Just War Theories Reconsidered: Problems with Prima Facie Duties and the Need for a Political Ethics," *Journal of Religious Ethics* 33(1), 2005, 119–137, 122.

[109] John Courtney Murray, "The Uses of a Doctrine on the Uses of Force as a Moral Problem," in *We Hold These Truths: Catholic Reflections on the American Proposition* (New York: Rowman and Littlefield, 2005), 246.

[110] Ramsey, *The Just War*, 309.   [111] Johnson, *Morality and Contemporary Warfare*, 21.

provide "principled guidance for both moral judgment and policy."[112] As Walzer puts it, just war thinking "is the doctrine of people who do expect to exercise power and use force."[113]

DEEPER LOGICS: NECESSITY AND ORDER

Clearly, realism and just war thinking (at least in its traditional, neoclassical, and Walzerian forms) share a great deal. Both traditions of statecraft view human nature and the potential for intergroup cooperation pessimistically and hence presume that war is a sad inevitability. Yet both realists and just war thinkers invoke two more underlying logics which we still need to consider. Although necessity and order are sometimes presumed to mark the points of divergence between the two traditions, they are actually fundamental to both.

As we shall see, necessity turns out to be a red herring – the famous Walzerian case for distinguishing realism and just war thought on the basis of the principle of necessity does not stand up to scrutiny. Order, however, is a more nuanced story. While both realists and just war thinkers care about order, they understand order slightly differently. Both traditions treat order and justice as separable goods, but only realists consistently value order above justice. In the following sections I sketch the argument in broad terms. The concepts of order and necessity will be addressed in greater depth in the subsequent chapters on the specific just war traditions.

On Necessity

Necessity is sometimes treated as the key distinguishing factor between realism and just war theory. Walzer, for example, imagines necessity as axiomatic to realism: realists do what is necessary, which is inherently in tension with what is moral. In this view, realists see war as a "realm of necessity and duress," in which norms are nothing more than "idle chatter."[114] Just war thought, by contrast, demands that norms be accounted for even in the extremes of war.

Admittedly, because realists see state behavior as largely conditioned by the structure of the international system, they are inclined to claim that ordinary morality should be "subordinated to interest."[115] But that

---

[112] Ibid.   [113] Michael Walzer, "The Triumph of Just War Theory," 935.
[114] Walzer, *Just and Unjust Wars*, 4.   [115] Waltz, *Theory of International Politics*, 172.

doesn't mean that anything goes. Treating the sphere of international relations as *amoral* is not akin to advocating immoral behavior. Indeed, many realists argue that limiting one's actions on the basis of necessity may lead to *more moral* outcomes than behavior motivated by morality. In other words, realists are (like Walzer) consequentialists "with limits."[116] American presidents' claims to seek "an end to conflict," despite their "humane and obvious good intention," should "worry us greatly," writes Waltz.[117] A concern with justice may be universal, but the content of justice is not. A great power tempted to seek its own kind of moral justice may end up fighting wars that are neither very successful nor very just.

Given the lack of international agreement about the content of justice, realists argue that the best a moral leader can aim for is to pursue his or her state's *necessary* interests. Chasing unnecessary interests is always costly and often risky. By contrast, a focus on the need to survive inevitably restrains state behavior. During the Cold War, prominent realists argued that preventing war between the nuclear-armed superpowers was a "clear-cut moral imperative," because a nuclear holocaust was clearly not in anyone's state interest.[118]

Just war thinking, too, frequently invokes necessity. For Walzer – as for Augustine and Aquinas before him – a just war is always fought out of necessity, forced upon us by the wrongdoing of others. The tyranny of war, as Walzer puts it, is that "those who resist aggression are forced to imitate, and perhaps even exceed, the brutality of the aggressor."[119] More concretely, the concept of necessity is embedded in the concept of double effect, which can be found in both the Christian and Islamic traditions. Vitoria, for example, deemed killing in war permissible when it was "necessary to victory."[120] He argued that cities could be attacked, even with indiscriminate weapons – if necessary – even though civilians would be harmed, because "it would otherwise be impossible to wage war against the guilty, thereby preventing the just side from fighting."[121] As we shall see in Chapter 5, the idea of necessity implicit in the concept of double effect is equally significant in the Islamic tradition.

---

[116] Russel Hardin and John Mearshiemer, "Introduction," *Ethics* 95(3), 1985, 411–423, 413.
[117] Waltz, *Theory of International Politics*, 302.
[118] Hardin and Mearsheimer, "Introduction." [119] Walzer, *Just and Unjust Wars*, 32.
[120] Cited in Richard Shelly Hartigan, "Francesco de Vitoria and Civilian Immunity," *Political Theory* 1(1), 1973, 79–91, 83.
[121] Francisco de Vitoria, "On the Law of War," 3.1, in Anthony Padgen and Jeremy Lawrance, eds., *Political Writings* (Cambridge: Cambridge University Press, 2003), 315.

Order, Stability, and Justice

Both realists and just war thinkers agree that order and justice are separable values. In other words, it is possible to have order without justice and justice without order (although such systems are likely to be unstable). This distinguishes both traditions from other international relations approaches that treat order and justice as inherently linked. Neoliberal institutionalists, for example, argue that shared norms matter for creating a stable order.[122] But not just any norms. The "right" norms are essential for generating stability, namely a certain set of democratic and human rights values. Likewise, the English school asserts that legitimacy is essential to the exercise of power.

For realists, a bright line exists between concerns about stability and concerns about justice. Order, in this context, isn't about peace or international hierarchy.[123] Instead, order for realists refers to the continued stability of the international system. Each state fights to prevent its own death but may also fight to maintain the stability of the system, in the sense of maintaining the balance of power. Thus, the anarchical structure of the international system itself creates a sort of order. States quickly discover that sovereignty does not actually mean they "can do as they please."[124] Instead, states "are always constrained" by the reactions – and threatened reactions – of others.[125] Although war is one option open to states for resolving their problems, its high costs and risks have a "sobering effect," discouraging states from engaging willy-nilly in war.[126] Although fear itself can drive conflict, "the constant possibility that force will be used limits manipulation, moderates demands, and serves as an incentive for the settlement of disputes."[127] Thus, in the interest of their long-term survival, states act in ways that uphold the order *without necessarily consciously intending to do so.* Order in this light emerges as a fact – the existence of "stable and regular" interactions, as opposed to "chaos, instability, or lack of predictability."[128]

---

[122] Charles Lipson, *Reliable Partners: How Democracies Have Made a Separate Peace* (Princeton: Princeton University Press, 2005), 5, 54. See also Joseph S. Nye, "Public Diplomacy and Soft Power," *Annals of the American Academy of Political and Social Science* 616(1), 2008, 94–109.

[123] Waltz, *Theory of International Politics*, 45.   [124] Ibid., 96.   [125] Ibid.

[126] Ibid., 114.   [127] Waltz, *Theory of International Politics*, 113.

[128] Andrew Hurrell, "Order and Justice in International Relations: What Is at Stake?" in Rosemary Foot, John Gaddis, and Andrew Hurrell, eds., *Order and Justice in International Relations* (Oxford: Oxford University Press, 2003), 24–38, 25.

Upholding order is thus fundamentally a self-centered act. States may attempt to justify their actions in terms of norms, sign on to versions of international law, or even work to establish international institutions. When states seek order intentionally, they treat it as a value.[129] But such efforts to create order are "not to be taken at face value, but to be seen as means of achieving ends."[130] As Carr put it, international peace is "a special vested interest of predominant Powers."[131] Powerful states seek to maintain international order because it suits them, not (at least primarily) because of any moral calling.

Furthermore, although justice *can* contribute to stability, it isn't necessary. In fact, pursuing justice can be dangerous, as both Machiavelli and Morgenthau remind us.[132] Using aggressive war to impose domestic values on the international sphere can have disastrous consequences. Conversely, an overly zealous commitment to peace can permit the rise of a hostile power. Once the newcomer is powerful enough to challenge the existing order, it may be too late – a war fought then may be more costly than a preventive war fought to maintain the status quo.[133]

Just war thinkers, too, distinguish order and stability from justice. Augustine, for example, does not hide his support for the Roman empire as an entity that provides significant stability domestically and internationally. At the same time, he makes it quite clear that the Roman empire – like any earthly government – falls short of accomplishing real justice. The conceptual separation between stability and justice can be seen as well in the way that Aquinas, Calvin, and Luther discuss rebellion. While all three decry tyranny, they simultaneously discourage subjects from rising up against a tyrannical government. Such a position is only logically coherent if stability is deemed a good independently of justice.

Although realists consistently rank the maintenance of order higher than justice, the case for just war thinkers is more nuanced. Traditional and neoclassical just war thinkers in particular tend to value order very highly, as the above discussion suggests. Better a bad tyrant than a bad war, they warn.[134] After all, "tranquility and peace are counted among the good things which men strive for; without security all the other good

---

[129] Ibid.   [130] Cox, "Multilateralism and World Order," 167.

[131] E. H. Carr, *The Twenty Years Crisis: 1919–1939* (New York: Perennial, 2001), 74.

[132] Morgenthau, *Dilemmas of Politics*, 52, 55.

[133] Mearsheimer, *The Tragedy of Great Power Politics*, 34. Niccolò Machiavelli, *The Prince*, ed. Quentin Skinner and Russell Price (Cambridge: Cambridge University Press, 1988), XIV. 52.

[134] Both Aquinas and Luther are particularly explicit about this.

things together cannot make happiness."[135] But the question of whether order is worth *more* than justice is always contextual. Just war thinkers imagine that there is such a thing as a *just order*, an order that permits human flourishing.

Consequently, the work of many just war thinkers is motivated not by a presumption against violence, but rather a presumption against *injustice*.[136] Nearly every iteration of just war theory begins with the premise that wars are fought for the sake of peace. This'can only make sense if "peace" in this context is something different than the mere absence of war. Although peace is a good, not every peace is worthy of the name. An unjust peace – characterized by instability, persistent threat, or tyranny – is no peace. As Augustine put it, "a man who has learnt to prefer right to wrong and the rightly ordered to the perverted, sees that the peace of the unjust, compared with the peace of the just, is not worthy even of the name of peace."[137] The appropriate aim of war is not simply peace, but peace with justice – in other words, the establishment of a just order.

SIMILAR ASSUMPTIONS, DIFFERENT CONCLUSIONS

Despite sharing similar assumptions about states and the nature of the state system, as well as underlying concerns with order and necessity, realism and just war thought reach different conclusions about the wisdom and permissibility of engaging in certain types of warfare. On the one hand, both camps would support most wars of self-defense, albeit for different reasons. For the realist, self-defense of one's sovereignty is an enshrined right, and the necessary building block for the world system of states. For the just war theorist, self-defense is a right because of what sovereignty enables the state to create within its own borders – in other words, because self-defense makes the maintenance of a justly ordered society possible.

While structural realists permit nondefensive wars to maintain the balance of power, just war theorists in the modern era would not explicitly do so. But there is nothing inherent within the various just war traditions that renders balance of power reasoning unacceptable. The rules of the game are generous enough to permit strong state powers

---

[135] Vitoria, *Political Writings*, 305.
[136] James Turner Johnson, *Morality and Contemporary Warfare* (New Haven, CT: Yale University Press, 1999), 35, 211; Morkevičius, "Just War."
[137] Augustine, *City of God*, XIX.12, 896.

to do (more or less) as they wish. Balance of power can be understood in some contexts as a broad form of self-defense (by preventing the rise of a potentially hostile power) or as righting a wrong (by turning back the territorial gains made by a hostile power).

Yet just war thinking's concern with justice leads it to radically different conclusions regarding nondefensive wars. To be clear: it is not a presumption in favor of peace that separates just war thinkers from realists. Neither tradition values peace per se. For realists, peace matters only in so much as it reflects a stable balance. It is desirable not so much as an end, but as a symptom of something potentially positive. For just war thinkers, peace is also not an ipso facto good. Many kinds of peace exist, and most are not peace at all. The peace of the dead after a genocide, the peace of silence under extreme oppression – these are not true peaces. Instead, just war thinkers are concerned about peace only when it represents *peace with justice*. To the extent that justice motivates just war thinking, just war thinkers partake of the perfectionism that characterizes liberalism.

This concern with justice works itself through the just war tradition on two different levels. On the most fundamental level, just war thinkers justify a state's forcible defense of itself through the language of justice. States have the *right* to defend themselves because states are the agents through which domestic justice is constructed. State governance is necessary to create stable human communities within which human individuals can flourish. This differs, of course, from the realist account in which states defend themselves because sovereignty is the necessary basis of the post-Westphalian world order in which they exist.

Justice claims on this first, fundamental level are linked to justice claims that reach beyond state boundaries. Justice on the second level argues that states not only have a right to defend themselves, but they also have the right (and perhaps a duty) to *right wrongs*. And there are a good many wrongs needing to be rectified. States may come to the defense of other states that have fallen victim to aggression. States may also respond directly to the peoples of other states, who suffer under tyrants. Here we wander onto the slippery slope to humanitarian intervention (and other forms of interventionism). What constitutes a legitimate effort to right a wrong changes over time within the Christian tradition, as it does within Islam and Hinduism as well. While the nature of the wrongs is disputed and shifting, the underlying principle – that states may use force to expand the sphere of justice internationally – has deep roots.

JUST WAR THINKING AND ITS CRITICS: ON FAILURES OF JUST
WAR THINKING TO RESTRAIN WAR

The linking of order and justice – which happens in just war thinking, but
not in realism – is the proximate cause of the tradition's "failure" to serve
as an effective brake on states' rush to war. Just war thinking's practical
potential to restrain violence is overlooked by both pacifists' and realists'
focus on the idealist aspects of the tradition. From the pacifist perspective,
just war theory too easily fails to reduce our appetite for war. John
Howard Yoder argues that the system is incapable of yielding a "a clear
and commonly accessible adjudication of contested cases," because not
only are the theories' terms contestable, the factual "data" that would be
used to make a determination is contestable (and often unavailable)
too.[138] Furthermore, just war thinking would have to deny the right to
go to war in certain hard cases – for example, when the cause is just, but
the war cannot be fought with just means – in order to be more than a
farcical attempt at moral justification. But in Yoder's view, "there is no
strong evidence for believing that most people using just-war language are
ready, either psychologically or intellectually, for that serious choice."[139]
In Yoder's judgment, part of the problem lies within the theory itself:
its loose terminology, the apparent separation between *ad bellum* and
in bello reasoning, and its unfalsifiable categories such as "just intent."
But as we have seen in this chapter, part of the problem lies within the
system just war theory helps create: a system where, because the recourse
to war is accepted as both necessary and moral, significant amounts of
money and time are invested in developing military options (as opposed
to nonviolent strategies).[140]

On the other end of the spectrum, realists are also skeptical about the
potential for just war traditions (or any moral or legal code, for that
matter) to restrict violence. On the most basic level, this derives from
pessimism about human nature. Machiavelli, for example, suggests that
the wise leader understands that "wars cannot really be avoided but are
merely postponed."[141] Emphasizing the importance of doing everything
necessary to protect the state (and his own power), Machiavelli boldly

---

[138] John Howard Yoder, "Just War Tradition: Is It Credible?" *Christian Century*, 108,
March 13, 1991, 295–298, 298.
[139] John Howard Yoder, *When War Is Unjust: Being Honest in Just-War Thinking*
(Maryknoll, NY: Orbis Books), 1996, 72.
[140] Ibid., 79–80.   [141] Machiavelli, *The Prince*, 11.

asserts that the ruler "must be prepared to act immorally when this becomes necessary."[142]

For realists, the problems inherent in human nature are only compounded by the nature of the international system itself. Without a hierarchical power structure to keep them in order, states remain in a state of nature. Hobbes's understanding of anarchy assumes that whenever a system lacks a power "to keep them all in awe," mankind is "in that condition which is called Warre."[143] War, for Hobbes, is not "actuall fighting; but ... the known disposition thereto, during all the time there is no assurance to the contrary."[144] Furthermore, for Hobbes, systems of ethics only emerge in a community – and by definition such a community cannot exist between states, only within them. International ethics is a meaningless category.

Morgenthau, writing in the waning days of World War II, carries this claim even further, arguing that infusing ethics into politics can be downright dangerous.[145] His own view owes much to Hegel, who saw the lack of one authority over all as foreclosing the possibility for truly moral or even legal relationships between states. Although individuals may have true rights toward each other, enforced by a sovereign power, states' rights "are actualized not in a universal will with constitutional powers over them, but in their own particular wills."[146] Therefore, any agreement among them "whether based on moral, religious, or other grounds or considerations, would always be dependent on particular sovereign rules, and would therefore continue to be tainted with contingency."[147] If agreement cannot be reached, war is the natural and inevitable result.[148] E. H. Carr sums up this position nicely: "One reason why a higher standard of morality is not expected of states is because states in fact frequently fail to behave morally and because there are no means of compelling them to do so."[149] In casting just war thinking in this light, realists fail to recognize the deeply realist aspects of just war thought.

---

[142] Ibid., 55.
[143] Thomas Hobbes, *Leviathan*, ed. Richard Tuck (Cambridge: Cambridge University Press, 1996), I:13:62, 88.
[144] Ibid., 89.
[145] Hans J. Morgenthau, *Scientific Man versus Power Politics* (Chicago: University of Chicago Press, 1952).
[146] G. W. F. Hegel, *Elements of the Philosophy of the Right*, ed. Allen B. Wood, trans. H. B. Nisbet (Cambridge: Cambridge University Press, 1991), III.B.333, 368.
[147] Ibid., 386.   [148] Ibid., III.B.334, 387.   [149] Carr, *The Twenty Years Crisis*, 161.

Were they to do so, it would raise very interesting questions about the potential for rational restraint in the international sphere.

PERSISTENT OPTIMISM: THE FALSE HOPE OF AN IMPROVED JUST WAR TRADITION

It is not only just war's critics who overlook its embedded realism. Even just war thinking's proponents frequently view it in idealist terms. Like Walzer, contemporary just war thinkers tend to believe that just war thinking – despite its roots in power politics – speaks truth to power, shaming statesmen into doing the right thing. As James Turner Johnson's introduction to his *Morality and Contemporary Warfare* explains, the "overall task" of his work and others' "is to bring the moral tradition of just war to bear on contemporary war so as to identify its particular injustices and to advance an argument as to how to respond to them and seek to remedy them."[150] The idea that "just war is a site of criticism" is often identified as one of the key strengths the tradition brings to the table.[151]

Just war thinkers have a tendency to think that if we could only "get it right" (i.e., elucidate the principles more clearly, close the loopholes, convince policymakers and citizens of its value, and so on), *then* fewer wars would be fought. In the forty years since Walzer's *Just and Unjust Wars* put just war thinking back on the map, an intellectual cottage industry has evolved to generate patches to fix what ails the tradition. Indeed, "it is commonplace to revisit the adequacy of elements of just war theory with each watershed war and each change in the character of warfare."[152] Sometimes, just war thinkers respond these changes by throwing up their hands, declaring a particular type of war (or technology of war fighting) unjust. If the type of warfare in question cannot simply be banned, such thinkers argue, we would do better to adopt pacifism as our principled stance.[153]

---

[150] Johnson, *Morality and Contemporary Warfare*, 7.
[151] Cian O'Driscoll, *Renegotiation of the Just War Tradition and the Right to War in the Twenty-First Century* (New York: Palgrave Macmillan, 2008), 97.
[152] Crawford, "Just War Theory," 6.
[153] See, for example, Richard Wasserstrom, "On the Morality of War: A Preliminary Inquiry," *Stanford Law Review* 21(6), 1969, 1627–1656; Norman C. Freund, "The Just War: Viable Theory or Moral Anachronism?" *American Journal of Theology and Philosophy* 3(3), 1982, 71–79.

Equally often, however, the just war tradition is kept alive by scholars who seek to improve the tradition through a process of incremental reform. These thinkers seek to make just war thinking more restrictive by closing what they see as loopholes within the traditional principles. One of the earliest of these patches emerged in response to a challenge from Yoder, who argued that proponents of the just war tradition needed pacifists to keep them honest, given their tendency to accept war too easily.[154] Yoder's critique emerged in the context of the Cold War fear that any conventional conflict between the great powers could escalate to the level of a nuclear confrontation. The patch that developed in response took the form of a meta-theoretical claim about the common origins of just war thinking and pacifism in the Christian context. Thus, James Childress, Richard Miller, and Lisa Cahill argued that contrary to customary assumptions, just war theory and pacifism did not derive from contradictory assumptions, but rather "rest upon overlapping and reinforcing modes of thought."[155] Specifically, they claimed that just war thinking is based on a presumption *against* war, *against* killing.[156] This conceptual shift was supposed to make "just war theory more effective by reducing recourse to war."[157] In addition to being a radically ahistorical reading of the tradition, as Johnson has argued, this move still doesn't fix the loophole – even a just war tradition inclined to judge against war "does not have the conceptual apparatus necessary to . . . [make] concrete judgments about the justness of particular wars."[158]

Another patch has emerged not from theology, but from philosophy. This view suggests that contemporary just war theory has given too much away by accepting the state as an ethically unique entity. Revisionist just war thinkers question whether the state should be treated as the locus of legitimate authority, and even whether the state is worthy of defense. In this case, the context is the ongoing war on terror, a war fought by states against a hodgepodge of nonstate actors, including transnational organizations (al Qaeda) and substate entities (the Taliban). The most elegant argument in this line is found in the work of David Rodin, who develops a powerful case for *individuals'* inherent right to self-defense,

---

[154] Yoder, *When War Is Unjust.*

[155] Baer and Capizza, "Just War Theories Reconsidered," 119.

[156] Richard B. Miller, "Aquinas and the Presumption against Killing and War," *Journal of Religion* 82(2), 2002, 173–204.

[157] Baer and Capizza, "Just War Theories Reconsidered," 120.

[158] Ibid., 132. See also James Turner Johnson, "Just War, As It Was and Is," *First Things,* January 2005.

but then finds no way to connect this basic right to any claim a state could make on its own behalf.[159] Similarly relying on the individual as the base of analysis, Jeff McMahan eviscerates much of traditional *in bello* just war thought by arguing that the rules of war should consider individuals' moral responsibility for the wars in which they participate, as well as the objective justness of those wars.[160] Likewise, James Pattison asserts that the "individual-centric approach" is superior to the customary communitarian one.[161] All three of these philosophers push toward a concept of individual responsibility that ultimately makes it difficult to imagine a case in which the recourse to war would be justified. As McMahan points out, if wars are unjust more often than they are just, when in doubt about the justice of a particular war, individuals would do well to presume against it.[162] Thus, this patch, too, is aimed at narrowing the possible scope for just wars.

The problem with these patches, and others, is that they can't work, not because they don't address important problems with the tradition, but because the tradition *as a whole was never meant to prevent war*. The just war tradition's failure to avoid war is not a problem that can be corrected by adding in new principles or amending old ones. Instead, the problem is with our own misunderstanding of the function of just war thinking. The just war tradition was meant to channel violence into socially acceptable directions.[163] After all, just war thinking is a *political theory*, a theory of statecraft. Originally conceived as advice for kings and diplomats, just war theory lays out norms for state behavior in the international sphere. This advice is built on assumptions about the nature of the international system and the capabilities and interests of the main actors in the system. I argue that rather than starting from a presumption against war, just war thinking begins from the assumption that war is an inevitable fact of life in a fallen world. Furthermore, while war is never a good in itself, war can be a *force for good*. As a result, just war thinkers are surprisingly unlikely to identify any particular war as unjust.

The prevalence of this mistaken understanding of just war theory owes much to the overly facile line usually drawn between just war thinking on one hand and realism on the other. Typically, just war thinking is

[159] David Rodin, *War and Self-Defense* (Oxford: Oxford University Press, 2005).
[160] Jeff McMahan, *Killing in War* (Oxford: Oxford University Press, 2009).
[161] Pattison, "When Is It Right to Fight?"   [162] McMahan, *Killing in War*, 153.
[163] Morkevičius, "Just War."

described as occupying the middle space on a continuum between realism on one side and pacifism on the other. Just war thinkers share with realists the understanding that war is a tool states use to pursue their goals, while denying the realist claim that war is *just* a tool, about which moral judgments are irrelevant. Like pacifists, just war thinkers value peace and human life, without accepting the pacifist argument that peace is always the highest value. The contemporary trend of treating the just war tradition as if it began from a presumption against war pushes just war thinking closer to pacifism, a move that I argue is not only disingenuous, but dangerous.

PART II

3

Power, Powder, Politics

Just War's Historical and Political Contingencies

This book is an argument in the just war tradition. I argue that power politics – relationships of power both within and between polities – molded just war principles over the centuries. Consequently, just war thinking as a tradition of statecraft reflects realist principles as much as, if not more than, idealist ones. In the end, I argue that there are good reasons for those of us who are interested in carrying just war thinking into the twenty-first century and beyond to resurrect this embedded realism, or at the very least, to think carefully about what we are doing and why we are doing it when we work in a more idealist vein.

To build this argument, I tell the story of the evolution of just war thinking within three distinct traditions: Christianity, Islam, and Hinduism. This requires answering the question "How is just war thinking, as an evolving tradition, affected by its political and historical environs?" This question not only gets to the heart of the realist aspects of just war thinking, but also raises questions about the degree to which we might consider just war thinking to be universal.

Although I will sometimes use the expression "just war thinking" to refer to patterns of ethical reasoning that legitimize war in certain circumstances and using certain means, I by no means intend to suggest that these three traditions are part of a single, coherent whole. For that matter, just war thinking *within* any one of these traditions is hardly monolithic. In the West, for example, there are at least three contemporary variants of just war thinking: the neoclassical, Walzerian, and revisionist veins. The particular principles we associate with just war thinking, and the ways in which we define and employ those principles, vary considerably across time and space. The content of just war thinking in any particular

43

tradition is full of thick norms that have been socially constructed in response to the concrete needs of unique human communities at specific moments in time.

While I do not believe that there is a deep consensus between or within these traditions as to what specifically constitutes the just recourse to war – or the just means for fighting – I nonetheless believe there is a pattern of thought that we can recognize cross-culturally and cross-temporally as "just war thought." As Walzer puts it, "whatever the origins of an idea of justice, whatever the starting point of the argument in this or that society, people thinking and talking about justice will range over a mostly familiar terrain and will come upon similar issues," and some aspect of that conversation, despite its cultural and political particularities, "will be immediately accessible to people who don't know anything" about those particularities.[1] Put simply, human beings as moral creatures ask moral questions about their world. And since that world is all too often at war, it seems likely that humans have always asked themselves questions about the ethical legitimacy of war. This moral question has many potential answers. So when I refer to "just war thinking" in general terms, I am referring to the just war *idea* – to the claim that war is sometimes (but not always) legitimate.

A WORD ABOUT METHOD: WHEN IS HISTORY NOT A HISTORY?

One way of approaching the history of any tradition of political thought is to treat it fundamentally as a history of *ideas*. This approach studies "the activity of thinking, of conceptualizing, of abstracting ideas from particular situations and traditions."[2] Simply put, this view treats political thought as "an aspect of intellectuality," of individuals' attempts to understand and explain their own experience within the bounds of a particular language of politics.[3] Methodologically, a history of ideas aims to decipher the author's linguistic context. Political languages are trad-itional languages. Writers must make use of already existing vocabularies to be intelligible. And yet the world around us changes. New groups claim

---

[1] Michael Walzer, *Thick and Thin: Moral Argument at Home and Abroad* (South Bend, IN: Notre Dame University Press, 1994), 5–6.
[2] J. G. A. Pocock. *Political Thought and History* (Cambridge: Cambridge University Press, 2009), 13.
[3] Ibid., 5.

political authority; new forms of social and political organization come into being. And so political languages evolve. Thus, the historian of ideas must carefully analyze "how traditional concepts are employed and modified in particular situations."[4] This, in turn, is a two-step process. The historian must first identify all the possible vocabularies that could have been used, before asking *why* this language, and not another, was invoked. The choice of a particular language lets us in on the author's intent.[5]

Alternately, the history of political thought can be told as a story of *action*. This approach is concerned with history not as a set of events, but as a set of ideas expressed in events.[6] Methodologically, a history of action considers "how ideas, beliefs, and arguments help us to understand the actions of men in particular situations."[7] Of course, this is not completely at odds with the study of ideas. After all, once we understand what an author meant, it's natural to want to know how that message was received, and what effect (if any) it had on those who read it.[8]

Although the study of the history of action is a valuable approach, the path is strewn with dangers. When we seek to uncover the relationship between texts and action, we can be tempted to see political thought too simplistically as the "'reflection' of a social structure or political situation.'"[9] Treating authors as simply the products of their times can blind us to the fact that "our concepts are not forced upon us by the world, but represent what we bring to the world in order to understand it."[10]

Despite these pitfalls, there are good reasons for thinking about how political contingencies shaped not only the questions just war thinkers asked, but also the responses they offered. We will be interested, of course, in how the authors we examine integrate past works of scholarship into their own as they formulate their own arguments. But this work is fundamentally motivated by the assumption "that political life itself sets the main problems for the political theorist, causing a certain range of

---

[4] Ibid., 13.

[5] Quentin Skinner, *Visions of Politics, Volume I: Regarding Method* (Cambridge: Cambridge University Press, 2002), 87.

[6] R. G. Collingsworth, *The Idea of History* (Oxford: Clarendon Press, 1964), 214.

[7] Ibid., 13.

[8] James Tully, "The Pen Is a Mighty Sword: Quentin Skinner's Analysis of politics," in James Tully, ed., *Meaning and Context: Quentin Skinner and His Critics* (Princeton: Princeton University Press, 1988), 10.

[9] Pocock, *Political Thought and History*, 16.   [10] Skinner, *Visions of Politics*, vol. 1, 46.

issues to appear problematic, and a corresponding range of questions to become the leading subjects of debate."[11] To be quite precise, rather than focusing on how ideas affect ideas, or how ideas affect action, this book will question how action might affect ideas.

This book is structured around three stories about the evolution of just war thinking in three distinct traditions. I use the historical context surrounding various canonical texts to suggest that as political contingencies changed, so too did thinking about just war. And yet this book is not a work of history. Instead, it is a philosophical argument with "historical illustrations," to borrow Walzer's term.[12] I cast the spotlight on the ways in which just war thinking in many times and places has been considerably more pragmatic than is commonly assumed. But my purpose is not to provide a definitive history of any of these just war traditions. I aim instead to raise questions about how we understand just war thinking today, and to caution against contemporary liberal tendencies in the tradition.

The claim that the past is worth exploring because the past is useful to our present is an old one. Thucydides and Machiavelli alike sought "to interpret the past for the purposes of the present, with a view to managing the future."[13] When we better understand the society of the past, we "increase [our] mastery over the society of the present."[14] By thinking about the ways in which past generations reacted to problems that may be similar to our own, we can learn from *their* experiences, becoming wiser and more effective thinkers ourselves.[15] Recognizing that past generations faced similar challenges can also help us put our own problems into context. It is worth asking just how uniquely fraught our own times are, rather than accepting such a claim at face value.

To learn well from the past, however, we must resist the temptation to overstate the similarities between our situation and those of people in the past.[16] We must also avoid presuming that the values we hold today

---

[11] Quentin Skinner, *The Foundations of Modern Political Thought, Volume I* (Cambridge: Cambridge University Press, 1978), xi. See also Skinner, *Visions of Politics*, 87.

[12] Rengger, similarly, identifies his work as a philosophical essay, rather than a contribution to history per se. See *Just War and International Order*, 5.

[13] John Lewis Gaddis, *The Landscape of History: How Historians Map the Past* (Oxford: Oxford University Press, 2002), 9.

[14] Ibid., 55.

[15] E. H. Carr, *What Is History?* (Harmondsworth, UK: Penguin Books, 1987), 114.

[16] Robert Jervis, *Perception and Misperception in International Politics* (Princeton: Princeton University Press, 1976), 228.

have been constant over time. Because we only speak the language of the present, when we read about the past, we consciously or unconsciously carry our contemporary values and assumptions about the structure of the world back in time with us.[17] When our present values and assumptions are challenged by what we find in the story of the past, we realize that our values, "supposedly absolute and extra historical . . . are in fact rooted to history."[18] The content of "hypothetical absolutes" – like justice, order, peace, and even natural law – varies "from period to period, or from continent to continent."[19] Rather than slamming us into the uncertain shoals of relativism, this recognition can help us come to recognize that our beliefs and standards of judgment are just as contextual and situational as those of those long-ago people we study.

Put simply, in this book I am offering a new way of thinking about the history of the just war idea, one that challenges many contemporary assumptions. Exploring what lies behind familiar expressions and concepts can help us see our world in a new light, loosening the apparent inevitability of the present's "hold on us by confronting us with the ways in which it is structured by unrecognized or willfully forgotten fictions."[20] My attempt to explain contemporary just war discourse and its all too frequent inability to serve as a serious brake on the recourse to war relies on what Foucault called a "genealogy" or "history" of the present.[21] Our understandings of contemporary just war criteria – and indeed the underlying principles themselves – are like any discourse "fabricated in piecemeal fashion" out of historical contingencies.[22] Recognizing that what appear to be "fixed oppositions" between concepts – in my case, between realism and just war thinking – are the result "of an established, rather than an inherent contrast" is the necessary first step to being able to rethink such theoretical arrangements.[23] In other words, my aim in revealing the pragmatism of past just war thinking is primarily to raise questions about our present.

---

[17] Carr, *What Is History?* 55.   [18] Ibid., 83.   [19] Ibid.

[20] Stephen K. White, *Political Theory and Postmodernism.* (Cambridge: Cambridge University Press, 1991), 27.

[21] Michel Foucault, *Discipline and Punish* (New York: Vintage Books, 1995), 22, 30.

[22] Michel Foucault, "Nietzsche, Geneaolgy, History," in Paul Rabinow, ed., *The Foucault Reader* (New York: Pantheon Books, 1984), 78.

[23] Helen Kinsella, *The Image before the Weapon: A Critical History of the Distinction between Combatant and Civilian* (Ithaca: Cornell University Press, 2011), 6.

ON TRADITIONS AND CANONS

Each of these just war stories spans a thousand years or more; the religious traditions from which they arose stretch back even farther. Of course, as Gaddis put it, "there's always a balance to be struck, though, for the more time the narrative covers, the less detail it can provide."[24] My attempt at striking such a balance is to concentrate only on the works of a handful of authors in each tradition. By focusing on these individuals' stories, rather than attempting to construct a systematic historical narrative, I follow Elshtain's lead, treating the just war discourse "as an authoritative tradition dotted with its own sacred texts."[25] When we work within a tradition, we study particular thinkers "to whom we have grown into the habit of paying attention." [26] Who we pay attention to is the product of historical circumstances: a mixture of chance, intellectual debate, and politics.

This approach relies on certain assumptions about the relationship between the canonical authors and their traditions, as well as the relationship between the canonical authors and their historical contexts. I presume that theorists reflect the norms and realities of their time. Partially, this is an unconscious reflex. Theorists are individuals, but human individuals are inherently social creatures. We can think our own thoughts, but at least some of our assumptions come from the society around us, as do most of our structures of logic and argument, and nearly all of our patterns of grammar and of course the very words themselves that we use to express all this.[27] Like jazz musicians, we can riff on the melody, within limits. Go too far, and we produce noise, not music. What is at stake is not so much a question of creativity or independence, but intelligibility.

Just war thinkers are historical personages, embedded in a time and place. Like us, they are shaped irrevocably by their social and political milieu. If this is true of humans in general, it is even more so for the just

---

[24] Gaddis, The Landscape of History, 14.

[25] Jean Bethke Elshtain, "Epilogue: Continuing Implications of the Just War Tradition," in Jean Bethke Elshtain, ed., *Just War Theory* (New York: New York University Press, 1992), 323.

[26] Pocock, *Political Thought and History*, 3.

[27] Consider, for example, Kwame Appiah's use of the "script" as a model for individuals' self-creation. We tell our own life stories, but the scripts that we can choose as models for our personal narratives are themselves social products. Kwame Appiah, *Ethics of Identity* (Princeton: Princeton University Press, 2005), 22.

war thinkers considered in this book's three historical chapters. They operate *within* a tradition of which they are keenly aware. Their canon's preexisting frameworks delineate what is considered ethical behavior (and what constitutes a good ethical argument).

Indeed, each tradition itself shapes what counts as an ethical problem in the first place. At first, this claim might seem a bit startling. We tend to assume that ethical problems simply emerge out of material realities. War, in this view, is a practical problem – it destroys lives and property, disrupts the ordinary flow of life, and places civilians, soldiers, and statesmen into unenviable moral quandaries. But so do criminals and natural disasters. In the West, we see war as occupying a fundamentally different ethical context than criminality and acts of nature. Hindu just war thinkers, by contrast, do not.[28] War as an *ethical* problem is socially constructed.

Just war thinkers operate *within* a tradition in the sense that they use preexisting ethical categories to address these problems. Indeed, the nature of what is perceived as a problem is itself framed by the tradition. In this sense, the just war principles in the various traditions behave something like symbols do for Geerz. The social meanings that are "stored" in these religious texts "are felt somehow to sum up, for those for whom they are resonant, what is known about the way the world is ... and the way one ought to behave while in it."[29] Because these texts combine explanatory and predictive theorizing, they "have an intrinsic double aspect: they give meaning ... to social and psychological reality both by shaping themselves to it and by shaping it to themselves."[30] Put differently, religious traditions provide a model that is replicated over time in a given society, from the level of the individual upward. The model is never – and can never – be reproduced exactly. Instead, the model works like a roadmap, offering a framework for moral choice. Some routes (moral options) may be blocked, but there is a dense network from which to choose.

But just war thinkers do not interact only with the world of ideas, whatever some may mutter about ivory towers. Following the pragmatic approach to religion and ethics, I presume that my subjects are "for the most part, rational agents, acting on what they take to be justified, true beliefs, in order to achieve goods, solve problems, and avoid

---

[28] See, for example, Torkel Brekke, "The Ethics of War and the Concept of War in India and Europe," *Numen* 52(1), 2005, 59–86.

[29] Clifford Geerz, *The Interpretation of Cultures* (New York: Basic Books, 1973), 127.

[30] Ibid., 93.

difficulties."[31] Morality serves an important function, fostering cooperation "among self-interested, competing, and conflicting persons and
groups."[32] Moral action guides have a *practical* purpose, prescribing
what constitutes appropriate behavior, as well as an *authoritative* component, establishing the language used to publicly justify behavior.[33]
Moral codes and religious codes have much in common. But while moral
action guides draw on what we might call secular reason – focusing on
what is good for human beings either as individuals or groups – religious
action guides are concerned with goods that transcend humanity. The
religious aspect of the Christian, Islamic, and Hindu just war traditions
means that our authorities will sometimes understand what is "good or
bad for human beings" in a very different way than a secular thinker
might, finding "in a supernatural order a whole extra dimension of
preeminently important gains and losses, benefits and harms."[34] This
does not mean that our authors cease to be historically grounded when
they invoke religious ends or justifications. It does mean, however, that
they may advocate pursuing ends – or using methods – that may differ
from what a secular political thinker might have considered.

Just as I assume just war thinkers are shaped by their traditions and
their historical contexts, I also assume that the works of certain authors
become canonical because they fit the needs of the time. In particular,
works that make it into the canon fit the needs of the dominant actors of
the age. This assumption is inspired by the neoliberal institutionalist claim
that hegemons develop institutions, such as norms, to meet their needs.
Norms are shared understandings about appropriate behavior. Successful
norms do not require actors to alter their identities or interests, but they
do serve to "constrain the behavior of states."[35]

Why might great powers care about establishing laws and norms?
They themselves don't seem to be particularly bound by them. Wouldn't
coercion be a quicker and easier way for great powers to get what they
want? Perhaps. Still, coercion is costly, and due to war's unpredictability,

---

[31] G. Scott Davis, *Believing and Acting: The Pragmatic Turn in Comparative Religion and
    Ethics* (Oxford: Oxford University Press, 2012), 175.
[32] David Little and Sumner B. Twiss, *Comparative Religious Ethics* (San Francisco: Harper
    & Row Publishers, 1978), 27. See also G. J. Warnock, *The Object of Morality* (London:
    Methuen, 1971), 26.
[33] Little and Twiss, *Comparative Religious Ethics*, 28–33.
[34] G. J. Warnock, *Contemporary Moral Philosophy* (London: Macmillan, 1967), 79. Cited
    in Little and Twiss, *Comparative Religious Ethics*, 68.
[35] Jeffery T. Checkel, "Norms, Institutions and National Identity in Contemporary
    Europe," *International Studies Quarterly* 43(1), 1999, 84.

it doesn't always work. True, some force (or threat of force) is inevitably required to assure compliance with laws and norms. Once the rules of the game are internalized, however, most of the players govern themselves most of the time. An initial investment in the creation of shared norms can lead to long-term payoffs for great powers, saving them blood and treasure in the end. Norms can do some of the heavy lifting, relieving the powerful from the burden of using coercion at every turn.

Although norms do not take the place of world government, broadly accepted norms do mitigate some of the pernicious effects of anarchy. A hegemon can ensconce itself in an international order that helps to reinforce its own power: "If it can establish international norms consistent with its society, it is less likely to have to change. If it can support institutions that make other states wish to channel or limit their activities in ways the dominant state prefers, it may be spared the costly exercise of coercive hard power."[36] While legitimacy bought through successful norm introduction is costly in the short run, "as a device of social control [it] has long-run efficiency advantages over coercion."[37]

Still, we should be quite clear – hegemons do not create norms because they are humane, or enlightened, or charitable. Hegemons create norms because norms reinforce their power. In other words, "norms themselves are dependent upon underlying power distributions."[38] A correlate of this is that when hegemons encourage the adoption of norms that suit their own interests, they do not necessarily intend to be bound by the norms themselves. To keep up appearances, they must pay lip service to the norms, which requires making plausible excuses for why they were obliged to violate the norms in some specific case or another. Weaker states may be punished by great powers for violating norms (by being excluded as rogue or pariah states, or by being subjected to an intervention or war). Great powers act as policemen, in a sense, but they themselves answer to no higher power. Thus, norms that are "actually obeyed and even enforced by almost everyone actually serve the powerful ... the strong support the norms because the norms support the strong."[39]

[36] Joseph S. Nye, Jr., "Soft Power," *Foreign Policy* 80, Autumn 1990, 153–171, 167.
[37] Ian Hurd, "Legitimacy and Authority in International Politics," *International Organization* 53(2), 1999, 379–408, 388.
[38] Checkel, "Norms, Institutions and National Identity in Contemporary Europe," 84.
[39] Robert Axelrod, "An Evolutionary Approach to Norms," *American Political Science Review* 80(4), 1986, 1095–1111. See also G. John Ikenberry and Charles A. Kupchan, "Socialization and Hegemonic Power," *International Organization* 44(3), 1990, 283–315.

JUST WAR THINKING AS NORMS OF POWER

The following chapters argue that the evolution of just war thinking in Christianity, Islam, and Hinduism can be read as a story of norm evolution, in which the norms reflect the interests of the great powers. The systemic variation within each tradition over centuries reflect changes in the political realities facing each society. While individuals' "cultural presuppositions" may direct their responses to various circumstances, "the worldly circumstances of human action are under no inevitable obligation to conform to the categories by which ... people perceive them. In the event they do not, the received categories are potentially revalued in practice, functionally redefined."[40] When the model does not fit the situation, depending on "the place of the received category in the cultural system ... and the interests that have been affected, the system itself is more or less altered. At the extreme, what began as reproduction ends as transformation."[41]

Changes in norms tend to be tied to changes in the distribution of power. New developments in military technology and organization and the emergence of new threats serve as exogenous shocks. These shocks "destabilize the prevailing wisdom, unsettle existing coalitions, and open the way for change."[42] The struggle between actors for dominance, whether within or between particular polities, also drives change.

Telling the complete story of the evolution of just war norms in three different religious traditions would require tomes. For example, contemporary Western just war thought formally relies on six or so *ad bellum* principles and two formal *in bello* principles. By the Middle Ages, just war thinking had come to coalesce around three key *ad bellum* principles. The decision about whether to go to war or not had to be made by a person possessing *legitimate authority* to do so, in the service of a *just cause* and motivated by a *right intention*. The three *ad bellum* prudential requirements, namely, *proportionality, likelihood of success*, and *last resort*, were added later.

Once the decision is made to go to war, Western just war thinking invokes two *in bello* principles to channel the use of force. *Proportionality*

---

[40] Marshall Sahlins, *Historical Metaphors and Mythical Realities: Structure of the Early History in the Sandwich Islands Kingdom* (Ann Arbor: University of Michigan Press, 2000), 67.

[41] Ibid.

[42] Deborah Avant, "From Mercenary to Citizen Armies: Explaining Change in the Practice of War," *International Organization* 54(1), 2000, 41–72, 42.

demands that the harms caused by any use of force must not outweigh the good end at which it is aimed. Traditionally, *discrimination* meant that innocents – persons who do not pose a threat – should not be harmed. (Revisionists now take the concept to mean that only persons liable to harm may be targeted, which leads to quite different interpretations.)

Furthermore, the broader discourse on just war thinking in the West – including Walzer's common sense approach and the more recent efforts of revisionists such as Rodin and McMahan – often draws on other moral concepts to better elucidate the content of these basic principles. The case is equally complex in the Islamic and Hindu traditions. To handle all of these principles and their corollaries in depth would simply be unwieldy.

And so, just as I have limited my story to a handful of influential thinkers in each tradition, I have likewise limited my analysis primarily to three particular just war principles that matter across all three traditions. Consequently, in the chapters that follow, I focus on two *ad bellum* issues: legitimate authority and just cause.[43] I also consider one *in bello* principle: discrimination, sometimes called noncombatant immunity. I treat discrimination quite broadly, to include concerns about protecting civilian property and appropriate treatment of prisoners of war.

ANALYZING JUST WAR THROUGH AN INTERNATIONAL RELATIONS LENS

A historian would approach this project quite differently, seeking to uncover the uniqueness of specific events and texts. As a political scientist, my aim is to emphasize the patterns in what we find.[44] Focusing on three broad trends as we explore these three basic just war principles across time and space can help us see the relationships between power and just war thinking more clearly. The power relationship between political and religious authorities, the degree of religious fractionalization within the state system, and the relative power of the just war thinker's state compared to other states are correlated with the type of just war principles that evolve. The sections that follow will consider each of these factors in turn.

---

[43] Just war thinking in the West draws a clear distinction between *ad bellum* questions, that deal with when to go to war, and *in bello* questions, that handle how war ought to be fought. Although this distinction is not made explicit in either Islamic or Hindu just war thinking, both types of issues are certainly addressed.

[44] In this I follow Levy's description of the role of political scientists. Jack S. Levy, "Too Important to Leave to the Other: History and Political Science in the Study of International Relations," *International Security* 22(1), 1997, 22–33.

Factor 1: Relationship between Political and Religious Authorities

First, the relationship between religious and political centers of power has a significant impact on the nature of just war thinking that emerges. Sometimes these relationships can be quite fraught, each party struggling for dominance and power in the domestic context. The Catholic Church's attempt to maintain the fiction of a Holy Roman Empire in Europe throughout the Middle Ages up through the early modern era is a case in point. Examples abound: Protestant churches in Catholic states prior to the peace of Westphalia, Shi'a *ulema* (religious scholars) in Sunni states, and even Sunni *ulema* of the wrong *madhab* (school) in the wrong place, or any religious thinker in a state that draws a bright line between the religious and political spheres. At other times, religious and political authorities interact cooperatively, in a mutually beneficial system. For much of history, such was the case between the English monarchy and the Church of England. (One could rather snarkily comment that that was precisely the point.) The Ottoman empire enjoyed such a relationship with its *ulema*, as did the Qajar dynasty in Iran. The Hindu model separating the spheres of responsibility of the kingly and priestly castes is also of this type. And at times, the boundaries between sacred and secular authority can blend, as in a theocracy. Calvin's Geneva approaches this model, as does the Umayyad caliphate and the early 'Abbasid caliphate.

I argue that more conflictual relationships between political and religious authorities generate a greater focus on *ad bellum* issues, while more cooperative ones tend to treat legitimate authority and just cause as settled, thus focusing more on just means. My claim is that just war theories serve as a mediator between the state, religion/theology, and external others. Although forcing just war traditions, which are an internally diverse lot, into boxes sacrifices conceptual richness for parsimony, I think it is important to the project of reimagining just war traditions to see them as political tools, capable of bridging the gap between (troublesome) state policies reflecting *realpolitik* concerns and norms about appropriate treatment of others.

Each tradition emphasizes different aspects of just war theory (either the *ad bellum* principles of just cause, or the *in bello* principle of just means/civilian immunity), depending on the political and theological needs of the society. I argue that the Christian just war tradition initially focused on just cause (especially self-defense), because of the peculiar conflict between secular state power and an essentially pacifistic religion. This tension made the question of whether it is ever possible to fight one of primary concern. Later, the focus shifts to just means, as the political environment of European warfare changed. Yet although just means become a more significant topic for authors from Aquinas onward, just cause – even today – still provokes the most commentary. Revisionist just war thinkers, for example, argue that without a just cause, there can be no possibility of acting justly *in bello*.

In early Islam, however, state and theology were not diametrically opposed, making the issue of just cause less problematic. Fighting to extend and defend the *dar al-Islam* was understood as much politically as religiously.[45] Still, at times when the Islamic polity was weaker than its neighbors, debates emerged as to what exactly the requirement to wage *jihad* entailed. While the discussion of what constitutes a just cause is not given much attention – and, in fact, is largely simply repeated from other sources – Islamic authors devoted considerable attention to establishing rules for how wars were to be fought, including protections of noncombatants, the treatment of prisoners of war, and the collection of booty.

In classical Hinduism, there is a clear separation between religious and political authority. And yet the tension between the two spheres does not appear as intense as it does in the Christian tradition. One might best understand the relationship between the two spheres as separate but generally cooperative. To be successful, a wise prince must follow the advice of his religious counselors – living a good and virtuous life is essential to achieving material success. Because political and religious powers were divided into different castes, a discussion of what could legitimate the prince's recourse to force was nevertheless important. Still, discussions of just cause did not entirely overshadow discussions of just means.

Thus, in these three traditions the relationship between religious and political power affects the choice to emphasize causes and means. The greater the tension, the greater the emphasis on causes, perhaps as a result

---

[45] In the modern context, there has also been a shift toward just cause, due again to a change in the nature of the political environment. In particular, the "secularization" of Islamic states in the modern era seems to generate the same tension between religion and politics as in the Christian world. On the one hand, fundamentalists claim that such a separation of religion and politics is impossible. On the other, liberal reformists argue that personal religious faith and state commitments to human rights and international law are indeed reconcilable. Consider, for example, the just war–related works of An-Na'im and Abu Sulayman, which recast *jihad* in nonaggressive terms fully compatible with international law. See Abdullahi An-Na'im, *Toward an Islamic Reformation* (Syracuse: Syracuse University Press, 1990), and 'AbdulHamid A. AbuSulayman, *Towards an Islamic Theory of International Relations: New Directions for Methodology and Thought* (Herndon, VA: International Institute of Islamic Thought, 1993).

of a desire to curtail state power. When relations are more amiable, just cause appears as a simpler issue, and *how* to fight becomes the focus. This relationship between sacred and secular authority is often – although not always – an issue that is internal to the state in which the just war thinker lives. The other two factors to consider, however, involve the relationship between the just war thinker's state and the international system. These factors seem to have an effect primarily on the degree to which the *in bello* rules place the onus of protection of civilians on the military.

Factor 2: Religious Fractionalization

Fractionalization in this context refers to the religious diversity of the international system, as that system is imagined by a particular author. The international system is, objectively speaking, made up of all the polities in existence at a particular time. Historically, however, just war thinkers have not always been conscious of the system as a whole, being aware of only their particular corner of it.

The key question, when thinking about fractionalization, is whether most of the religion's adherents live in a single polity, or whether they spread out across several polities. For example, before the collapse of Rome, most Christians lived within a single polity; with the split between Rome and Byzantium, they came to inhabit two (and later many more). Likewise, during the early Islamic caliphates, most Muslims lived (at least ostensibly) under a single authority, a fact that changed quite dramatically by the ninth century. Fractionalization gives us an idea of whether wars would be expected to occur among co-religionists, or against "others."

This factor has a greater impact on *in bello* issues. When the state system is united, and thus fighting occurs mostly against others, just war thinkers tend to have a very pragmatic attitude toward civilian protections. At best, certain classes of civilians should be protected, but only if it is convenient for the army's operations. Military necessity trumps civilian protections. On the other hand, a divided state system, with wars arising among co-religionist powers, is more likely to produce just war theories that are more protective of civilians, who are no longer seen so starkly as others. This shifts the onus of protection of civilians onto the military.

It is unsurprising that the degree to which warfare is understood to be an act carried out against members of an out-group, rather than a group more or less like one's own, affects what means are deemed permissible. After all, social distance has been identified as an important variable in determining the degree to which warfare is regulated. When cultural differences are minor, the "conduct of war will be more comprehensively subject to limiting rules," but is generally more brutal, "the more the parties concerned perceive each other as ideological foes."[46] The same has been found for civil wars, which tend to be bloodier where religious differences are involved.[47] Perhaps as a consequence of this tendency, just war thinkers concerned primarily with intracommunal conflict elaborate more precise and more restrictive *in bello* rules.

Factor 3: State Power

The relative power of the just war thinker's state is the third significant consideration. Is it relatively powerful and secure? Does it have the capability to expand? Or is it weak and in danger of occupation?

Just war thinkers in relatively powerful states or state systems express greater ambivalence about civilian protection, perhaps because their states are better able to protect their own compatriots. But thinkers in a weak state or system generate more specific protections, perhaps because they are more acutely aware of their own vulnerabilities. At first, this may seem counterintuitive. If we presume that powerful states also possess superior forces and technology, wouldn't they be better able to live up to a higher standard? This is the argument made by those contemporary just war thinkers who claim that the availability of precision technology and drones should make it possible for militaries to fight in ways that pose less of a risk to civilians in war.[48] But capability and willingness may be distinct. Domestic political concerns may pressure more capable states to seek to end wars more quickly, using maximum force.[49]

LAST THOUGHTS

In the following three chapters, I emphasize these three factors – the relationship between political and religious authorities, the degree of

[46] Daniel Frei, "The Regulation of Warfare: A Paradigm for the Legal Approach to the Control of International Conflict," *Journal of Conflict Resolution* 18(4), 1974, 620–633.

[47] Monica Duffy Toft, "Getting Religion? The Puzzling Case of Islam in Civil War," *International Security* 31(4), 2007, 97–131, 98.

[48] Ronald C. Arkin, *Governing Lethal Behavior in Autonomous Robots* (New York: Taylor and Francis, 2009), 29.

[49] Robert W. Tucker, *The Just War* (Baltimore: Johns Hopkins University Press, 1960), 21. Tucker argues that at least in the American case, the initial aversion to resorting to force in the first place is not coupled with restraint in how that force is employed.

religious fractionalization, and the relative power of the author's state – as a way of emphasizing the role of the political in shaping the ways in which just war thinking has evolved. My purpose in using these overarching frameworks to shape the stories we explore is not to suggest that this is the only way to read these histories.

I use this history as a way to question the present.[50] Historically, just war thinking has been the province people who have thought realistically about what is necessary. And, I would argue, it is exactly this underlying realism that has made just war thinking so durable across time and cultures. It is a political tradition that serves political ends. If my argument is right – if the history of just war thinking is the story of the development of a morally concerned realism – then we should think long and hard about what we expect of just war theory today.

[50] O'Driscoll, "Divisions within the Ranks?," 54.

4

Between Two Kingdoms

The Christian Just War Traditions

Understanding the Christian roots of the Western just war tradition is important for both the tradition's supporters and its critics. Some of the most thoughtful criticism of the tradition has come from Christian pacifists, who argue that the just war tradition has failed miserably in its attempt to speak truth to power.[1] Such thinkers point to the early days of the Church, invoking an ideal of neighborly love that precludes the use of force. Drawing on the New Testament, critics argue that those who embrace the just war tradition have strayed far from their roots, and what's more – they have little to show for it. If just war thinking is supposed to curb states' appetite for violence, why don't we see much improvement in state behavior despite centuries of development of just war thought?

The Western just war tradition's contemporary supporters also appeal to its history, albeit to different ends. Jean Bethke Elshtain uses Augustine to argue that our desire for peace should not be permitted to trump our responsibility to pursue justice.[2] James Turner Johnson and Cian O'Driscoll invoke the tradition to critique the underlying assumptions of some of the contemporary philosophical approaches to just war thinking – often termed the *revisionist approach* – and to suggest fresh ways of reimagining the old categories of thought.[3]

---

[1] Yoder, When War Is Unjust, 3–6. See also Stanley Hauerwas, "Should War Be Eliminated," in *The Hauerwas Reader*, John Berkman and Michael Cartwright, eds. (Raleigh, NC: Duke University Press, 2001), 410–417.

[2] Jean Bethke Elshtain, *Just War against Terror* (New York: Basic Books, 2003), 125.

[3] James Turner Johnson, "Thinking Historically about Just War," *Journal of Military Ethics* 8(3), 2009), 247. O'Driscoll, "Divisions within the Ranks?," 49.

This chapter explores the just war thinking of some of the traditions' greatest names: Augustine of Hippo, Thomas Aquinas, and Francisco de Vitoria. It also includes the early Protestant thinkers Martin Luther and John Calvin. As we turn our attention to each thinker in turn, I will highlight the similarities between their assumptions about human nature, the state, and the state system and those of the realists we have already met. The traditional just war thinkers have a rather dim view of human nature. Humans are social creatures, dependent on each other for survival, and yet tragically unable to cooperate peacefully. Political authority is both a necessity and a good. Without it, there would be no order and human existence would be miserable. These thinkers also draw parallels between the domestic and the international contexts. Just as force must be used domestically to uphold order, so too is it essential for the maintenance of even a minimal international order. Thus, the use of force internationally is justified not only by states' need to defend themselves, but also their roles as judges and police officers.

By placing each author in his historical context, I argue that these thinkers are deeply realist in another sense. They approach the problem of just war *pragmatically*. Rather than aiming to create an ideal theory of just war, they address specific problems that plague their contemporary world. This deliberate focus on real-world concerns means that Christian approaches to just war change in tandem with shifts in the international system, as well as changes in the domestic structure of states. Thus, a tradition that begins as pacifist in response to what it perceives to be a pagan state comes to accept war as an appropriate tool of statecraft. Likewise, the degree of emphasis placed on particular concerns – just cause, rebellion, civilian protections – reflects the political problems plaguing a particular time and place.

CHANGING RELATIONS TO STATE POWER: CHRISTIAN JUST WAR TRADITIONS

Christianity traces its roots to first-century Judea, an outpost of the Roman empire. When Jesus was born, the Romans had already occupied it for sixty years; the province of Judea was incorporated into the Roman empire by 6 CE. Although Jews at the time had considerable freedom of religion (which, among other things, excluded them from forced conscription into the military), they had little direct political influence. The loss of the state was still felt acutely – the New Testament contains numerous references to the popular expectation that if Jesus was indeed the awaited

Messiah, then a political revolution (the restoration of the Kingdom of Israel) should shortly be underway.

During Jesus' lifetime, the province was relatively stable, but undercurrents of dissent against Roman rule and fractionalization within the Jewish community ran deep. The execution of the disciple Simon as seditious zealot and Jesus' crucifixion between two zealots tell us something about the underlying insecurities of the age.[4] This instability only grew with time. Just thirty years after Jesus' death, the zealots led an uprising against the Roman occupiers, destroying the Roman garrison in Jerusalem, and establishing a provisional Jewish government. (Their success was short lived. By 70 CE, the Temple lay in ruins, and the Roman forces soon mopped up the last outposts of resistance.)

Despite the charged atmosphere, Jesus' message, although certainly not apolitical, did not presage the reestablishment of a Jewish state, nor did it lay out a clear political ideology or legal code for such a state. In fact, Jesus explicitly denied any desire for earthly power.[5] Instead, he described an ideal heavenly kingdom. The Gospels' authors suggest that Jesus' message was so revolutionary because it *spiritually* overthrows all earthly rulers, even if they remain *physically* in positions of power (which ought to be respected). His followers will be spiritually liberated, albeit still politically bound. Writing just a decade or so after the failed zealot rebellion, the author of the gospel of Luke emphasized Christians' loyalty to the Roman government. Aiming to distance Jesus from the zealots, he engaged in a bit of historical anachronism by portraying Jesus' family as willingly submitting to the Emperor Augustus' census in 6 CE.[6] (The zealots, after all, had refused to participate, sparking a brief rebellion in Judea.)[7]

Proclaiming themselves disarmed by Christ, early Christians denied posing a secessionist threat. The internal stability of the Roman state made the apostle Paul's missionary journeys across the Gentile world possible.[8] And although the Gospel message revolutionarily challenged

---

[4] Reuven Firestone, *Holy War in Judaism* (Oxford: Oxford University Press, 2012), 42.

[5] Consider for example Jesus' trial before Pilate, where he claims that his "kingdom does not belong to this world. If my kingdom did belong to this world, my attendants [would] be fighting to keep me from being handed over"; John 18:36.

[6] Paul W. Walasky, *'And So We Come to Rome' – The Political Perspective of St. Luke* (Cambridge: Cambridge University Press, 2005), 26. See also Allen Brent, *A Political History of Early Christianity* (London: T&T Clark International/Continuum, 2009), 172, 174.

[7] Firestone, *Holy War in Judaism*, 42.

[8] Bainton, *Christian Attitudes toward War and Peace*, 55.

prevailing class and ethnic norms, it explicitly ceded political authority to Rome. Thus, Paul writes:

Let every person be subordinate to the higher authorities, for there is no authority except from God, and those that exist have been established by God. Therefore, whoever resists authority opposes what God has appointed ... For rulers are not a cause of fear to good conduct, but to evil ... But if you do evil, be afraid, for it does not bear the sword without purpose; it is the servant of God to inflict wrath on the evildoer. Therefore, it is necessary to be subject not only because of the wrath but also because of the conscience. This is why you also pay taxes, for the authorities are ministers of God ... Pay to all their dues, taxes to whom taxes are due, toll to whom toll is due, respect to whom respect is due, honor to whom honor is due.[9]

In a similar vein, the author of Luke and Acts portrayed centurions – Roman citizens and military officers – favorably, respecting their political authority and their genuine interest in Jesus' message.[10] All in all, Luke's gospel seems aimed at promoting "an accord between the church and the state," or at the very least, opening the possibility of official toleration.[11]

For the next few centuries after Jesus' death, Christians imagined themselves as outside of earthly political concerns. They refused to serve in the military and to avail themselves of the civil legal system.[12] While the Roman government increasingly doubted such abstention was really apolitical, Christian theologians of the time insisted that opting out was not a form of political protest. Instead, they stressed their loyalty to the state. Consequently, Christian scholars counseled their flocks to patiently wait out this life, in expectation of the next. While this pacifism (coupled with a refusal to participate in emperor worship) frustrated the Romans, it also shielded the sect from an even harsher political crackdown – such as that which befell the Jews, who were exiled from Judea by 73 CE.[13]

---

[9] Romans 13:1–7.   [10] Walasky, '*And So We Come to Rome,*' 31.

[11] Ibid., 35, and Brent, *A Political History of Early Christianity.*

[12] Paul encouraged Christians to settle disputes among themselves, rather than turning to the courts in I Corinthians 6:1–11.

[13] On an interesting side note, in exile most Jewish diaspora scholars also upheld a strict pacifist position, reinterpreting the events of both the Great Revolt in 66 CE and the earlier Maccabean Revolt in 167 BCE in spiritual, rather than political, terms (see Firestone, *Holy War in Judaism*). This shift to pacifism supports my claim that political contingencies shape religiously inspired thinking about war. While Old Testament history is replete with wars fought by the Israelites, and explicit rules of war are found in Numbers and Deuteronomy, later scholars opted for a pacifistic stance. The difference between these two sets of authors is not faith, but politics: the loss of the state of Israel.

Later, the Talmud did develop two categories of war, based on the Old Testament histories (namely, "commanded wars" and "optional wars"), but "the regulations on war in the Talmud and the Medieval codes were purely theoretical, with no practical application."

After all, while Nero's persecution of Christians captured the attention of Roman and Christian commentators alike (and resulted in the execution of Paul himself in 67 or 68 CE), it was limited in both time and geographical scope.

And so, the community of Christians – viewed skeptically by Jews and Romans alike – continued to grow. But despite the expanding membership, there is little evidence of Christian participation in the Roman military prior to 170 CE, apart from Cornelius (baptized by Peter at Caesarea around 40 CE) and the jailor (baptized by Paul at Philippi around 49 CE).[14] From that time onward, references to Christians in the military increase. It has been wisely observed, however, "the lack of references to enlistment proves there is a lack of references to enlistment – nothing more."[15] The lack of mention of Christian soldiers could imply that it was taken for granted that Christians should abstain from military service, but it could just as well imply that military service was so commonplace that it warranted no mention.[16] After all, during a battle against invading barbarians in blistering summer heat along the Danube, soldiers of the Twelfth Legion knelt in prayer. Twenty years later, Tertullian credited Christian soldiers with bringing forth the thunderstorm that refreshed the Romans and terrified the enemy; pagan accounts from the time credit an Egyptian magician, pagan gods, and the emperor himself.[17]

The early Church fathers were virtually silent on the issue of military service. Only Tertullian and Origen discuss the issue of Christian military participation at length. Both men wrote as the Church was facing increasing

See Robert Gordis, *Judaic Ethics for a Lawless World* (New York: Jewish Theological Seminary of America, 1986), 173. Lacking a state, Jewish scholars did not develop a military ethic of statecraft. Instead "their very powerlessness reinforced the lessons of Talmudic tradition: that they should despise violence and war, love mercy and justice." See Stuart Gottlieb, "Judaism, Israel and Conscientious Objection," *Christian Century*, September 3, 1969, 1136. The Talmud instead urged pacifism and patient suffering. Consider the following Talmudic declarations: "If someone should say to the kill, or I will kill thee, it is better that thou should be killed" and "One should always be one of the persecuted rather than of the persecutors." See Arthur Meyerowitz, *Social Ethics of the Jews* (New York: Bloch Publishing Company, 1935), 26, 51.

[14] Cecil John Cadoux, *The Early Christian Attitude to War* (New York: Seabury Press, 1982), 97.

[15] John Helgeland, "Christians and the Roman Army AD 173–337," *Church History* 43(2), 1974, 150. See also James J. Megivern, "Early Christianity and Military Service," *Perspectives in Religious Studies* 12(3), 1985.

[16] Éric Rébullard, *Christians and their Many Identities in Late Antiquity, North Africa, 200–450 CE* (Ithaca: Cornell University Press, 2012), 29.

[17] J. Daryl Charles and Timothy J. Demy, *War, Peace, and Christianity* (Wheaton, IL: Crossway, 2010), 111.

pressure from the Roman government. From 180 to 197, there were only "scattered incidents of persecution," at least in North Africa, which both Tertullian and Origen called home.[18] Much of the harassment of Christians at this time came not from imperial authorities, but from local leaders and townspeople, who tended to blame Christians for every public disaster. As Tertullian put it, "If the Tiber rises to the walls, if the Nile does not rise to the fields ... if there is an earthquake, a famine, a plague, immediately the cry arises, 'The Christians to the lion!'"[19] After 197, officially sanctioned persecution increased, and both Tertullian and Origen encouraged the Christian community to stay the course, even if it meant death.

In the face of such social and political pressures, both authors strove to portray Christians as loyal Romans. In many ways, Tertullian and Origen were exactly the sort of "good Romans" their works described. Tertullian, born in Carthage, was the son of a centurion, converting to Christianity only in adulthood. Origen, by contrast, was just sixteen when his father died a martyr under Septimius Severus. That his father was beheaded suggests that he was a Roman citizen, or at least a man of high social standing – decapitation was considered less painful and less humiliating than other common forms of capital punishment, including crucifixion.[20] Origen himself managed to obtain an audience with the imperial court to plead for the emperor's mother to intervene to settle an intra-church dispute over his ordination in his favor.[21] Despite unflagging efforts to court the ruling class, Origen was imprisoned and tortured under Decius, during the "first truly universal" persecution.[22]

Despite these personal hardships, both men valued the order and security the empire provided. Tertullian supported "the legitimate and necessary function of the state and its rulers," positioning himself as "a pacifist but not a separatist."[23] He accorded the Roman state the "right of the sword," arguing that "by fear of vengeance ... all iniquity is restrained."[24] When the Roman authorities suppressed Christianity out of fear of dissent,

---

[18] Rébullard, *Christians in Their Many Identities*, 36.

[19] Tertullian, *Apologeticum*, 40.1, in ibid., 37.

[20] Elizabeth DePalma Digeser, *A Threat to Public Piety: Christians, Platonists, and the Great Persecution* (Ithaca: Cornell University Press, 2012), 51. See also Henri Crouzel, *Origen* (San Francisco: Harper & Row, 1989), 5.

[21] Digeser, *A Threat to Public Piety*, 67.   [22] Crouzel, *Origen*, 34.

[23] Lisa Sowle Cahill, *Love Your Enemies: Discipleship, Pacifism, and Just War Theory* (Minneapolis: Augsburg Fortress, 1994), 48.

[24] Lester L. Field, *Liberty, Dominion, and the Two Swords: On the Origins of Western Political Theology* (South Bend, IN: University of Notre Dame Press, 1998), 47. Tertullian, *Five Books against Marcion*, IV.XVI.

Tertullian did not criticize those who imprisoned or killed Christians on the grounds that the policy was unjust. Instead, he chided the judges for failing to maintain "order and the punishment of disorder" and for being unable to constrain "violence within the empire."[25]

Regardless of its imperfections, Christians had good reason to hope that the Roman empire would last. The Roman government – through its military – kept the roads and seas safe for domestic travel and the barbarians at bay. Travel, not coincidentally, was crucial to the Christian mission. Origen credits the peace established by Augustus' imperial reach for creating the environment in which Jesus' message could spread "through the whole world."[26] And Origen himself traveled far afield, visiting Rome, Antioch, and Caesarea seeking the favor of powerful imperial family members.[27] Unsurprisingly for one who benefited from Roman public security, Origen saw in "the Roman peace a providential provision for the dissemination of the gospel," and so he "did not wish to see the empire overthrown."[28] Tertullian, too, valued the security of Rome:

There is another and a greater need for us to pray for the emperor, and indeed, for the whole estate of the Empire and the interests of Rome. For we know that the great upheaval which hangs over the whole earth, and the very end of all things, threatening terrible woes, is only delayed by the respite granted to the Roman Empire. Because we would not experience these things, we favor Rome's long continuance.[29]

Christians thus had "a clear ruling to be subject in all obedience, according to the Apostles' command, to magistrates and princes and those in authority; but within the limits of Christian discipline, that is, so long as we keep ourselves free of idolatry."[30]

Therein lay the catch. Participation in military service – or any administrative office, including teaching school – was synonymous with idolatry. Teachers were required to teach pagan texts; administrators were expected to lead sacrifices, preside over festivals, take oaths, and try criminals on

---

[25] David A. Lopez, *Separatist Christianity: Spirit and Matter in the Early Church Fathers* (Baltimore: Johns Hopkins University Press, 2004), 20.

[26] Origen, *Contra Celsum*, trans. Henry Chadwick (Cambridge: Cambridge University Press, 1953), §30.92.

[27] Digeser, *A Threat to Public Piety*, 62, 66–68. Crouzel, *Origen*, 14, 17.

[28] Bainton, *Christian Attitudes toward War and Peace*, 75.

[29] Tertullian, *Apologia*, c. 32, cited in Karl Frederick Morrison, "Rome and the City of God: An Essay on the Constitutional Relationships of Empire and Church in the Fourth Century," *Transactions of the American Philosophical Society* 54(1), 1964, 12.

[30] Tertullian, *On Idolatry*, §15, in S. L. Greenslade, trans. and ed., *Early Latin Theology: Selections from Tertullian, Cyprian, Ambrose and Jerome, vol. 5* (Philadelphia: Westminster Press, 1956), 101.

capital charges.[31] Soldiers were compelled "to offer sacrifices or impose capital sentences."[32] How could a soldier "make war, indeed how will he serve in peacetime, without a sword – which the Lord took away?"[33] Could "a Christian, taught to turn the other cheek when struck unjustly, guard prisoners in chains, and administer torture and capital punishment?"[34] Tertullian concludes that as no man can serve two masters, soldiers must immediately leave military service upon becoming a Christian. Origen took a slightly different approach. Believing each Christian to be a member of the priesthood, he reminded his pagan audience that their own priests were not expected to fight, so as to remain "undefiled."[35] Christians, he argued, comprised a "special army of piety," more than doing their part by praying to God "for those who fight in a righteous cause and for the empire who reigns righteously."[36]

Tertullian's prohibition on military service hinged not on the moral dangers of violence, but on the problem of idolatry. Origen argued Christians' special role in working for the salvation of mankind meant that their energies were better spent on the divine than the political.[37] Yet while both Tertullian and Origen forbade Christians to shed blood, they never denied the right of the Roman state to make war. On the contrary, they emphasized the good Roman order provided. They even claimed that Christians were good citizens who assisted the empire's war efforts through their commercial activities and prayers. Arguably, Tertullian and Origen had the luxury of ceding the defense of Rome to others, because there were more than enough non-Christians available to fill the military's ranks.[38] The survival of the Roman state did not depend on their small community. In contemporary realist terms, they had the luxury of buck-passing.

AUGUSTINE: THE KINGDOM OF GOD AND THE CITY OF ROME

By the time of Augustine, the situation had changed. International stability and order could no longer be taken for granted. The century

---

[31] Tertullian, *On Idolatry* (§10, §15) in Greenslade, *Early Latin Theology*, 92, 102.
[32] Ibid., §19, 105.   [33] Ibid.
[34] Tertullian, *The Chaplet* (§2), in Rudolph Arbesmann, Sister Emily Joseph Daly, and Edwin A. Quain, trans., *Tertullian: Disciplinary, Moral and Ascetical Works* (New York: Fathers of the Church, 1955), 255.
[35] Origen, *Contra Celsum*, §73, 509.   [36] Ibid.   [37] Ibid. §74, 510.
[38] Robert Emmet Meagher makes a similar argument in *Killing from the Inside Out: Moral Injury and Just War* (Eugene, OR: Cascade Books, 2014), 65–66.

between Tertullian and Augustine was characterized by "great instability on the Empire's borders."[39] Germanic tribes pressed in from the north. Parthian forces, from today's Iran, advanced into the empire's eastern territories. This external instability was intimately tied to the political instability within the Roman empire itself. In the third century, regime change was frequent and almost always involved assassination. Not surprisingly, imperial policy aimed to restore domestic unity. A united front, in this case, linked political and religious concerns. The shared practice of religion – namely, sacrifices to the empire's gods – was deemed to be useful not only in pleasing the gods (who might then protect Rome) but also in binding together the empire's peoples (who might then not revolt).[40] Political contingency and religious conviction thus overlapped.[41] Growing Christian populations, particularly in North Africa where in some towns they may have already been in the majority, came to be seen as more of a threat – and a convenient scapegoat. Christians under the Emperor Decius, for example, were required to offer sacrifices to Rome's gods – and to provide certificates from witnesses testifying to their faithful participation. Some Christians went through with it, treating it as a necessity akin to paying taxes. Others paid servants or friends to do it for them. But those who refused were punished with death.

By Augustine's time, however, the relationship between Christianity and Rome had changed dramatically. No longer a persecuted sect, Christianity had become the religion of the realm. Constantine's conversion and the subsequent Edict of Milan offered official toleration of Christianity; Theodosius would declare it to be the state religion.[42] Christians now received "public recognition and protection that were wholly unanticipated by the earlier pacifist theologians."[43] The early converts had mostly been simple folk who could not even have dreamt of holding the reins of power. These new converts *already* held them. This put them in the difficult position of needing to reconcile their earthly role with their spiritual beliefs. By the late fourth century, Christian service

---

[39] Morwenna Ludlow, *The Early Church* (New York: Palgrave Macmillan, 2009), 98.
[40] Ibid., 99.   [41] Ibid., 103.
[42] The distinction is significant. While Constantine regarded Christianity as a "favored cult," he tolerated other religions within the empire and still served as the head of the pagan Roman religion; Theodosius ended state support for Roman paganism entirely and made the Nicene version of Christianity the "true religion over 'all peoples which the government ... rules.'" Morrison, "Rome and the City of God," 20.
[43] Cahill, *Love Your Enemies*, 69.

to the state in professions ranging from soldier to judge to emperor had come to be seen as permissible. Yet actually serving such functions was still seen as inherently involving sin.[44] Late fourth- and early fifth-century Christian writers remained concerned about the shedding of blood, just as Origen had been. Consequently, Christians "sullied by the sins of public affairs" had to perform public penance if they wished to return "to the pristine innocence of their postbaptismal state."[45]

Augustine was writing in a Christianized empire, in which service to the state was understood to be permissible, and yet tainted. But Augustine's concern with preserving order – no doubt colored by Rome's ongoing insecurity – led him to take the radical step of denying that service to the state inherently involved sin, even if that service involved killing.[46] In Augustine's day, cross-border raids were frequent, and the peoples to the Empire's north and east were growing more restive. Pushed westward by the rise of the Huns even farther east, Germanic tribes sought to resettle within the territory of Rome. In 378 the Roman army attempted to confront the Visigoths in the Balkans, but instead found itself defeated, its emperor killed in battle. For the next thirty years, the Romans struggled unsuccessfully to bring the German threat under control. Germanic tribes flooded over the Rhine and into the Roman Empire during the harsh winter of 406, and just four years later, Alaric the Visigoth sacked Rome.[47] Refugees seeking out the comparative peace and security of North Africa carried the shock of the hitherto unimaginable thought of barbarians sacking the empire's heart to Augustine's ears. But Hippo's sanctuary was soon to be shattered. The Vandals swept across France, carving out a new kingdom in Spain, invading North Africa shortly before Augustine's death. As Augustine lay on his deathbed, Hippo itself was under siege.

---

[44] Philip Wynn, *Augustine on War and Military Service* (Minneapolis: Fortress Press, 2013), Kindle version, chapter 3.

[45] Ibid.

[46] Ibid., chapter 6. Wynn convincingly argues that "few principles appear more often in his works ... or seem more fundamental to his thinking" than order.

[47] Ludlow, *The Early Church*, 181. The irony of Alaric's story bears mentioning. While he went down in history as a barbarian invader, Alaric was actually a disgruntled commander of a barbarian force allied to Rome, comprising largely Arian Christians (as soldiers tended to follow the religion of their commanders). While Roman Christians saw Arians as heretics, one has to wonder if this distinction mattered much to Augustine's pagan compatriots. For a discussion of Alaric's turbulent career, see Guy Hastell, *Barbarian Migrations and the Roman West, 376–568* (Cambridge: Cambridge University Press, 2007).

If Rome were to survive, it would need all hands on deck. The recent past had made it clear that Rome's enemies were more than willing to exploit her internal divisions. Pagans could not turn their back on their civic duties to spite their newly Christianized ruling elite. But even more importantly, the newly Christianized ruling elite would need to step up and defend the state against its enemies at home and abroad.

Augustine wrote *The City of God* to deal with these concerns. Begun just three years after the sack of Rome by Alaric and the Goths, *The City of God* was his reply to those who "blamed the Christian religion for the disaster and began to blaspheme the true God more sharply and bitterly than usual."[48] Critics of Christianity saw "the mishaps of their own time" as unique and causally related to the prohibition on pagan worship; Augustine was "therefore bound to prove that the facts were very different, from the evidence of the books in which their own authors ... recorded the history of the past."[49] Early in his career, Augustine had understood history to be the story of progress – an idea borrowed from his pagan Roman predecessors. In this view, Rome had a key role to play in sacred history. By becoming the world's first Christian empire, Rome was setting the stage for the establishment of God's kingdom on earth. Had things gone differently, Augustine might have been seen as the father of liberalism, rather than realism.

But the events of 410 shook this worldview to its core. Sacred history was now confined to the scriptures, and the rest of history became "starkly secular."[50] Rome's success (or failure) was no longer to be seen as the result of God's favor (or disdain), and was certainly not to be read as the tale of God's *response* to the particular virtues (or lack thereof) of Rome's citizens. Witnessing the changing fortunes of Rome, Augustine came to believe that the accomplishment of God's purposes did "not stand or fall with the fate of Rome, or indeed, with the fate of any particular earthly society."[51]

Augustine held a similarly tragic view of mankind, believing that the Fall had left man scarred, corrupted, and bent on sinning. This translated into a tragic view of politics in the international arena. Man's corrupted

---

[48] Augustine of Hippo, *Retractations*, II.43, in Ernest L. Fortin, Roland Gunn, and Douglas Kries, eds., *Augustine: Political Writings* (Indianapolis: Hackett, 1994), 1. See also Augustine, *City of God*, IV.1, 135.

[49] Augustine, *City of God*, IV.1, 135.

[50] Robert A. Markus, *Saeculum: History and Society in the Theology of St. Augustine* (Cambridge: Cambridge University Press, 1988), 43.

[51] Ibid., 53.

nature leads him to crave power for the sake of dominating others, a twisted desire that distracts him even from seeking what passes as true glory in human terms: the "good opinion of enlightened judges."[52] Rare is the ideal statesman who seeks to rule for the good of the city. Individual corruption generates tyrants; state-level corruption produces empires seeking aggrandizement. Thus, the earthly city desires "victories and an earthly peace, not with a loving concern for others, but with lust for domination over them."[53]

War, under such circumstances, is inevitable. "The earthly city is generally divided against itself by litigation, by wars, by battles, by the pursuit of victories that bring death with them or at best are doomed to death," Augustine writes, "for it will not be able to lord it permanently over those whom it has been able to subdue victoriously."[54] Considering the vast reaches of the empire, Augustine describes the security dilemma that Rome's own success has generated. Might not Rome have been better off as a more moderately sized state? "Why must an empire be deprived of peace, in order that it may be great? In regards to men's bodies, it is surely better to be of moderate size, and to be healthy, than to reach the immense stature of a giant at the cost of unending disorder."[55] Is Rome the collective equivalent of the human glutton with an insatiable appetite, bringing about its own downfall?

Augustine quotes the historian Sallust in response: "as soon as [the Romans'] power advanced, thanks to their laws, their moral standards, and the increase of their territory, and they were observed to be very flourishing and very powerful, then, as generally happens in human history, prosperity gave rise to envy."[56] And envy motivated barbarian invasions. In response to such external threats, Augustine argues that "obviously the Romans had a just excuse for undertaking ... those great wars. When they were subjected to unprovoked attacks by their enemies, they were forced to resist not by lust for glory in men's eyes but by the necessity to defend their life and liberty."[57] In Augustine's estimation, Rome's expansion was driven as much by the pursuit of security as it was by a desire for greatness. In modern parlance, we might call him a defensive realist.

Because of the security dilemma, Augustine reasoned, war is inevitable and necessary – a fact of life for the earthly city. But if Christians were meant to be mere wayfarers through the earthly city on their way to the heavenly one, what role could they legitimately play in all of this? After

[52] Augustine, *City of God*, V.19, 212.   [53] Ibid., XV.7, 604.   [54] Ibid., XV.4, 599.
[55] Ibid., III.10, 97.   [56] Ibid., III.10, 98.   [57] Ibid.

all, Tertullian and Origen certainly permitted pagan Roman authorities to go on maintaining domestic order and defending the empire against outside threats, while denying that Christians themselves had any business assisting them. Although Christian participation in the secular sphere was given by Augustine's time, some pacifists still claimed that the New Testament message of love and redemption rendered violence impermissible and meant Christians should abstain from killing.

In response to such concerns, Augustine turns the idea of neighbor-love on its head. Love could explain how the use of force could be permitted – and, indeed, might even be at times desirable – within a Christian community. For Augustine, the use of force could express love in two ways. First, love generated a responsibility to protect. While defense of one's self was impermissible, because one's natural instinct for self-preservation could too easily be mixed with anger and hatred, defense of one's neighbor was not only permissible, but perhaps even a duty. Thus, a selfless intent to serve others could justify the use of force.

Love could also be expressed in a second, less intuitive way. Force could be used not only to restrain someone engaged in harm, but also to punish him or her. A good Christian ought to look out for his or her neighbor's best interests, not out of a sense of moral superiority, but out of true, selfless love for the other. So great is the virtuous man's "righteousness ... that he loves even his enemies; and such is his love even for those who hate and disparage him, that he wishes them to be reformed so that he may have them as fellow citizens, not of the earthly city, but of the heavenly."[58]

Love requires action: punishing and reforming the wayward other. In Augustine's terms, "the duty of anyone who would be blameless includes not only doing no harm to anyone but also restraining a man from sin or punishing his sin, so that either the man who is chastised may be corrected by his experience, or others may be deterred by his example."[59] Here, too, the intent is not to harm, but to reform. Hence, the wise judge does not act "though a will to do harm," or a desire for vengeance, but rather with the aim of "healing the wounds of sin."[60] He acts out of a "certain benevolent harshness," correcting wrongdoers as a father corrects his son.[61]

---

[58] Ibid., V.19, 212.   [59] Ibid., XIX.16, 876.

[60] Ibid., XIX.6, 860. Augustine, "Letter 133, to Marcellinus," in Fortin et al., *Augustine: Political Writings*, 246.

[61] Augustine, "Letter 138, to Marcellinus," in Fortin et al., *Augustine: Political Writings*, 209. Indeed, Augustine returned frequency to the image of the loving father punishing with the rod, including in *Sermones* 13.9 and *De Sermone Domini in Monte* I, 20 (63). See Wynn, *Augustine on War and Military Service*, chapter 6.

This is not, of course, love operating at its most ideal. Instead, when Augustine imagines love operating this way through corporeal or capital punishments – or through war – he sees it as love operating in the realm of necessity:

In view of this darkness that attends the life of human society, will our wise man take his seat on the judge's bench, or will he not have the heart to do so? Obviously, he will sit; for the claims of human society constrain him and draw him to this duty; and it is unthinkable to him that he should shirk it.[62]

The tragedy of necessity is that even a good judge will – out of ignorance – occasionally torture and even execute the innocent. The guilty will sometimes get away. But "all these serious evils our philosopher does not reckon as sins; for the wise judge does not act in this way through a will to do harm, but because ignorance is unavoidable – and yet the exigencies of human society make judgment also unavoidable."[63] For Augustine, this unavoidable necessity is "a mark of human wretchedness," part of the tragedy of human relationships after the Fall.[64]

Augustine sees soldiers, like judges, filling positions made necessary by the weakness of human nature. To argue for the moral legitimacy of such work, Augustine argues directly against Origen and Tertullian. There is nothing in the Gospels that disarms *all* soldiers; the various centurions Jesus encounters are not required "to throw down their arms and quit the military completely."[65] Instead, they are told not to terrorize anyone. Likewise, Augustine reassures his correspondent Boniface, the governor of the Roman province of Africa, that it is not "impossible for anyone serving in the military to please God."[66] Instead, Boniface should strive to "be a peacemaker, then, even by fighting, so that through [his] victory [he] might bring those whom [he defeats] to the advantages of peace."[67] Clearly, what is important for Augustine is not the outward act of killing, but rather the inward intention: "Let necessity slay the warring foe, not your will."[68]

Furthermore, the soldier, like the judge, is carrying out the law – a law made necessary by fallen man's corrupted will. Thus, for Augustine,

one who owes a duty of obedience to the giver of the command does not himself "kill" – he is an instrument, a sword in its user's hand. For this reason, the commandment was not broken by those who have aged wars on the authority

[62] Augustine, *City of God*, 860. XIX.6, 860.   [63] Ibid.   [64] Ibid.

[65] Augustine, Luke 3:14, in "Letter 138, to Marcellinus," in Fortin et al., *Augustine: Political Writings*, 209.

[66] Augustine. "Letter 189, to Boniface," in Fortin et al., *Augustine: Political Writings*, 219.

[67] Ibid., 220.   [68] Ibid.

of God, or those who have imposed the death penalty on criminals when repre-
senting the authority of the State in accordance with the laws of the State, the
justest and most reasonable source of power.[69]

Here we come to the next step in Augustine's argument. Augustine's claim
about the compatibility of love and punishment hinges on the idea that
the judge, the executioner, and the soldier are acting *on God's command*.
But Augustine does not claim that such individuals act on direct orders
from heaven. Instead, those serving the state have presumptive authority
to use force because God has created the institution of the state.

Although the earthly city is far from perfect, it serves an essential role.
Paraphrasing Cicero, Augustine describes a republic as the "affair of
a people," a "multitude of human beings joined in a certain bond of
concord."[70] The fact that the state creates order – an essential good – is
not lost on Augustine. "It would be incorrect to say that the goods which
this city desires are not goods, since even that city is better, in its own
human way, by their possession," Augustine explains; "for example, that
city desires an earthly peace, for the sake of the lowest goods; and it is that
peace which it longs to attain by making war."[71] To create earthly order,
the state seeks to ensure "a kind of compromise between human wills
about the things relevant to mortal life," a sort of "harmonious agreement
of citizens concerning the giving and obeying of orders."[72] The goods the
earthly city can provide – order, security, and human justice – "are goods
and undoubtedly they are gifts of God."[73] Thus, "even the Heavenly City
in her pilgrimage here on earth makes use of the earthly peace and defends
and seeks the compromise between human wills in respect of the provisions
relevant to the mortal nature of man."[74]

Because the goods the earthly city provides are decidedly human,
Augustine draws a bright line between secular and religious authority.[75]
The exact nature of these earthly institutions does not matter to Augustine,
as long as they present "no hindrance" to the practice of the true faith.[76]
The religious, moral, and personal attributes of the leader are relatively
unimportant. Given the brevity of "this mortal life ... what does it matter
under whose rule a man lives ... provided that the rulers do not force him

---

[69] Augustine, *City of God*, I.21, 32.
[70] Augustine, "Letter 138, to Marcellinus," in Fortin et al., *Augustine: Political Writings*, 206.
[71] Augustine, *City of God*, XV.4, 599.   [72] Ibid., XIX.17, 877.   [73] Ibid., XV.4, 600.
[74] Ibid., XIX.17, 878.   [75] Markus, *Saeculum*, 71.
[76] Augustine, *City of God*, XIX.17, 878.

to impious and wicked acts?"[77] Because God instituted *all* authority, Augustine argues, Christian soldiers did the right thing in following the military commands of a wicked emperor (while ignoring his orders to worship idols), thus making "a distinction between their eternal and their temporal lord."[78]

Augustine even finds some moral qualities in the state, at least in Rome itself. In the *City of God* he aims to "show for what moral qualities in the Romans, and for what ends, the true God ... deigned to assist the growth of the Roman Empire."[79] His argument here is twofold. First, the Christian God uses Rome for good (a novel concept for once persecuted Christians). Second, Rome's old pagan gods were not behind Rome's past successes. If Rome is generally a good realm (an implication woven throughout the text), then God will bless it with territory and stability, for "it is beneficial that the good should extend their dominion far and wide, and that their reign should endure ... This is for the benefit of all, of the subjects even more than the rulers."[80] After all, even when Rome was pagan, "these conquerors" suffered a great deal, and holding a high "regard for such virtues" they deserved the glory they won; "therefore the citizens of so great a country should not suppose that they have achieved anything of note if, to attain that country [the City of God], they have ... endured some ills, seeing that those Romans did so much and suffered so much for the earthly country they already possessed."[81] Rome – despite its imperfections – is the best chance for a virtuous *earthly* community, and as such warrants protection.

The responsibility for preserving the city falls to its leaders, who have the authority to wage war. For Augustine, "the natural order, which is suited to the peace of mortal things, requires that the authority and deliberation for undertaking war be under the control of a leader."[82] Indeed, Augustine emphasized that one of the key defining characteristics of a just war was that it be initiated and led by "the good," who find that their duty demands that they inflict punishment on wrongdoers.[83] After all, for Augustine one of the duties that a king owes not only his people

---

[77] Ibid., V.17, 205.
[78] See also Augustine, *Enarrationes in Psalmos*, 124.7, in Wynn, *Augustine on War and Military Service*, chapter 7.
[79] Augustine, *City of God*, IV.2, 137.   [80] Ibid., IV.3, 138.   [81] Ibid., V.17, 206–207.
[82] Augustine, *Against Faustus the Manichaen*, XXII. 73–79, in Fortin et al., *Augustine: Political Writings*, 222.
[83] Ibid., 74, in Fortin et al., *Augustine: Political Writings*, 222.

but his God is "sanctioning with suitable vigor laws that enjoin just behavior and prohibit its opposite."[84]

The emphasis that Augustine places on the right of the ruler to wage war is made clear by his recommendation that soldiers should not worry too much about whether or not the king has a just cause. Instead, Augustine suggests that

a just man, if he should happen to serve as a soldier under a human king who is sacrilegious, could rightly wage war at the king's command, maintain the order of civic peace, for what he is commanded to do is not contrary to the sure precepts of God, or else it is not sure whether it is or not. In this latter case, perhaps the iniquity of giving orders will make the king guilty while the rank of a servant in the civil order will show the soldier to be innocent.[85]

Augustine's willingness to encourage Christians to serve even under a dubious leader differentiates him from both Tertullian and Origen. While they, too, valued earthly order, they held Christian purity as a higher good. For Augustine, living in such tumultuous times, purity seems to come second to maintaining order.

What Augustine understood to be a just cause can be teased out from his discussion of the value of the earthly city. If the earthly city is a good because it provides the civil order necessary for human flourishing, then defense of that city must also be a good. War is just when it punishes a wrong against the city, whether that be an invasion by a foreign power or an uprising from within. Simply put, it is "the injustice of the opposing side that lays on the wise man the duty of waging wars," in Augustine's view.[86]

Just as right intent undergirds Augustine's justification of domestic judgment and punishment, it also points to the way in which war should be carried out. For Augustine, the problem with war is not that involved death and killing – how can it be a problem "that those who will die someday are killed so that those who will conquer might dominate in peace?"[87] Instead, the real tragedy is "the desire for harming, the cruelty

---

[84] *Epistolae* 185.19, in Wynn, *Augustine on War and Military Service*, chapter 7.

[85] Augustine, *Against Faustus the Manichaen*, XXII. 73–79, in Fortin et al., *Augustine: Political Writings*, 223.

[86] Augustine, *City of God*, XIX.7, 862. This formulation of just cause as a response to a wrong is following Cicero. Augustine reiterates the same point elsewhere, in *Quaestions in Heptateuchum*, 6.10 (see Wynn, *Augustine on War and Military Service* chapter 7).

[87] Augustine, *Against Faustus the Manichaen*, XXII, 73–79, in Fortin et al., *Augustine: Political Writings*, 221.

of revenge, the restless and implacable mind, the savageness of revolting, the lust for dominating, and similar things" brought about by war.[88]

This translates into the idea that war should be conducted with restraint. Augustine argues that "if this earthly republic kept the Christian precepts, wars themselves would not be waged without benevolence, so that, for the sake of the peaceful union of piety and justice, the welfare of the conquered would be more readily considered."[89] Because the good of the other must always be at the forefront of the soldier's mind, Augustine asserts that just as "violence is returned to one who rebels and resists, so should mercy be to one who has been conquered or captured, especially when there is no fear of a disturbance of peace."[90] After all, "it is an established fact that peace is the desired end of war."[91] To this end, tactics that would undermine future reconciliation cannot be employed. Augustine has little to say about specific *in bello* restrictions on the use of force. He does counsel Boniface, however, that "when fidelity is promised it must be kept, even to an enemy against whom war is being waged."[92] If peace is the end goal, acts that harden the heart are counterproductive.

Another example of Augustine's thinking about *in bello* restraint comes across in his discussion of the sack of Rome by Alaric and his men. These "barbarians" (some of whom were Germanic Christians) respected the sanctuary of the churches. Those who sheltered there, including pagan Romans, were spared. To Augustine, this reveals God's mercy, which "even in the midst of the horrors of war ... bestowed through the name of Christ ... consolations foreign to the normal usage of war, granted to good and bad alike."[93]

Although the contemporary principle of civilian immunity can be read back into Augustine's account, the lack of specificity regarding the conduct of war suggests that his main concern lies in the *ad bellum* problem of justifying the recourse to force in the first place. This makes a great deal of sense, given the political context. The need to legitimize the use of force by the newly Christianized Rome for its own defense seems to have superseded any concerns Augustine may have had about how that force would be used in practice.

---

[88] Ibid.

[89] Augustine, "Letter 138, to Marcellinus," in Fortin et al., *Augustine: Political Writings*, 209.

[90] Augustine, "Letter 189, to Boniface," in Fortin et al., *Augustine: Political Writings*, 220.

[91] Augustine, *City of God*, XIX.12, 866.

[92] Augustine, "Letter 189, to Boniface," in Fortin et al., *Augustine: Political Writings*, 220.

[93] Augustine, *City of God*, IV.2, 137.

Aquinas: The Roman Empire Recast

Nearly one thousand years of dramatic political change separate Augustine from Aquinas. Rome fell and Christendom splintered, yet the *ideal* of a unified Christian world remained. Political entities of various types and sizes jostled with each other for greater influence. The feudal system remained the dominant form of political organization, and as a result, would-be heads of state (and the Church itself) were dependent on armies provided by their inferiors – lesser princes, dukes, and barons – who were plenty busy fighting among themselves. Domestic rebellion was a perennial problem, as were inter-European wars. Islamic and Mongol powers also threatened the edges of the European sphere of influence.

In contrast to earlier periods, religious and temporal authority were increasingly concentrated in separate hands. At the end of the eleventh century, Pope Gregory VII had declared the Church to be politically and legally independent of all earthly authority, a revolutionary change from Augustine's era when the spiritual and secular realms had overlapped, "with emperors calling Church councils and promulgating new theological doctrine, and with archbishops, bishops and priests being invested by emperors, kings, and lords."[94] And yet, "to the medieval Christian mind, the public welfare did not immediately indicate a sphere independent of religious considerations; right ordering of social life included its subordination to the divine intention."[95] Thus, political struggles were happening on three planes: between church and state over temporal jurisdiction, between various states over physical jurisdictions, and within states, between petty princes and the growing power of kings.

Emblematic of the times, the titanic conflict between Pope Gregory IX and the Holy Roman Emperor Frederick II spiraled across Europe and into the Levant. Having inherited both the Holy Roman Empire and Sicily, Frederick dreamed of a Mediterranean empire. Aquinas's eldest brother joined Frederick on his Crusade to recover Jerusalem in 1228.[96] (Taken prisoner on the way home, he was ransomed by the Pope, to whom he thereafter remained loyal.)[97]

---

[94] Harold J. Berman. "The Influence of Christianity upon the Development of Law," *Oklahoma Law Review* 12, 1959, 86–101, 92.

[95] Cahill, *Love Your Enemies*, 91.

[96] David Decosimo, *Ethics as a Work of Charity: Thomas Aquinas and Pagan Virtue* (Stanford, CA: Stanford University Press, 2014), 34.

[97] Jean-Pierre Torrell, *Saint Thomas Aquinas, Volume I: The Person and His Work*, trans. Robert Royal (Washington, DC: Catholic University of America, 2005), 3.

While Frederick celebrated his victory, the Pope's forces invaded his Italian lands. Frederick promptly regained control of his territory and pushed back, seeking to unify large portions of Italy. Aquinas's father and older brothers served as knights in Frederick's forces. Over the course of twenty some years of war, Frederick won several significant victories in the North, and even threatened Rome itself in 1240. He also helped the Teutonic Knights relocate from the Holy Land to Poland, and encouraged them to launch the Prussian crusades – ostensibly to bring Christianity to the pagan Balts, but also to reinforce his eastern frontier.[98] Frederick interpreted his own policies as not merely political, but theological, and urged other secular princes to join him in his campaign to return the church to the spiritual sphere.[99] For obvious reasons, the Pope was *not* pleased, and Frederick was excommunicated not once, but three times.

While Frederick championed secular power, his contemporary and competitor, the French king Louis IX, earned sainthood for his crusades. In 1248 Louis attempted to exploit the instability caused by the death of the Ayyubid sultan by launching a crusade against Egypt, but his army lost and he was taken prisoner. After being ransomed, Louis spent four years visiting the Frankish kingdoms in today's Israel, investing his personal funds in the construction of new defenses and engaging in diplomacy with the Islamic rulers of Syria and Egypt, as well as the Mongols, who represented a rising threat. In 1270, shortly before Aquinas's death, Louis launched one final crusade. Most of his ships never arrived, and the king died (along with most of his army) from dysentery.

Of Aquinas himself, little is known. His father was a minor noble in the Sicilian lands of Emperor Frederick II.[100] His family was no stranger to international politics, and all his brothers pursued military careers. As the youngest son, Thomas could expect no inheritance, and so "he was destined for the highest ecclesiastical office that diplomatically cultivated connections in the right quarters and an appropriate education could buy."[101] Thus, in 1229, at the age of five, his parents installed him at the Benedictine abbey of Monte Cassino, where his uncle was abbot. The Benedictines were well-established, conservative, and wealthy – "fully integrated into the systems of power and patronage of the Middle

[98] Eric Christiansen, *The Northern Crusades* (London: Penguin Books, 1998), 83, 109.
[99] Brian Tierney, *The Crisis of Church and State 1050–1300* (Toronto: University of Toronto Press, 1988), 142, 145.
[100] Bernard McGinn, *Thomas Aquinas' Summa Theologiae: A Biography* (Princeton: Princeton University Press, 2014), 17.
[101] Denys Turner, *Thomas Aquinas: A Portrait* (New Haven: Yale University Press, 2013), 9.

Ages."[102] Thomas's parents had done their best to ensure their youngest son a chance at a comfortable and influential position. If he played his cards right, he might even become Abbot one day.

But politics intervened. Monte Cassino became the latest flashpoint in the rivalry between the Pope and Frederick II. Shortly before the abbey was occupied by the emperor's forces in 1239, Aquinas's worried parents withdrew the fourteen-year-old and sent him to study at the University of Naples.[103] Recently founded by Frederick II – for the purpose of generating a cohort of lawyers to argue in his defense – it was the first secular university in Europe, and the first to permit the study of Greek, Hebrew, and Arabic texts.[104] At university, Aquinas readily partook of the liberal arts curriculum, focusing in particular on Aristotle, whose work had recently been reintroduced to the West by Jewish and Muslim scholars.[105]

And then, Aquinas met the Dominicans. Unlike the Benedictines, the Dominicans were a new order – and poor. Even worse, they had the wrong politics – they supported the Pope, rather than Frederick.[106] Thomas's family was shocked. His mother scurried to Naples to make Thomas see sense. On discovering that he had already fled the city with his new Dominican brothers, she organized her other sons into a raiding party. They intercepted Thomas and effectively placed him under house arrest at his family castle at Roccasecca.[107] When their desperate entreaties – including sending a naked prostitute to his room – failed to deter him from his commitment to the Dominicans, his family at last relented.

Thomas went on to the University of Paris in 1245. That same year, his second oldest brother shifted allegiances and joined a conspiracy against Frederick II, for which he was executed.[108] At Paris, Aquinas continued to study Aristotelian ethics, but he also read the Islamic scholars Avicenna (ibn Sina) and Averroes (ibn Rushd), as well as the Jewish philosopher Maimonides. By 1256, Aquinas – now tall, corpulent, balding, and prone to "disappear into fits of abstraction" – had become a master himself at the University of Paris.[109] (That Thomas was apt to lose track of the world around him is unsurprising, giving his prodigious scholarly output.)

---

[102] Ibid., 10.
[103] Thomas Aquinas, *On Evil*, ed. Richard J. Regan and Brian Davies (Oxford: Oxford University Press, 2003).
[104] McGinn, Thomas Aquinas' Summa Theologiae, 18.
[105] Decosimo, *Ethics as a Work of Charity*, 19.   [106] Torrell, *Saint Thomas Aquinas*, 3.
[107] Turner, *Thomas Aquinas*, 12.   [108] Torrell, *Saint Thomas Aquinas*, 3.
[109] Turner, *Thomas Aquinas*, 35.

Over the next decade, he taught at various Italian Dominican institutions training preachers, before returning to Paris as a professor for the
second time in 1269. The *Summa Theologiae*, for which he is most
famous, dates to this period and was likely composed to serve as a
textbook for his students.[110] In 1272 he was ordered to Naples to
establish a school of theology. A year later, in December 1273, Thomas
would experience a mysterious vision – and, afterwards, never put pen to
paper again. He would be dead by spring.

At first glance, Aquinas's views on war seem to be a restatement of
Augustine in the style of Gratian, a "resynthesis of previous works."[111]
But Aquinas's rediscovery of Aristotle leads him to reread the tradition in
a radically new way. Augustine's view of humankind after the Fall was
dark and pessimistic. What humble goods the earthly city offered were
mere shadows of the true goods to come in the next life. The state did
serve a purpose – providing a modicum of order so as to minimize human
suffering in this life – but the very fact that man needed a state was a sign
of how far he had fallen.

Aquinas, on the other hand, embraced Aristotle, recovering some of the
more optimistic aspects of Greek political theory.[112] "Man," cribbed
Aquinas, "is by nature a social and political animal, who lives in a community."[113] Aquinas argued that Augustine had treated dominion, or the idea
that "man is subject to man" in a political community, as something
"introduced as a punishment for sin."[114] But for Aquinas, political dominion in which a leader directs "a free subject ... either towards his own
good, or towards the common good" could have existed in the state of
innocence, before the Fall.[115] Because man "is by nature a social animal,"
even in the state of innocence he would have led a social life – which by
definition requires "someone who is to look to the common good."[116]
Individual interests and the common good do not always overlap, and so
without a king to organize men's diverse interests toward a common end
"the community would break up into its various parts."[117]

---

[110] Brian Davies, *Thomas Aquinas on Good and Evil* (Oxford: Oxford University Press,
2011), 12.
[111] Richard Shelly Hartigan, *The Forgotten Victim: A History of the Civilian* (Chicago:
Precedent Publishing, 1982), 40. See also Frederick Russell, *The Just War in the Middle
Ages* (Cambridge: Cambridge University Press, 1975), 264.
[112] Tierney, *The Crisis of Church and State*, 165.
[113] Aquinas, De regimine principum I.1, in Dyson, Aquinas: Political Writings, 5–6.
[114] Aquinas, *Summa theologiae* Ia 96, art. 4, ob. 2, in Dyson, *Aquinas*, 3.
[115] Ibid., Ia 96, art. 4, responsio, in Dyson, *Aquinas*, 4.   [116] Ibid.
[117] Aquinas, *De regimine principum*. I.1, in Dyson, *Aquinas*, 7.

The state is thus necessary for Aquinas, but in a different sense than it had been for Augustine. Man's distance from God did not make the state necessary. Instead, it is necessary *because of man's social nature.* Here Aquinas appeals to reason, using a nautical analogy. Every ship needs a captain, for "a group of men in a boat cannot pull together as one unit unless they are in some measure united."[118] If the job of a captain is to guide the ship to safe harbor, the role of the king is to preserve the unity of a community for its "good and wellbeing."[119] For Aquinas, peace is the result of such unity.

In Aquinas's time, political communities came in many forms. Aquinas accords special attention to kings, or those who rule a "perfect community."[120] Perfection, in this sense, has nothing to do with quality. Instead, Aquinas understands perfection as completion. A perfect community is self-sufficient "in all the necessaries of life."[121] A sovereign state is dependent on no external power.

Because sovereign states are no one's subjects, each state has a "need for common defense and mutual assistance against enemies."[122] Thus, "it pertains to the duty of government to protect what is governed."[123] Kings, therefore, have the authority to punish domestic criminals and to wage wars. Tellingly, when Aquinas lays out the three requirements for a just war in the *Summa Theologiae*, the very first is right authority, followed by just cause and right intent. Aquinas is adamant that "it does not pertain to a private person to declare war, because he can prosecute his rights at the tribunal of his superior; similarly, it does not pertain to a private person to summon the people together, which must be done in time of war."[124] For a private individual to use or organize the use of force for his or her own ends undermines the unity of the community, and is therefore unacceptable. The prince however, is entrusted with the "care of the commonwealth" and has no higher authority from whom to demand justice. It is lawful for him to use the sword both "in defense of the commonwealth against those who trouble it from within," and "to protect the commonwealth against enemies from without."[125]

In his very explanation of just authority, Aquinas identifies both internal and external threats to the state. Unlike some contemporary

---

[118] Ibid., I.1 and I.3, in Dyson, *Aquinas*, 5, 11.   [119] Ibid., I.3, in Dyson, *Aquinas*, 10.

[120] Ibid., I.2, in Dyson, *Aquinas*, 10.

[121] Ibid., I.2, in Dyson, *Aquinas*, 9. Aquinas is drawing here on Aristotle's *Politics*, I:2.

[122] Ibid., I.2, in Dyson, *Aquinas*, 10.

[123] Ibid., I.14, in Dyson, *Aquinas*, 37. See also Aquinas, *Summa Theologiae*, IIaIIae 40, responsio, in Dyson, *Aquinas*, 240.

[124] Aquinas, *Summa theologiae*, IIaIIae 40, in Dyson, *Aquinas*, 240.   [125] Ibid.

Western just war thinkers who draw a bright line between the use of force domestically and internationally, Aquinas treats both as two sides of the same coin. Domestically, force can be used to punish criminals and suppress rebellion. After all, at times "some people are negligent in carrying out the duties which the commonwealth requires," and they may "even damage the peace of the community when they transgress against justice and disturb the peace of others."[126] The king must therefore establish a domestic system of laws, courts, and punishments to maintain order.

Maintaining order goes beyond punishing common criminals to preventing and suppressing rebellion. The topic concerned Aquinas enough that he dealt with it in four different works, ranging from the first to the last of his writings. Indeed, during his lifetime Sicily was affected by several small-scale rebellions (and much grumbling over Frederick II's high taxes); one of his brothers was executed for his role in a conspiracy against the emperor.[127] Over time, Aquinas presents a "bleaker and bleaker gaze on rebellion."[128] While he acknowledged that tyrannical rule was unjust, he felt that efforts to resist or overthrow that rule often led to greater injustices. In the *Summa Theologiae*, he argues that tyranny is unjust, and that "disruption of such a government therefore does not have the character of sedition, unless perhaps the tyrant's rule is disrupted so inordinately that the community subject to it suffers greater detriment from the ensuing disorder than it did from the tyrannical government itself."[129] If the leader in question were not a tyrant, then sedition would be a "mortal sin," because it is "contrary to the common good of the community."[130] A leader had the right to use force to put down any rebellion.[131]

External threats also legitimated the use of force. "When the peace is undone by the invasion of enemies," Aquinas argued, "it is the king's task to furnish the community subject to him with protection against enemies; for taking measures against internal perils will bring no benefit if it is not possible for it to be defended against external ones."[132] Just cause for war

---

[126] Aquinas, *De regimine principum*, I.16, in Dyson, *Aquinas*, 44.

[127] David Abulafia, *Frederick II: A Medieval Emperor* (Oxford: Oxford University Press, 1992), 377.

[128] Thomas A. Fay, "Thomas Aquinas on the Justification of Revolution," *History of European Ideas* 16(4–6), 1993, 501.

[129] Aquinas, *Summa Theologiae*, IIaIIae42, art. 2, ad 3, in Dyson, *Aquinas*, 250.

[130] Ibid.   [131] Ibid, IIaIIae40, art. 1, responsio, in Dyson, *Aquinas*, 240.

[132] Aquinas, *De regimine principum*, I.16, in Dyson, *Aquinas*, 44.

requires that "those against whom war is to be waged must deserve to have war waged against them because of some wrongdoing."[133] Aquinas cites Augustine to explain that "a just war is ... one which avenges injuries, as when a nation or state deserves to be punished because it has neglected either to put right the wrongs done by its people or to restore what it has unjustly seized."[134] This turns war into a form of extended lawsuit, much as the ancient Greeks and Romans understood it.

Although a modern reader may be tempted to read self-defense into the phrase "what it has unjustly seized," two words of caution are in order. First, the phrase itself has a broader meaning, encompassing, for example, the seizure of merchant shipping or naval vessels in a foreign harbor. Second, and more significantly, although a defensive war would be justified in Aquinas's eyes, it would be legitimate not because of its defensive nature, but instead because it was *righting a wrong*. Thus, the permission to fight a defensive war arises from the king's responsibility to protect the commonwealth, rather than from a right to self-defense.[135]

Aquinas does rule out one potential just cause – the use of force to spread the faith. This was a bold statement in a world where popes and secular kings alike engaged in crusades – not only in the Mediterranean region, but also in the Baltics – motivated by faith, glory, and economics. For Aquinas, belief cannot logically be compelled because faith is an internal act of the will. But Aquinas's views here are subtle. While denying the right to use force to compel belief, Aquinas nonetheless encourages resistance against unbelievers who would actively persecute the faith:

These are in no way to be compelled into the faith ... for belief is an act of will. If the means to do so are present, however, they should be coerced by the faithful lest they hinder the faith by blasphemies or evil persuasions, or, indeed, by open persecutions. And it is for this reason that Christ's faithful frequently wage war against unbelievers: not, certainly, to coerce them to believe, for even if they were to conquer them and take them captive they should still leave them the liberty to believe if they wish; but to prevent them from hindering the faith of Christ.[136]

Specifically, he argues that Christian territories should be defended against incursions by non-Christian powers. The dominion over believers by unbelievers "established for the first time" (i.e., through conquest) "should not by any means be permitted, because it would give scandal

---

[133] Aquinas, *Summa Theologiae*, IIaIIae40, responsio, in Dyson, *Aquinas*, 240.
[134] Ibid.
[135] James Turner Johnson, *Sovereignty: Moral and Historical Perspectives* (Washington, DC: Georgetown University Press), 32.
[136] Aquinas, *Summa Theologiae*, IIaIIae10, art. 8, responsio, in Dyson, *Aquinas*, 268.

and imperil the faith."[137] But if the non-Christian authority already rules, then it may continue, for dominion is an institution of natural law. In this, Aquinas can be read as more of a defensive than an offensive realist. He is willing to permit defense of the existing boundaries for the sake of the survival of the polity, but not to allow preventive or expansionary war to create ostensibly safer boundaries.

For Aquinas, the third requirement for a just war is right intention. The correct intent is righteous, "to promote a good cause or avert an evil."[138] It is theoretically possible for a prince to have a just cause, but for the war to be "rendered unlawful by a wicked intent," such as a lust for domination or a desire for revenge.[139] We can only guess what Aquinas would have said about Frederick's unending wars and crusades, but it seems quite unlikely that he would have approved.

Aquinas's lack of comment on the conduct of war itself is somewhat perplexing. For Augustine, the oversight could be explained by his primary concern with a systematic justification of the Christian resort to force in the first place. But Aquinas had no need to justify Christian rule (which was taken for granted in Europe), nor to legitimate the use of war by Christians – pacifism as a moral alternative had been relegated to a few small religious communities, and was not endorsed by the Church.[140] Even the question of whether Christian polities could rightfully wage war against each other had been settled nearly two hundred years earlier, during the Investiture Conflict.[141]

There are several potential explanations for Aquinas's apparent lack of interest in the problem of just conduct. One is that he followed his sources, Augustine and Aristotle, so closely that the issue did not occur to him. After all, Aristotle is concerned only with cause.[142] As we have seen, Augustine, too, focused on cause. But this answer is less than satisfactory. If the *Summa Theologiae* was meant to provide practical guidance to preachers facing tough questions from their congregants, why wouldn't Aquinas expect the problem of killing in war to come up?[143]

---

[137] Ibid., IIaIIae 10, art. 10, responsio, in Dyson, *Aquinas*, 207.
[138] Ibid., IIaIIae 10, art. 10, responsio, in Dyson, *Aquinas*, 240.   [139] Ibid.
[140] Keith Haines, "Attitudes and Impediments to Pacifism in Medieval Europe," *Journal of Medieval History* 7, 1981, 369–388.
[141] Joseph R. Strayer, *On the Medieval Origins of the Modern State* (Princeton: Princeton University Press, 2005), 22.
[142] By contrast, Plato does mention the idea that Greeks ought not to burn the homes and fields of fellow Greeks during war.
[143] Aquinas wrote the *Summa Theologiae* in Rome, at the request of his Dominican superiors, who were concerned with the low standard of theological training. See Turner, *Thomas Aquinas*, 25.

A second possible response is that Aquinas didn't feel the need to comment on a subject already well covered by the existing secular and sacred literature. Some three hundred years earlier, the Peace of God and the Truce of God movements had incorporated the old Germanic rules of chivalry into Church proclamations. These rules made it clear that women, children, and unarmed peasants were not to be harmed during war. Fighting was also to be avoided on certain feast days and Sundays. Indeed, these rules even became part of canon law at the Second Lateran Council in 1123.

This explanation, too, is only partially satisfactory. While Aquinas skips over the issue of noncombatant protections, he does take up two specific points about *in bello* conduct. The first is the problem of fighting on holy days. Drawing a parallel between the ruler and a doctor – who must of course care for sick people whenever they need him – Aquinas declares that it is "lawful to wage just war on holy days, provided only that it is necessary to do so."[144] Preserving the "health of the commonwealth – to prevent the slaughter of many and innumerable other ills both temporal and spiritual" – makes acting in its defense an inexorable necessity.

The second *in bello* concern that Aquinas handles directly, ambushes, is also colored by necessity. While Augustine had declared that faith must be kept even with one's enemies, Aquinas suggests that an important distinction can be made between deliberate attempts to deceive and failure to reveal one's hostile intentions. While lying or breaking covenants is never permissible, "someone may be deceived by what we say or do because we do not reveal our thoughts or intentions to him."[145] Thus ambushes are not deception – hiding something from others is "the art of concealment" and not akin to dishonesty.[146]

A third possibility for Aquinas' relative silence on *in bello* matters is that Aquinas felt that a soldier acting with right intent would naturally show restraint.[147] If the correct motivation for killing in war is to protect the commonwealth and restore peace, then brutality toward noncombatants would be not only unnecessary, but counterproductive. The fact that Aquinas takes up the problem of killing the innocent in his discussion of homicide, rather than war, adds weight to this possibility. Aquinas unequivocally rules out the intentional killing of the innocent as

---

[144] Aquinas, *Summa Theologiae*, IIaIIae 40, art. 4, responsio, in Dyson, *Aquinas*, 247.
[145] Ibid., *Summa Theologiae*, IIaIIae 40, art. 3, responsio, in Dyson, *Aquinas*, 246.
[146] Ibid., in Dyson, *Aquinas*, 246.
[147] James Turner Johnson, *Ideology, Reason, and the Limitation of War: Religious and Secular Concepts, 1200–1740* (Princeton: Princeton University Press, 1975), 40.

unlawful.[148] Aquinas's concerns in this section are explicitly murder and the imposition of capital punishment. But by extension, the killing of noncombatants in war would also fall under the category of killing the innocent. This is not a great leap to make, as Aquinas justified the recourse to war and the imposition of justice through the courts on the same basis – the defense of the commonwealth.

Further evidence for this possibility can be found in Aquinas's analysis of self-defense, embedded in his discussion of homicide. Augustine had forbidden killing out of self-defense. But Aquinas claims that Augustine misunderstood the nature of the intent involved in the act. Drawing on Aristotle, Aquinas argues that all living beings naturally seek to survive. Self-defense is thus a natural, and permissible, instinct. It becomes problematic only when other intentions cloud the act. Thus, Aquinas concludes that "if a man uses more violence in self-defense than is necessary, this will be unlawful, whereas if he repels force with force in moderation, his defense will be lawful."[149]

Aquinas's justification of personal self-defense hinges on a new loophole, the principle of double effect. Since an act derives its moral nature from its intent, if it has two (or more) results, only the intended one matters.[150] Later scholars took this to mean that if civilians are killed in consequence of an act whose intent was to target military personnel then the action is not morally culpable. While this view is often attributed to Aquinas, he never tied double effect to his discussion of warfare at all, invoking it only in the case of individual self-defense. The idea took on a life of its own, however, as we shall see in the work of Vitoria.

FRANCISCO DE VITORIA: TAKING STOCK OF A BROADER WORLD

The two hundred years after Aquinas's death were a period of rapid change in Europe. States as we know them in the modern sense had emerged in England, France, and Spain. Kings were developing sources of power independent of their nobles, seeking to consolidate their domestic power. The Italian Wars, a series of struggles for control over the prosperous Italian states of Milan and Naples, were the background of Vitoria's life. The first Italian War began in 1494, when he was just ten, and they continued with short periods of truce even after his death in

---

[148] Aquinas, *Summa Theologiae*, IIaIIae 64, art. 6, in Dyson, *Aquinas*, 261–262.
[149] Ibid., IIaIIae 64, art. 7, responsio, in Dyson, *Aquinas*, 264.   [150] Ibid.

1546. The external parties to these wars read like a who's-who list of European powers: England, Scotland, France, Spain, the Holy Roman Empire, and the Papal States. The Ottoman Empire was involved, too, allying with the French and even invading Hungary.

The old feudal economic order had also begun to fade. Serfs were becoming free peasants – whether *de facto* or *de jure* – and with their newfound economic might came political power. Mercantile trade bustled in the rapidly growing cities, marking the dawn of modern capitalism. European merchants' trade connections stretched as far as Asia, and the drive to corner the market on trade goods motivated a sudden burst of sea-faring exploration. Vitoria was born in Spain around 1485, just a few years before Christopher Columbus made landfall in the Americas. This event dramatically changed Spain's fortunes in ways that Vitoria could not fail to notice. Indeed, Vitoria penned *On the American Indians* in 1539 to expresses concern that the Spanish conquest "may have gone beyond the permissible bounds of justice and religion,"[151] contending that Spanish rule in the Americas must be "for the benefit and good of the barbarians, and not merely for the profit of the Spaniards."[152] Central to his argument was the claim that the peoples of the new world were true and full subjects of the king, entitled to equal benefits and protection. Despite Vitoria's critique of imperial policy, Charles V, King of Spain and Holy Roman Emperor, frequently consulted him on questions of colonial and foreign policy.[153]

Public religion took on new political overtones at the end of the fifteenth century, foreshadowing the emergence of modern nationalism. Domestic political order began to be seen again – as it had in Roman times – as dependent upon a unity of religious belief. Spain's new political theology, for example, linked Catholic belief with the nation and the state. The Spanish monarchs Ferdinand and Isabella instituted the Spanish Inquisition in 1478, creating their own institutions to suppress Jews and Muslims (and *conversos*, or converts) and, later, Protestants. The idea of the Inquisition was not new, but the medieval version had been firmly under the control of the Pope. In Spain, however, the Inquisitor General was appointed by the crown. The Alhambra Decree, ordering

---

[151] Francsico de Vitoria, "On the American Indian," 3.2, in Anthony Padgen and Jeremy Lawrance, eds., *Political Writings* (Cambridge: Cambridge University Press, 2003), 286.

[152] Ibid., 3.8, 291.

[153] James Brown Scott, *The Spanish Origin of International Law: Francisco de Vitoria and His Law of Nations* (Oxford: Clarendon Press, 1934), 85–86.

the expulsion of Jews from Spain, was issued in 1492, and the most intense period of persecution lasted until the 1530s. Vitoria himself participated in a meeting of the Inquisition in 1527, called as an expert to discuss the orthodoxy of the writings of Erasmus, whose *Handbook of a Christian Knight* had recently been translated into Spanish.[154]

In this highly charged context, it is not surprising that Vitoria looks for religious justifications for Spanish foreign policy. What is more interesting is that he consistently reminds his readers that conquest cannot be justified in the name of religion *alone*. Conquest can be legitimate to rescue people from tyranny (even against their will) or because a people wrongfully persecutes Christian missionaries – but it cannot be justified for the sake of spreading religion. Indeed, Vitoria's resistance to the dominant political theology of the time may stem not only from his cosmopolitan reading of the Christian tradition, but also from his personal background. While little is known about Vitoria's youth, he seems to come from *converso* Jewish parentage.[155]

The influence of the Protestant Reformation on Vitoria is also great. Vitoria emerged as one of the leading Dominican figures in the Counter-Reformation. Interestingly, Vitoria entered the Dominican order at the monastery of San Pablo, Burgos, the same year that Luther became an Augustinian in Erfurt. After four years in the monastery at Burgos, Vitoria was sent first to the Collège de Saint-Jacques, and later to the University of Paris – Aquinas's old alma mater – where he spent thirteen years studying and teaching.[156] In 1523, he returned to Spain, assuming the Prime Chair of Theology at the University of Salamanca in 1526. He died, as did Luther, in 1546.

Vitoria's response to this age of rapid change, religious strife and great power wars is conservative. Like Aquinas, Vitoria invokes Aristotle, identifying man as a social animal. For Augustine, it was man's willful sinfulness after the Fall that made the institution of the state necessary. But for Vitoria the cause lies in nature. Some creatures have been given thick furs, fleet feet, and powerful jaws, but "to mankind Nature gave

---

[154] Anthony Pagden, Introduction to Vitoria, *Political Writings*, xxx.

[155] Bruce Rosenstock, "Against the Pagans: Alonso de Cartagena, Francisco de Vitoria, and *Converso* Political Theology," in Amy Aronson-Friedman and Gregory Kaplan, eds., *Marginal Voices: Studies in Converso Literature of Medieval and Golden Age Spain* (Boston: Brill, 2012). See also Salo Wittmayer Baron, *A Social and Religious History of the Jews: Late Middle Ages and the Era of European Expansion, 1200–1650* (New York: Columbia University Press, 1970), 80.

[156] Pagden, Introduction to Vitoria, *Political Writings*, xxix.

'only reason and virtue', leaving him otherwise frail, weak, helpless and vulnerable, destitute of all defence and lacking in all things."[157] This weakness propels man into relationships, both to acquire necessities and also out of a real need for fellowship.

The family may be the first institution to provide for our physical and social needs, but for Vitoria, "the city is ... the most natural community, the one which is most conformable to nature."[158] After all, even a large family is not "whole and self-sufficient, especially in defence against violent attack."[159] Vitoria claims that the "origin of human cities and commonwealths was not a human invention or contrivance ... but a device implanted by Nature in man for his own safety and survival."[160] The city, therefore, is by definition necessary *for the purpose of defense.* Without a city, there can be no order, and without order, mankind suffers.

For Vitoria, the need for a polity generates the need for a "public power," that is, for political authority. Human societies "cannot exist without some overseeing power or governing force."[161] In terms very similar to those used by Aquinas, he argues that any body needs a head to direct its various members. Without a political head, each individual in the city would strive "against the other citizens for his own advantage to the neglect of the common good."[162] This, for Vitoria is "the final cause, and the most potent, of secular power, namely utility and necessity so urgent that not even gods can resist it."[163]

The fact that the commonwealth is by definition self-sufficient "and therefore cannot be subject to anyone outside itself" means for Vitoria that its prince can be "in no way subject to another in temporal matters."[164] Thus, temporal and sacred power are necessarily separate. Princes do not have an obligation "to frame their policy on the best grounds for a Christian life," nor to work to advance the Christian religion.[165]

Vitoria denies the pope the right to interfere in the cases of princes or to depose them, at least not "in ordinary circumstances."[166] Above all, Vitoria argued, the pope had no business punishing violators of natural law. To expand the pope's authority in this way would only lead to "chaos and anarchy, not order and stability, the goals of the natural

---

[157] Vitoria, "On Civil Power," 1.2, §3 in *Political Writings*, 7.   [158] Ibid., 1.2, §4 9.
[159] Ibid.   [160] Ibid., 1.2, §5   [161] Ibid.   [162] Ibid., 10.   [163] Ibid.
[164] Vitoria, "On the Power of the Church," 5.3, §4 in *Political Writings*, 87.
[165] Ibid., 5.9, §14, 95.   [166] Ibid., 5.3, §5, 87.

political order."[167] After all, if the pope could make war on any country where people (or the rulers) behaved sinfully, "kingdoms could be exchanged everyday."[168]

Nonetheless, in extraordinary circumstances, the pope is empowered to critique wrong-headed policies in *Christian territories*, "where there is obvious error or fraud," or where the commonwealth threatens "harm in spiritual matters."[169] For example, if Christians were to elect an unbeliever as prince "of whom it might justly be feared that he would lead the people from the Faith," the pope would have the "duty to exhort, or indeed to order, the people to depose such a prince."[170] This would be true, argues Vitoria, even though the prince is a true ruler in terms of both divine and natural law. Because the pope has an obligation to care for the spiritual needs of Christendom, he has authority to interfere if the temporal powers act contrary to the law of Christ. Princes who do so forfeit their right to sovereignty. If the people refused or were unable to remove their prince, then "the pope would be empowered to depose the prince on his own authority."[171] The threat to reform-minded kings, such as Henry VIII of England, is clear. Kings have a right to domestic sovereignty, so long as they do not use that right to interfere in matters of religion.

For Vitoria, the rights of the commonwealth stem from the rights of its constituents. Individuals have a right to self-defense; therefore, the commonwealth, too, can claim such a right. Individuals can sacrifice a diseased limb for the sake of their overall health; correspondingly, the commonwealth has "the same power to compel and coerce its members as if they were its limbs for the utility and safety of the common good."[172] "Nothing can be more natural than to repel force with force," writes Vitoria, and the right to self-defense is one of the most basic that he accords the commonwealth.[173] This includes the right to punish domestic lawbreakers, and also to wage war against aggressive outsiders. Vitoria defines the concept of defense more carefully than his predecessors. He writes that "self-defence must be a response to immediate danger ... once the immediate necessity of defence has passed, there is no longer any license for war."[174]

---

[167] James Muldoon, "Francisco de Vitoria and Humanitarian Intervention," *Journal of Military Ethics* 5(2), 2006, 128–143, 139.

[168] Vitoria, "On the American Indians," 2.5, §40in *Political Writings*, 274.

[169] Vitoria, "On the Power of the Church," 5.8, §13 and 5.9, §14 in *Political Writings*, 94–95.

[170] Ibid., 5.8, §13, 94.   [171] Ibid.

[172] Vitoria, "On Civil Power," 1.4, §7, in *Political Writings*, 11.   [173] Ibid.

[174] Vitoria, "On the Law of War," 1.2 §5, in *Political Writings*, 300.

This understanding of self-defense, if taken to its logical extent, would be a drastic limitation on the state's recourse to war. First, this definition eliminates the possibility of preventive war, and essentially rules out preemption as well. It could, in principle, limit things even further. Imagine a case in which an invader seizes a piece of territory but makes no further inroads. Under this narrow definition of sovereignty, the defending state might be required to accept the new status quo.

But Vitoria argues that states have the right to go beyond basic self-defense in ways that would not be permissible for individuals. Vitoria asserts that the commonwealth "has the authority not only to defend itself, but also to avenge and punish injuries done to itself and its members."[175] After all, if a state stopped at immediate self-defense, it would not be able to "sufficiently guard the public good and its own stability ... since wrongdoers become bolder and readier to attack when they can do so without fear of punishment."[176] This formulation owes much to Aquinas, of course, but goes further, "shifting the focus from the maintenance of justice ... to the stability of the commonwealth itself, that is, its use of force to protect itself as a political community able to ensure the public good for its members."[177]

Vitoria so privileges the polity over individuals that he suggests that an injustice carried out by its monarch could warrant punishing an entire commonwealth. Thus, "if a sovereign wages an unjust war against another prince, the injured party may plunder and pursue all the other rights of war against that sovereign's subjects, even if they are innocent of offense."[178] Having delegated power to the sovereign, the members of the commonwealth become responsible for its actions. Vitoria counsels that the commonwealth should thus take care to entrust "its power only to a man who will justly exercise any authority or executive power he may be given."[179] After all, it is the public who will have to pay off the debts of war, in the form of reparations, if their prince wages an unjust war (and loses).

In certain cases, the wrongs committed by another prince may justify deposing him, in what is now popularly termed "regime change." Vitoria cautions that deciding to remove a prince is a serious business, and that even among the category of princes who wrong their enemies, not all deserve to be deposed. The "punishment should not exceed the crime," cautions Vitoria, "therefore, although the harm done by the enemy may

---

[175] Ibid.   [176] Ibid.   [177] Johnson. *Sovereignty*, 49.
[178] Vitoria, "On Civil Power," 1.9, §12, in *Political Writings*, 21.   [179] Ibid.

be a sufficient cause of war, it will not always be sufficient to justify the extermination of the enemy's kingdom and deposition of its legitimate native princes."[180] Sometimes, however "the number or atrocity of the injuries and harm done by the enemy" warrant such drastic actions; likewise, it may be permissible "when failure to do so would cause a dangerous threat to the commonwealth."[181] War, for Vitoria, should generally have a status quo end. Only in extreme cases can the victor demand regime change.

For Vitoria, wars of self-defense – "in which property is defended or reclaimed" – rather naturally morph into offensive war.[182] Defining offensive wars as those that seek "vengeance for an injury," Vitoria declares that "even defensive war could not conveniently be waged unless there were also vengeance inflicted on the enemy for the injury they have done, or tried to do."[183] After all, security emerges from deterrence – it is the fear of punishment that prevents enemies from invading again.[184] In sum, Vitoria identifies the "sole and only just cause for waging war" as a harm inflicted by the enemy.[185] This, of course, rules out several types of causes as unjust. Difference of religion alone cannot justify war, as faith cannot be compelled.[186] Furthermore, desire for territorial aggrandizement cannot be a just cause, nor can the "personal glory or convenience of the prince."[187]

A just cause is not enough. Vitoria introduces an *ad bellum* form of proportionality that was only implied in Augustine and Aquinas. Because "all the effects of war are cruel and horrible – slaughter, fire, devastation," it would be wrong to pursue "trivial offenses" using such means.[188] The injury must be sufficiently grave, due war's high costs. Furthermore, the war must further the commonwealth's interest. Thus, Vitoria argues that "no war is legitimate if it is shown to be more harmful than useful to the commonwealth."[189] Because the right to wage war is given to the commonwealth only "for the protection and benefit of itself and its affairs, it follows that where these are prejudiced and damaged rather than promoted by war, that war will be in itself unjust."[190] This prudential reasoning is familiar to modern realists.

But then Vitoria makes a move that would be surprising to any contemporary realist. *Ad bellum* proportionality is not simply a matter

---

[180] Ibid., 3.9, §58, 326.   [181] Ibid. 3.9, §59.
[182] Vitoria. "On the Law of War," 1.1, §1, in *Political Writings*, 297.
[183] Ibid., 1.1, §1, 298.   [184] Ibid.   [185] Ibid., 1.3, §13, 303.
[186] Ibid., 1.3, §10, 302.   [187] Ibid., 1.3, §11–§12, 303.   [188] Ibid., 1.3, §14, 304.
[189] Vitoria, "On Civil Power," 1.10, §13, in *Political Writings*, 21.   [190] Ibid.

of calculating the costs of a particular war in light of the state's broader strategic interests. "I would go further," he writes, "since any commonwealth is part of the world as a whole, and in particular since any Christian country is part of the Christian commonwealth, I should regard any war which is useful to one commonwealth or kingdom but of proven harm to the world or Christendom as, by that very token, unjust."[191] Vitoria's claim is that a moral state must take into account *global* security and justice concerns. The hypothetical example Vitoria offers is telling. If Spain were to fight France, even if the cause were just and even if the war were beneficial to Spain's interests, if the war enabled the Turks to occupy new Christian territories "then hostilities should be suspended."[192] To be clear, Vitoria does not mean to say that a prince has a duty to "to look after the good of another commonwealth, even a greater good, if it is to the harm of his own commonwealth."[193] Vitoria's concern is more limited: a state ought not pursue its own good at the expense of others.

In such cases, Vitoria accords the pope an extraordinary right to act temporally, just as he did in the case of princes who act domestically against the law of Christ. Thus, "if princes should war amongst themselves over some territory to the obvious detriment and harm of religion, the pope may not only forbid them to fight, but may also, if there is no other way of bringing them to agreement, make a judgment between them by his own authority."[194]

Unlike his predecessors, Vitoria devotes considerable attention to the appropriate conduct of war. Changes in norms often "emerge from the stresses of human necessity."[195] And Vitoria's age was certainly one of stress. The intersection of emerging national identities and shifting religious ones had rendered wars bigger and bloodier than they had ever been before. Armies had grown, and peasants and mercenaries, rather than the noble knights of the Middle Ages, now made up their rank and file. They fought with cannons and handguns, which were seen as "inhumane" and degrading, "putting as they did the noble man-at-arms at the mercy of the vile and base born."[196] War's increasing technological destructiveness is reflected in Vitoria's heightened concern with *in bello* principles.[197]

[191] Ibid.   [192] Ibid.
[193] Vitoria, "On the Power of the Church," 5.6, in *Political Writings*, 90.
[194] Ibid., 5.8, §13, 94.   [195] Hartigan, *The Forgotten Victim*, 93.
[196] Michael Howard, *War in European History* (Oxford: Oxford University Press, 1977), 14. See also Gilpin, *War and Change in World Politics*, 62.
[197] Johnson, *Sovereignty*, 48.

Just conduct for Vitoria, as for contemporary just war thinkers, is bound by necessity, discrimination, and proportionality. Just as necessity restrains the initial recourse to war, it also restricts conduct during war. Indeed, necessity is so important to Vitoria's thought that he mentions it twice in response to the question of how much may be done in a just war. "In the just war one may do everything necessary for the defence of the public good," Vitoria writes, adding later that "a prince may do everything in a just war which is necessary to secure peace and security from attack."[198]

At first glance, necessity seems permissive. Much can be legitimated under the guise of military necessity, after all. And indeed, Vitoria's initial treatment of plunder, for example, seems to belie this fact. Vitoria asserts that plundering the territory of the enemy, including innocent people's property, is permissible: "we may take the money of the innocent, or burn and ravage their crops or kill their livestock; all these things are necessary to weaken the enemies' resources."[199] Vitoria's logic is chillingly clear. "There can be no argument about this," he writes, "it is lawful to plunder the enemy indiscriminately, both innocent and guilty, since the enemy rely upon the resources of its people to sustain an unjust war, and their strength is therefore weakened if their subjects are plundered."[200]

Yet necessity does not mean that everything goes. One may do what is *necessary*, but *no more*. Vitoria asserts that "if the war can be satisfactorily waged without plundering farmers or other non-combatants, *it is not lawful to plunder them*."[201] Necessity here functions a restraint, much as it does for the realists discussed in Chapter 1.

Vitoria similarly uses necessity to claim that the unintentional killing of innocents in war does not make the responsible combatants guilty of homicide. Like his predecessors, Vitoria makes it quite clear "it is never lawful in itself intentionally to kill innocent persons."[202] The "innocent person has done you no harm," and so just as it would be unthinkable domestically to punish the innocent for the crimes of the guilty, deliberately killing "innocent members of the enemy population for the injury done by the wicked among them" is also forbidden.[203] Thus, "even in wars against the Turks" – even in desperate wars against those whom Vitoria specifies that children cannot be killed (they are "obviously innocent"), nor women ("who are presumed to be innocent ... unless,

---

[198] Vitoria, "On the Law of War," 1.4, §15, in *Political Writings*, 304.
[199] Ibid., 3.2, 317.   [200] Ibid.   [201] Ibid.   [202] Ibid., 3.1, §35, 314.
[203] Ibid., 3.1, §36, 315.

that is, it can be proved of a particular woman that she was implicated in guilt"), nor travellers, nor visitors, nor clergy, nor monks, "unless there is evidence to the contrary or they are found actually fighting in the war."[204]

But the innocent can be killed *unintentionally*, even "with full knowledge of what one is doing, if this is an accidental effect."[205] Vitoria describes the storming of a city where one knows that innocents are present, but where artillery could not be used without harming them. It must be permissible to use indiscriminate force in this case, reasons Vitoria, "since it would otherwise be impossible to wage war against the guilty, thereby preventing the just side from fighting."[206] Even in this case, however, necessity limits the scale of the violence. This loophole – now termed "double effect" in the just war discourse – cannot be used "except when it advances a just war that cannot be won in any other way."[207]

Proportionality is the final limit to what may be done *in bello*. It is important "that care be taken to ensure that the evil effects of the war do not outweigh the possible benefits sought by waging it."[208] To return to the hypothetical city, if it is "full of innocent inhabitants" but "not of great importance for eventual victory in the war, it does not seem ... permissible to kill a large number of innocent people by indiscriminate bombardment in order to defeat a small number of enemy combatants."[209] To do so would be disproportionate, and morally culpable. (One could also argue that it would be unnecessary.)

PROTESTANTISM: RETHINKING AUTHORITY

Martin Luther (1483–1546) was the most prominent reformer of his time. Born in Saxony, his father was a peasant, but prosperous enough to send young Luther away to school at the age of fourteen, and then on to university, to study law.[210] The elder Luther was so proud of his son's graduation from the University of Erfurt in 1501 that he presented him a "copy of the *Corpus Juris* and addressed him no longer with the familiar Du but with the polite Sie."[211]

---

[204] Ibid. [205] Ibid. [206] Ibid. [207] Ibid., 3.1, §37, 316.
[208] Ibid., 3.1, §37, 315. [209] Ibid., 316. [210] Cahill, *Love Your Enemies*, 101.
[211] Roland Herbert Bainton, *Here I Stand: A Life of Martin Luther* (Nashville: Abingdon Press, 2013), 8.

In 1505, however, after a close call with lightening during a stormy walk, Luther abruptly entered an Augustinian monastery, against his father's wishes. To a father who had pinned his retirement hopes on his talented son, the young man's decision to give up a potentially prosperous career for a life of poverty was unfathomable. (In the end, the two Luthers did reconcile – Hans attended the service when Martin was ordained, and later seems to have reacted surprisingly cheerfully to his son's decision to leave the monastery and ultimately start his own family.) But Luther never gave up on scholarship. After taking his vows, he completed his doctorate in theology at the University of Wittenberg.

Luther eventually left the backwaters of Germany, in 1510, on a mission to Rome as part of a delegation seeking Papal assistance in the settlement of a dispute within the Augustinian order.[212] But rather than being impressed with Renaissance Rome, Luther seems to have been struck by its decadence, its irreverence, its sensuality.[213]

When he returned home, Rome followed, in a matter of speaking. The Pope wished to construct a new, grander St. Peter's basilica. But, as always, money was short. Albert of Brandenburg (one of the Hohenzollerns) had been made a bishop at just twenty-three years old. Now twenty-eight, he wanted to be archbishop of Mainz, which would make him the most powerful ecclesiastical figure in Germany. The fee to be installed in such a high office was more than he – or the parish – could afford, so Albert borrowed cash from a prominent banker.[214] To recoup the investment, Albert obtained permission from the Pope to sell indulgences in his diocese, so long as half the monies went toward the financing of the basilica.

Luther was infuriated by the ditty used by Albert's spokesman, Johann Tetzel, to advertise the indulgences: "as soon as the coin in the coffer rings, the soul from purgatory springs."[215] How could the church offer for sale what only God could grant? In anger, Luther dashed off a letter to Albert, which later became known as the *Ninety-Five Theses*, in 1517. What might have remained a minor doctrinal conflict assumed larger than life dimensions. This was, of course, partially due to Luther's intransigence. But Luther's critique of the church in Rome and its demands for cash hit a German political nerve. Why should Germans pay to finance a church in a faraway place they would never visit? Couldn't that money be better spent at home? And why did the German heads of the churches not resist such demands? By January of 1518, one of Luther's friends had

---

[212] Ibid., 33.   [213] Ibid., 34–36.   [214] Ibid., 62.   [215] Ibid., 72.

translated the letter from Latin into German, and copies were widely distributed, thanks to the relatively new printing press. By 1519, Luther's critique had reached France and England, touching off a pan-European debate not only over theology, but over the right relationship between religious and secular authorities.

Unsurprisingly, Luther's critique of the indulgence system did not go down well with Church authorities, and Luther was excommunicated in 1521. He was, however, protected by Frederick III, the Elector of Saxony. Although Frederick III remained a Catholic, he relished the chance to carve out a German sphere of influence against the decidedly Spanish Charles V, the Holy Roman Emperor. Thus Luther was, from the moment he set off the sparks of the Reformation, a highly politicized figure. Many of his works were written in direct response to political concerns of the day. The "Admonition to Peace: A Reply to the Twelve Articles of the Peasants in Swabia" and "Against the Murderous, Thieving Hordes of Peasants" both respond to the Peasant Rebellion in Germany.[216] His essay, "Whether Soldiers, Too, Can Be Saved," was written in December 1526, after Charles V had called on all Catholic rulers to forcibly suppress the Protestant heresy.[217]

Clearly, rampant political instability left Luther longing for peace and order. He likens a prince who engages in a just war to a surgeon who amputates a diseased limb, sacrificing a few for the common good. If princes could not use force, "everything in the world would be ruined . . . Therefore, such a war is only a very brief lack of peace that prevents an everlasting and immeasurable lack of peace."[218] Order is fundamentally important, and the prince's primary duty is to provide it.

Like Augustine, Luther draws a stark contrast between the ideal, loving relationships that characterize the kingdom of God and relationships in the earthly kingdom, which rely on law and force to remain well-ordered. But while Augustine did not believe that much evidence of the heavenly kingdom could be seen on earth, Luther thought that its reflection could be seen in relationships between true believers. Those who "belong to the kingdom of God" are in need of "neither secular

---

[216] Martin Luther, *Luther: Selected Political Writings*, J. M. Porter, ed. (Philadelphia: Fortress Press, 1974), 71.

[217] Valerie Ona Morkevičius, "Protestant Christianity," in Gregory M. Reichberg, Henry Syse, and Nicole M. Hartwell, eds., *Religion War and Ethics: A Sourcebook of Textual Traditions* (Cambridge: Cambridge University Press 2014), 245.

[218] Luther, "Whether Soldiers, Too, Can Be Saved," trans. Charles M. Jacob, in Porter, ed., *Luther: Selected Political Writings*, 103.

Sword nor law."[219] If the world were populated with true Christians, "there would be neither need nor use for princes, kings, lords, the Sword or law ... because the just man of his own accord does all and more than any law commands."[220]

But Luther was no optimist. "No man is by a nature a Christian or just," writes Luther, "but all are sinners and evil."[221] Luther's judgment of human nature is as dim as Augustine's. Because of man's fallen nature, there are few – if any – true Christians around. "There are few who believe, and even fewer who behave like Christians and refrain from doing evil [themselves], let alone not resisting evil [done to them]."[222] It is for the sake of all "the rest" that God instituted human government.[223] Luther sees the imposition of the death penalty in Genesis after the Flood as the moment in which "God establishes government and gives it the sword, to hold wantonness in check, lest violence and other sins proceed without limit."[224]

The government's function is to create and enforce laws, to restrain man's sinful nature. At the very least, government serves "to create outward peace and prevent evil-doing."[225] Luther describes man as "a wicked, fierce animal" who must be "chained and bound so that it cannot bite or tear, as its nature would prompt it to do."[226] Earthly law is all that stands between man and a brutish state of nature:

If there were [no law and government], then seeing that all the world is evil and ... scarcely one human being in a thousand is a true Christian, people would devour each other and no one would be able to support his wife and children, feed himself and serve God. The world would become a desert.[227]

By giving government the sword, however, God creates a "hedge" a set of "walls" that protect "our life and possessions" against evil men.[228]

The state's significance for earthly order is so great that Luther takes a very dim view of rebellion. Rebellion is "the worst disaster," like a great fire it "attacks and devastates a whole land ... it makes widows and

---

[219] Martin Luther, "On Secular Authority," in Harro Höpfl, ed., *Luther and Calvin on Secular Authority* (Cambridge: Cambridge University Press, 2010), 9.

[220] Ibid.   [221] Ibid., 10.   [222] Ibid.   [223] Ibid.

[224] Luther, "Genesis 9:6," in Jaroslav Pelikan and Helmut T. Lehmann, eds., *Luther's Works* (St. Louis: Concordia, 1955–1986), 2:141, cited in David M. Whitford, "*Cura Religionis* or Two Kingdoms: The Late Luther on Religion and the State in the Lectures on Genesis," *Church History* 73(1), 2004, 41–62, 48 (f. 22). See also Luther, "Genesis 49:3," in Whitford, "*Cura Religionis* or Two Kingdoms," 52 (f. 36).

[225] Luther, "On Secular Authority," 12.   [226] Ibid., 10.   [227] Ibid.

[228] Luther, "Genesis 9:6," in Whitford, 48 (f. 22).

orphans, and turns everything upside down."[229] Ultimately, "a wicked tyrant is more tolerable than a bad war."[230] Luther's view of rebellion reflects his times. Regarding the 1525 Peasant's War, Luther recognized that the peasants were suffering grave injustices at the hands of their princes. (Specifically, the princes had overstepped their temporal authority by demanding particular religious practices.) Before the violence began, Luther wrote to the princes, begging them to consider the peasants' concerns.[231] The peasants possessed legitimate grievances, but lacked right authority. Consequently, Luther thought they could defend themselves if attacked. But they had no right to initiate conflict. So when the peasants took matters into their own hands, Luther roundly condemned them. By contrast, when the Diet of Augsburg proclaimed in 1530 that all Reformation heresy should be removed from the empire, Luther counsels Protestants that self-defense is not rebellion and urges soldiers not to obey the emperor if he orders them to forcibly suppress the movement.[232] In this latter case, it is the Diet that has overstepped its authority, by interfering in spiritual matters.

The right to political authority lies squarely with the princes, regardless of their creed. Because political authority comes from God, "even a heathen ruler has the right and the authority to punish."[233] Such authority not only applies to non-Christians living in such territories, but to Christians as well. Unlike his predecessors, who forbade the clergy from shedding blood, Luther declares that "even if I served a Turk and saw my lord in danger, I would forget my spiritual office and stab and hew as long as my heart beat. If I were slain in so doing, I should go straight to heaven."[234]

Political authority for Luther, however, is strictly secular. While Vitoria had opened a narrow window for papal critique of (and

---

[229] Luther, "Against the Robbing and Murdering Hordes of Peasants," in *Luther: Selected Political Writings*, 86.

[230] Luther, "Whether Soldiers, Too, Can Be Saved," in *Luther: Selected Political Writings*, 109.

[231] Luther, "Admonition to Peace: A Reply to the Twelve Articles of the Peasants in Swabia," in *Luther: Selected Political Writings*, 72–74.

[232] Luther, "Dr. Martin Luther's Warning to His Dear German People," in *Luther: Selected Political Writings*, 136, 139.

[233] Against the Robbing and Murdering Hordes of Peasants," in *Luther: Selected Political Writings*, 87.

[234] Luther, "An Open Letter on the Harsh Book against the Peasants," in *Luther: Selected Political Writings*, 97–98. For an excellent discussion of ritual purity and the exemption of Christian clergy from war, see Meagher, *Killing from the Inside Out*, 58–59, 84–85.

intervention in) secular political affairs, Luther squarely rules out such a possibility. In a biting critique of "the sophists at universities," Luther claims that they must have been possessed by the devil to go "so far as to allow the [use of the] Sword and secular authority to the 'perfect estate' of bishops, and even to the 'most perfect' estate of all, that of the pope."[235] While the papal supporters claimed that spiritual authority trumped secular authority (and hence, secular authorities should bow to the counsel of the Church), Luther argued that the two spheres were entirely distinct, and neither should interfere in the other.[236]

The function of secular authority for Luther is to create a stable order on earth, both by punishing domestic wrongdoers and by protecting against external enemies. "What else is war but the punishment of wrong and evil? Why does anyone go to war, except because he desires peace and obedience?"[237] Like Augustine, Luther ties the right to use force in this way not only to the right to authority, but also to the duty to love one's neighbor. "Now slaying and robbing do not seem to be works of love," Luther admits, "In truth, however, even this is a work of love ... [When] I think of how it protects the good and keeps and preserves wife and child, house and farm, property, and honor and peace, then I see how precious and godly this work is ... For if the sword were not on guard to preserve peace, everything in the world would be ruined because of lack of peace."[238] War is a "small lack of peace" that must be used to "set a limit to this universal, worldwide lack of peace which would destroy everyone."[239]

War for Luther, as for his Catholic contemporaries, could be used both for defense and to right wrongs. Like Vitoria, he vehemently denied that war should advance religious ends. Thinking about the wars against the Ottoman Turks, Luther asserted in 1526 that self-defense was certainly legitimate, but that the war should not be treated as a crusade. Condemning the use of crusading rhetoric to encourage Europeans to fight, Luther questioned the Christian credentials of most of the soldiers and even the pope – were they really claiming to live up to the title of true

---

[235] Luther, "On Secular Authority," 4.
[236] Johnson, *Sovereignty*, 61–62. Although Luther's call for the state to punish Anabaptists may seem to contradict the rule, his concern is not with their religious heresy per se so much as with the political consequences of their doctrine, which he saw as questioning the legitimacy of government. Thus, he declared them "rebels ... attacking the rulers and their government." See Luther, "Psalm 82:4," in Pelikan and Lehmann, *Luther's Works*, cited in Whitford, 56.
[237] Luther, "Whether Soldiers, Too, Can Be Saved," 102.   [238] Ibid.   [239] Ibid.

Christians?[240] And even if they were true Christians, "where the soul is concerned, God neither can nor will allow anyone but himself to rule. And so, where secular authority takes it upon itself to legislate for the soul, it trespasses on [what belongs to] God's government, and merely seduces and ruins souls."[241]

While suffering an injustice could generate a just cause, Luther cautions that war should only be entered into out of necessity. War should be the last resort, not the first. "Wait until the situation compels you to fight when you have no desire to do so," counsels Luther, for "no war is just, even if it is a war between equals, unless one has such a good reason for fighting and such a good conscience that he can say, 'My neighbor compels and forces me to fight, though I would rather avoid it.'"[242] Wars of necessity are permitted, "wars of desire" are not.[243] Put differently, Luther advises that "you are not to consider your own advantage, and how you can remain ruler, but your subjects, whom you owe help and protection, so that the work is done out of love . . . even if you cannot help making some widows and some orphans, you must at least prevent total ruin."[244]

In discussing the importance of necessity as a limiting principle, Luther develops something akin to the contemporary concept of last resort. War is necessary when an enemy attacks "and refuses to cooperate in settling the matter according to law or through arbitration and common agreement, or when one overlooks and puts up with the enemy's words and tricks, but he still insists on having his own way."[245] One should first offer one's opponent "justice and peace," but "if he will not settle, then do the best you can and resist force with force."[246] Necessity acts here as a restraint, rather than a permission.

Luther has very little to say about *in bello* protections. In a just war "it is a Christian act, and an act of love, to kill enemies without scruple, to rob and to burn, and to do whatever damages the enemy, according to the usages of war, until he is defeated."[247] Nonetheless, he warns that soldiers should "beware of sins and of violating women and maidens."[248] This is a far cry even from Vitoria, who despite his realistic appraisal of siege warfare still calls for civilian immunity to be respected. But it is

---

[240] Luther, "On War against the Turk," in *Luther: Selected Political Writings*, 123, 129.
[241] Luther, "On Secular Authority," 23.
[242] Luther, "Whether Soldiers, Too, Can Be Saved," 113.   [243] Ibid., 114.
[244] Luther, "On Secular Authority," 40.
[245] Luther, "Whether Soldiers, Too, Can Be Saved," 114
[246] Luther, "On Secular Authority," 39.   [247] Ibid., 40.   [248] Ibid.

important to keep in mind the context. Luther, an excommunicated ex-priest condemned as an outlaw by Charles V, relied on the good graces of the Elector of Saxony. His interest in affirming his patron's right to put down the rebels threatening him seems to overwhelm his concern with avoiding the punishment of the innocent.

JOHN CALVIN

If Luther can be considered lucky by virtue of enjoying powerful patronage, John Calvin had to make his own luck. Born in 1509 in Noyon, France, his father intended him for the priesthood. A bright lad, he was employed by the local bishop as a clerk by the age of twelve and had his hair cut short to symbolize his intention of joining the priesthood. His father had originally enrolled him at the Collège de Montaigu in Paris to prepare for a career in the priesthood, but withdrew him in 1526 to study law at the University of Orléans. He hoped Calvin might make more money as a lawyer, perhaps to help support the religious careers of his younger brothers. The 1520s, after all, were a rough time for France, as fears of social unrest grew in the face of poor harvests, grim wars, and outbreaks of plague.[249]

Calvin entered the University of Bourges in 1529 and studied for a time under a humanist lawyer. Intrigued by the classics, he learned Greek and began to study the New Testament in its original language. He earned a law license in 1532. But a year later, Calvin was struck by a sudden religious conversion. At the same time, while on a visit to Paris, Calvin's friend Nicolas Cop was inaugurated as rector of the University of Paris. Cop's inaugural lecture, calling for the reform of the Catholic Church, caused an uproar. He was denounced as a heretic. Calvin was implicated due to his friendship and spent the next year in hiding in France. In 1534, however, a violent backlash against Protestants in France forced Calvin into exile in Switzerland.

Two years later, Calvin's *Institutes of the Christian Religion* were published, intended as a defense of the reformers' position.[250] Calvin dedicated the work to the French king, "with a view to the hearing of

---

[249] Bruce Gordon, *Calvin* (New Haven: Yale University Press, 2011), Kindle version, location 267, chapter 1.

[250] The *Institutes* were revised frequently, each reflecting "the historical moment in which it was created," both in terms of Calvin's spiritual development and his earthly cares. See Bruce Gordon, *John Calvin's Institutes of the Christian Religion: A Biography* (Princeton: Princeton University Press, 2016), 17.

our cause, to mollify your mind, now indeed turned away and estranged from us – I add, even inflamed against us – but whose good will, we are confident, we should regain, would you but once ... read this our Confession."[251] Shortly thereafter, Calvin returned home to France briefly, to settle his affairs and to bring his only surviving brother back to Switzerland with him.[252] Forced by civil violence to take a different route back, he ended up in Geneva. According to Calvin's modest account, he had no intention to stay, but William Farel – another French reformer living in the city – entreated him so vehemently that he had no choice. He "surrendered himself to the disposal of the Presbytery and magistrates," who appointed him not only preacher, but professor of divinity.[253]

Just a year later, Calvin and Farel presented the city council with articles for the organization of the church. These were immediately accepted, launching Calvin's first theocratic experiment. But it was not smooth sailing. The council proved reluctant to enforce the terms of the articles, as only a few citizens had subscribed to the Protestant confession of faith. After a riot over what type of bread to use for the Easter Eucharist, Farel and Calvin fled. Despite pleading their case to both church officials in Bern and Zurich, they could not win readmission to Geneva. Instead, Calvin accepted a position as a minister in Strasbourg, where he worked on revisions to the *Institutes*. The French version was instantly popular and quickly banned by the Paris parliament.[254]

By 1541, however, the council in Geneva reconsidered their expulsion of Calvin. Without his zeal, Geneva struggled to deal with the rising tensions both within the city and between the city and its neighbors. Upon Calvin's return, the city council passed the Ecclesiastical Ordinances, which proposed a "mixed form of government in which ministers and laity were bound together under mutual responsibility for building the godly society."[255] Calvin had wanted to keep "theologically untrained politicians" out of doctrinal discussions, but the interests of the civil magistrates prevailed, and the ecclesiastical court – the Consistory – was staffed with both clerical and lay officials.[256] The ministers, as paid

---

[251] John Calvin, *Institutes of the Christian Religion*, trans. Henry Baeveridge (Grand Rapids, MI: Eerdmans, 2001), 19–20.

[252] Thomas Beza, *The Life of John Calvin* (Lindenhurst, NY: Great Christian Books, 2012), Kindle version, location 123.

[253] Ibid., location 146.

[254] Gordon, *John Calvin's Institutes of the Christian Religion*, 28.

[255] Gordon, *Calvin*, location 1861, chapter 8.   [256] Ibid., locations 1876–1882.

officials of Geneva, were subject to the civil magistrates. Still, the division of labor between secular and religious authority was never as clear as either Calvin or the magistrates would have wanted.

Tensions ran high, especially when the Consistory punished Genevans of high social standing, or when ministers (including Calvin) called out specific individuals from their pulpits for public shaming. Calvin soon ran afoul of the city council again. Yet when Calvin handed in his resignation in 1553, the council refused to accept it, recognizing that the political costs of banishing him would be too high. Within two years Calvin's supporters had the majority of the seats in the council, and opposition largely ceased.

Luther's focus had been the reform of the German church, but Calvin's approach was international. Calvin, of course, was interested in furthering the Reformation in his native France. Under his leadership, Reformist tracts and missionaries poured over the Swiss border into France. When the French government complained that this was unneighborly meddling, the Genevans pointed out that the church supplied the funds, not the city council – a case of probable deniability. Geneva also opened its arms to exiles fleeing the Catholic rulers of England and Scotland. Among the notables who took refuge in Geneva was John Knox, who spearheaded a Protestant Revolution against Mary of Guise upon his return to Scotland in 1559 and later fomented trouble for her daughter, Mary Queen of Scots. But although Calvin sought unity among the various Reformed churches emerging at the time, doctrinal differences with Luther made the overall unity of the Reformation impossible.

Despite spearheading the creation of a church that clearly extended its reach into disciplining secular society, Calvin nonetheless relies on the image of a "twofold government in man," one internal and dealing with the soul, one relating to external life, as a way of explaining the importance of secular authority.[257] Like Augustine, he finds himself needing to refute the idea that Christians must withdraw from the world, as some pacifist Protestant sects advocate. Calvin calls Anabaptists and others who insist that "after we are dead by Christ to the elements of this world ... it is unworthy of us ... to be occupied with those profane and impure cares," and who suppose "that the whole scheme of civil government is matter of pollution, with which Christian men have nothing to do."[258] Equally wrong are those who claim that the liberty "promised in

---

[257] Calvin, *Institutes of the Christian Religion*, I.XX.1, 651.   [258] Ibid., IV.XX.2, 652.

the gospel, a liberty which acknowledges no king and no magistrate among men, but looks to Christ alone" means that "nothing will be safe until the whole world is changed into a new form, when there will be neither courts, nor laws, no magistrates, nor anything of the kind to interfere, as they suppose, with their liberty."[259]

Instead, Calvin argues, we must recognize that earthly government is not merely necessary. It also "begins the heavenly kingdom in us, even now upon earth, and in this mortal and evanescent life commences immortal and incorruptible blessedness."[260] After all, earthly government is concerned with earthly peace, and so aims "to foster and maintain the external worship of God, to defend sound doctrine and the condition of the Church, to adapt our conduct to human society, to form our manners to civil justice, to conciliate us to each other, to cherish common peace and tranquility."[261] The object of governance is to provide for both man's temporal and spiritual needs. Of course, government must see "that the public quiet be not disturbed, that every man's property be kept secure, that men may carry on innocent commerce with each other, that honesty and modesty be cultivated," but it must also prevent idolatry, blasphemy, and heresy.[262] In short, the state must ensure that "a public form of religion may exist among Christians, and humanity among men."[263]

This view separates Calvin radically from Augustine, Aquinas, and Luther. For Calvin, the earthly city can and should serve the heavenly one. Thus he argues that "no polity can be successfully established unless piety be its first care."[264] Unsurprisingly, Calvin emphasizes the divine authority of princes to a greater degree. Magistrates "have a commission from God ... they are invested with divine authority, and, in fact, represent the person of God, as whose substitutes they in a manner act."[265] God established just governments for the good of mankind, "not owing to human perverseness."[266] Thus Calvin asserts that "no man can doubt that civil authority is, in the sight of God, not only sacred and lawful, but the most sacred, and by far the most honourable, of all stations in mortal life."[267]

Of course, some rulers are incompetent, some are self-serving, and some are even tyrants. For Calvin, the existence of such imperfect rulers does not discredit the office, only the man who holds it. Calvin asserts that the people owe "reverence, and even ... piety" to their rules, "be their

---

[259] Ibid., IV.XX.1, 651. [260] Ibid., IV.XX.2, 652. [261] Ibid.
[262] Ibid., IV.XX.3, 653. [263] Ibid. [264] Ibid., IV.XX.9, 658.
[265] Ibid., IV.XX.4, 653. [266] Ibid. [267] Ibid., IV.XX.4, 654.

characters what they may."[268] Although rulers do owe mutual duties to their subjects, their failure to uphold those duties does not mean that the people have a right to disobey or to rebel. Instead, Calvin suggests that "if we are cruelly tormented by a savage, if we are rapaciously pillaged by an avaricious or luxurious, if we are neglected by a sluggish, if, in short, we are persecuted for righteousness' sake by an impious and sacrilegious prince, let us first call up the remembrance of our faults, which doubtless the Lord is chastising by such scourges."[269] We must "curb our impatience," recognizing "that it belongs not to us to cure these evils," but rather to plea to God for help.[270]

What subjects themselves may not do, God can, through the actions of "manifest avengers" whom he commands "to punish accursed tyranny, and deliver his people from calamity when they are unjustly oppressed."[271] Sometimes these leaders are lesser magistrates from the troubled state; at other times God employs the "fury of men who have other thoughts and other aims," namely outside princes.[272] Private men have only "to obey and suffer," but "popular magistrates" have an obligation to "check the undue licence of kings."[273] While this forecloses populist revolutions, it implies that an elite-led revolt would be not only permissible, but possibly requisite against tyrannical kings.

Public authorities have a duty to protect the innocent and to ensure peace, both domestically and with foreign powers. Their role is to "provide for the peace of the good, and to restrain the waywardness of the wicked."[274] The just ruler therefore provides "for the common peace and safety" and acts "to avenge the afflictions of the pious."[275] For Calvin, this necessarily involves the use of force:

Now, if it is true justice in them to pursue the guilty and impious with drawn sword, to sheath the sword, and keep their hands pure from blood, while nefarious men wade through murder and slaughter, so far from redounding to the praise of their goodness and justice, would be to incur the guilt of the greatest impiety.[276]

Consequently, it is permissible and necessary "for kings and states to take up arms in order to execute public vengeance."[277] Princes have a positive duty to "maintain the tranquility of their subjects, repress the seditious movements of the turbulent, assist those who are violently oppressed."[278] To fail to oppose the "fury of the wicked" is to permit "universal destruction."[279]

---

[268] Ibid., IV.XX.29, 673.   [269] Ibid.   [270] Ibid., IV.XX.29, 674.
[271] Ibid., IV.XX.30, 674.   [272] Ibid.   [273] Ibid., IV.XX.31, 675.
[274] John Calvin, *Romans 13*, 281. 13.3.
[275] Calvin, *Institutes*, IV.XX.9 and IV.XX.10, 659.   [276] Ibid., IV.XX.10, 660.
[277] Ibid., IV.XX.11, 661.   [278] Ibid.   [279] Calvin, *Romans 13*, 13.3, 281.

Calvin, like Luther, has next to nothing to say about *in bello* concerns. Drawing on Augustine, he asserts that when force is necessary, it "must not be borne headlong by anger; nor hurried away by hatred, nor burn with implacable severity."[280] Most importantly, the soldier should not allow himself "to be carried away by any private feeling," but to "be guided solely by regard for the public."[281] To act with any intent other than to defend the public and punish wrongdoing is to act wickedly. It is public service alone that justifies force. Like Aquinas before him, Calvin relies on the discretion of the soldier to restrain violence in war – the proper attitude should lead to the proper behavior.

CONCLUSION

The authors explored in this chapter share deep concerns with the maintenance of order. Looking out into a world that they see as insecure and conflict ridden, there is little sign of hope that humanity can find a new way of settling its political disputes. Thus, the just war theories they advance do not seem aimed at preventing states from using war in general, but rather at restricting the causes for which states and peoples may fight. Each author's view of justice both *ad bellum* and *in bello* varies, however. It is possible to tell a plausible story that suggests these variations, particularly those dealing with just cause, rebellion, and civilian protections, reflect the political contingencies of the time.

For example, while Augustine's belief that faith cannot be compelled implies that war to expand Christendom would be unacceptable, he seems to have found no reason to discuss the issue explicitly, given that the Roman empire was in no position to expand, whatever the cause. But Aquinas and Vitoria – considering the Crusades and colonial expansion, respectively – seek to curtail just cause, specifically forbidding the use of war to convert nonbelievers. Calvin, heading an essentially theocratic state, sees a place for the use of force by the state to enforce the right practice of religion domestically. He even hints that magistrates might launch a rebellion to change the government if the king does not permit the right practice of religion or does not enforce its tenets. But yet Calvin does not deal explicitly with the question of expansive wars to bring more territory under the rule of a properly religious government. Given Geneva's weakness in comparison to its Catholic neighbor, France, this is not surprising.

---

[280] Calvin, *Institutes*, IV.XX.12, 662.   [281] Ibid.

On a similar note, a story about political considerations can be told by looking at the ways in which these authors approach the problem of rebellion. Unsurprisingly, none of the authors surveyed express very positive views of rebellion. And yet all three of the authors of the Reformation era – Vitoria, Luther, and Calvin – are more preoccupied with rebellion than their predecessors. Each responds to rebellion in a way that reflects their domestic political realities. Vitoria condones it, if the king tries to lead the people away from the one true Church. Luther, reliant on his local prince for protection, has no stomach for it at all. And Calvin, who had emerged on the upside of what was effectively a revolution by the ballot box in Geneva, thought that rebellion by civil authorities could be justified.

In bello considerations also seem tied to time and place. Augustine has the least to say about just means. It is hard to imagine his political interlocutors, busy fighting barbarian incursions, having much patience with rules meant to limit the destructiveness of war. Vitoria, writing during the early sixteenth century as gunpowder has begun to democratize both killing and being killed in war, advances the most specific set of *in bello* prescriptions out of the authors surveyed here. It may be that Vitoria, like many contemporary just war thinkers, was shocked by the increasingly destructive technology of war into clarifying the rules that had been treated as custom in the past.

There is no smoking gun here, no absolute proof that these canonical authors sought to make their theories politically relevant. But the correlation between their concerns and claims, and the real-world political issues of the age, certainly lends credence to such a claim. Likewise, the fact that *these* authors became part of the canon is significant in itself. Pacifists and crusaders alike were edged out of the canonical tradition, in favor of a group of thinkers whose work relies heavily on a familiar realist principle: necessity. It is not the case that justice doesn't matter to these Christians just war thinkers. Each has a very clear idea of what an ideal society would look like, and how an earthly government might best go about improving the spiritual and material lives of its people. But these ideals of justice are never permitted to drive political action uninhabited. The unmistakable running theme across the tradition is that one should do what is necessary for maintaining order – but not more. The pragmatic aspects of the tradition, especially in its *ad bellum* concerns, promise to help leaders find the wise balance between pursuing justice and pursuing order. It is likely this pragmatic aspect of the tradition that has made it so appealing to so many political leaders for so long.

5

Taming the World of War

The Islamic Just War Traditions

The broad parallels between the Christian and Islamic just war traditions are striking. Both Abrahamic traditions share a similar view of human nature. While created in God's image, mankind struggles to submit to God's will, and as a result conflict ensues. God has offered the Qur'an to the people to show them the way, "but man is more contentious than any other creature."[1] Indeed, "God wishes to lighten [mankind's] burden," but "man was created weak."[2] From this familiar assumption of mankind as a work in progress, Islamic scholars have historically held a view of the state and the state system that treats conflict and war as endemic.

This chapter provides a broad overview of just war thinking within the classical Islamic tradition. Our exploration will lead us into the works of scholars from the four major schools of Sunni Islamic *fiqh*, or jurisprudence. While *shari'a*, or divine law, is the divine duty of mankind as revealed by God, we can understand it only through a form of interpretation.[3] The *fiqh* represents humans' best attempts to understand and codify the divine law in human terms. These four dominant traditions of legal reasoning – Maliki, Shafi'i, Hanafi, and Hanbali – take their names from the authors of their earliest texts. Unlike Christian denominations, which tend to compete with each other demanding exclusive loyalty, the Sunni tradition has generally accepted all four of these legal schools as legitimate. Indeed, individual believers may consult judges from multiple traditions when faced with a dilemma, and it is not unheard

[1] M. A. S. Abdel Haleem, trans., *The Qur'an* (Oxford: Oxford University Press, 2005), 18:54.
[2] Ibid., 4:28.   [3] An-Na'im, *Toward an Islamic Reformation*, 11.

of to shift allegiances from one school to another, or to follow the rules of different schools for different purposes. No school is treated as holding the monopoly and correct interpretation of *shari'a*.

The Shi'i tradition has its own schools of *fiqh*, which rely heavily on their Sunni predecessors. The fundamental schism between Sunni and Shi'i ways of thinking hinges on whether political and religious authority were passed on together from the Prophet Muhammad to his successors, and specifically on who these successors actually were in history. This difference has significant consequences for Shi'i political thought. Simply put, legitimate authority in Shi'ism has a genealogical component. True Imams must be descended from Fatima and Ali, the Prophet's daughter and son-in-law. By contrast, Sunni imams are selected by the community.

The analysis in this chapter begins with three jurists from the Golden Age of Islamic law in the eighth and ninth centuries – Malik ibn Abas (from whom the Maliki school takes its name), Muhammad ibn Idris al-Shafi'i (the eponym of the Shafi'i school), and Muhammad ibn al-Hasan al-Shaybani (a disciple of Abu Hanifa). In the eleventh century, we will take on Abu al-Hasan al-Mawardi, a legal scholar in the Shafi'i tradition. In the tumultuous thirteenth century, we will explore the works of Ahmad ibn Taymiyya, a Hanbali scholar.[4] For comparative purposes, this chapter also introduces the work of a Shi'i jurist, Najm al-Din Ja'far ibn al-Hasan al-Hilli (al-Muhaqqiq), who, like Taymiyya, responded to the Mongol invasions of the era.[5] Al-Muhaqqiq was a scholar in the Twelver tradition, the largest contemporary Shi'a sect. Last, we will consider the work of Ahmad ibn Naqib al-Misri, working within the Shafi'i tradition in the early fourteenth century.

Just as in the Christian just war tradition, Islamic thought about the ethics of war reflects response to historical and political realities. The earliest Muslim community was largely pacifistic, while it remained outside the circles of power. Although Christianity did not acquire state power for centuries, the Prophet Muhammad became a political leader in

---

[4] Ibn Taymiyya's political thought has proven immensely influential in the modern age, as he is cited frequently by groups ranging from the Muslim Brotherhood to the Jama'at al-Jihad, to al-Qaeda and ISIS. To be fair, his use by extremists relies both on misreading of Ibn Taymiyya and a misreading of the contemporary circumstances. For a discussion of this in the Egyptian context, see Mona Hassan, "Modern Interpretations and Misinterpretations of a Medieval Scholar: Apprehending the Political Thought of Ibn Taymiyya," in Yossef Rapoport and Shahab Ahmed, eds., *Ibn Taymiyya and His Times* (Oxford: Oxford University Press, 2010), 338–366.

[5] Al-Muhaqqiq al-Hilli is sometimes also referred to as al-Muhaqqiq al-Awwal.

his own lifetime. This made the question of using force more immediate. Rather than questioning whether force is ever permissible, the Islamic debate emphasizes the problems of *who* may direct the use of force, as well as *how* and *against whom* it may be used.

THE ERA OF THE PROPHET: RESISTANCE AND EXPANSION

The political environment facing the Prophet Muhammad was quite different from that of first-century Judea. The Western Roman empire had already collapsed. While the eastern Mediterranean remained largely under Byzantine control, Persian and Turkish incursions had begun to seriously erode its underpinnings. The Arabian peninsula itself was outside the direct control of either the Byzantine or Sassanid empires. Governed by various tribes, many of whom followed Bedouin principles of organization, it lacked kings or other formal institutions beyond the clan councils.[6] Justice was enforced through a system of blood feuds, both between tribes and between clans within the same tribe. The Arab peninsula was as fractured religiously as it was politically. Some of the important tribes subscribed to Christianity, Judaism, or Zoroastrianism (often for political reasons), while others remained polytheistic.

Within Muhammad's lifetime, two Islamic responses emerge to the question of violence. The first, during the Meccan period, encourages Muslims to avoid responding to force with force. The second, dating to the Medinan era, permits the use of defensive force. The verses of the Qur'an revealed to Muhammad during the period of the first Islamic community, at Mecca between 610 and 622, focus on "the discovery of transcendent God, the gathering of the first community, the appeals and injunctions for generosity toward the poor and unfortunate, and ... conflict with the hostile environment of Mecca – but never organized, armed conflict."[7]

Instead, the verses dealing with conflict during this era enjoin Muslims to patiently practice self-restraint (*sabr*) in the face of injustices committed by their non-Muslim neighbors. The third chapter of the Qur'an lays out the similarities between the Islamic message and the earlier Christian and

---

[6] Marshall G. S. Hodgson, *The Venture of Islam: Conscience and History in a World Civilization, Vol. 1: The Classical Age of Islam* (Chicago: University of Chicago Press, 1988), 155.

[7] Michael Bonner, *Jihad in Islamic History: Doctrines and Practice* (Princeton: Princeton University Press, 2006), 41.

Jewish traditions, encouraging Muslims to spread the new message through peaceful argument: "You who believe, be steadfast, more steadfast than others; be ready; always be mindful of God, so that you may prosper."[8] Later exegetes use this verse to emphasize the duty of Muslims to patiently suffer whatever is necessary while maintaining their faith. In addition to being steadfast (*sabr*), the verse also tells believers to be ready (*rabitu*).[9] While *ribat*, or patient waiting, at the time of Muhammad referred to the practice of prayer multiple times a day, this passage was reinterpreted by later Quranic scholars "in the context of belligerent Umayyad-Byzantine relations" to refer to vigilance on the borders.[10] But in Mecca, it meant quite simply to wait in anticipation.

Rather than responding to provocations with force, the Qur'an encourages believers to struggle (*jihad*) against disbelievers by following God and preaching his message nonetheless.[11] Steadfast patience is a recurring theme, emphasizing God's demand that Muhammad invite all people to the new way:

Argue with them in the most courteous way ... If you [believers] have to respond to an attack, make your response proportionate, but it is best to stand fast. So [Prophet] be steadfast: your steadfastness comes only from God.[12]

Peaceful struggle is thus clearly preferred to the use of force. Indeed, *jihad* did not have a combative meaning in this era, instead referring to the struggle to obey God.[13]

As Muhammad's message developed and his following grew, relations with the leading clans deteriorated.[14] Eventually, he fled with his followers to Medina. This event, called the *hijra*, marks such a significant moment in the development of Islam that it became year one in the Muslim calendar. After the *hijra*, Muhammad's tactics shifted. Welcomed and supported by the city of Medina, Muhammad became a political leader, and the young Muslim community began to fight against its oppressors. Still, only defensive war was understood to be justified at the time.

---

[8] Qur'an 3:200.

[9] Asma Afsaruddin, *Striving in the Path of God: Jihad and Martyrdom in Islamic Thought* (Oxford: Oxford University Press, 2013), 25. *Sabr* and *ribat* are not linked to their military meanings by Quranic scholars until the ninth century, nearly three hundred years after the Qur'an was revealed (ibid., 271).

[10] Ibid., 34–35.   [11] Qur'an 25.52 and 29.69.   [12] Qur'an 16:125–128.

[13] Afsaruddin, *Striving in the Path of God*, 270.

[14] Albert Hourani, *A History of the Arab Peoples* (New York: Warner Books, 1991), 17.

The first verse addressing armed conflict in the Medinan period offers reassurance to the refugee community:

God will defend the believers ... Those who have been attacked are permitted to take up arms because they have been wronged – God has the power to help them – those who have been driven unjustly from their homes only for saying "Our Lord is God." If God did not repel some people by means of others, many monasteries, churches, synagogues, and mosques, where God's name is much invoked, would have been destroyed.[15]

The term for fighting here is *qital*, and not *jihad*, which simply means to struggle. Early scriptural exegetes understood these verses as purely defensive.[16] Furthermore, the idea of defense in this passage refers not only to Muslims, but to the Peoples of the Book. All of God's followers are entitled to the same degree of protection. Even the verse from a few years later, giving Muslims divine permission to defend themselves even inside the Ka'aba at Mecca, emphasizes that force is to be used only in *response* to an attack by others.[17]

Fight in God's cause against those who fight you, but do not overstep the limits: God does not love those who overstep the limits. Kill them wherever you encounter them, and drive them out from where they drove you out, for persecution is more serious than killing. Do not fight them at the Sacred Mosque unless they fought you there. If they do fight you, kill them ... but if they strop, then God is most forgiving and merciful. Fight them until there is no more persecution, and worship is devoted to God. If they cease hostilities, there can be no [further] hostility, except towards aggressors ... So if anyone commits aggression against you, attack him as he attacked you, but be mindful of God and know that he is with those who are mindful of Him.[18]

Three key themes emerge from this passage. Two involve justifications for using force, while the third calls for restraint *in bello*. First, war can be used against aggressors. Their violence justifies the *defensive* use of force in response. Second, fighting can be used to restore order and justice – to end persecution. Third, even in war one should not "overstep the limits." Islamic thinkers, both scriptural exegetes and the legal scholars this chapter emphasizes, expand upon this concept by developing specific *in bello* rules about what constitutes just combat.

When the word *jihad* appears in the Qur'an in this later period, it occasionally appears in military contexts, rather than referring to spiritual struggle. Although *jihad* was used in the Mecca period only in a spiritual

[15] Qur'an 22:38–40.   [16] Afsaruddin, *Striving in the Path of God*, 35.   [17] Ibid., 43.
[18] Qur'an 2:190–194.

sense, "the *jihad* of Medina refers to an organized and total effort of the community – if necessary through war – to overcome the hurdles in the way of the spread of Islam. Indeed, in Medina, it is often equivalent to *qital* or to active war."[19] The Medina Constitution "is clearly founded more for war than for any other recognizable purpose, even though the text ... does not name the adversary."[20] The last decade of Muhammad's life, starting with a raid against a Meccan caravan in the second year after his exile, was punctuated by war.

While the Medinan verses permit political violence, a careful reading of makes it clear that only defensive war is allowed, not offensive war. For example, today Qur'an 9:5 is often cited as advocating offensive war. This verse declares that except during the sacred months, when fighting is forbidden, "wherever you encounter the idolaters, kill them, seize them, besiege them, wait for them at every lookout post; but if they turn [to God], maintain the prayer, and pay the prescribed alms, let them go on their way, for God is most forgiving and merciful."[21] This includes not only fighting against pagans, but also against the People of the Book "who do not [truly] believe in God and the Last Day, who do not forbid what god and His Messenger have forbidden, who do not obey the rule of justice."[22] Such people should be fought until they "pay the tax and agree to submit."[23]

But the context of *sura* 9:5 tells a different story. Indeed, early Quranic scholars believed that this verse referred only to a specific situation in Muhammad's time.[24] The *sura* itself refers to people who have "broken their oaths, who tried to drive the Messenger out, who attacked [the Muslims] first."[25] By contrast, the community is urged to "be true" to those nonbelievers who keep their treaty obligations.[26] These obligations include paying the *jizya*, but this tax was not meant to be punitive. Instead it took the place of the mandatory military service required of Muslims. Because Peoples of the Book were committed to monotheism and the Ten Commandments, they could be relied upon to uphold treaties and contracts.[27] Polytheists, by contrast, could not be reliable allies. Thus, if the Islamic community fought against them – in response to their

---

[19] Fazlur Rahman, *Major Themes of the Qur'an* (Minneapolis: Bibliotheca Islamica, 1994), 160.
[20] Bonner, *Jihad in Islamic History*, 40.   [21] Qur'an 9:5.   [22] Ibid., 9:29.   [23] Ibid.
[24] Afsaruddin, *Striving in the Path of God*, 276.   [25] Qur'an 9:12.   [26] Ibid. 9:7.
[27] Peoples of the Book were understood to include Christians, Jews, Zoroastrians – and after the Mughal conquest of India, Hindus.

aggression – they could not be permitted to carry on their traditional religious practices. However, the expansion of the Islamic *polity* was not seen as synonymous to the expansion of the Islamic faith: "what was spread by the sword was not the religion of Islam, but the *political domain* of Islam, so that Islam could work to produce the order on the earth that the Qur'an seeks."[28] The underlying belief was that Islam offered a fundamentally important service to humanity, by providing a stable, secure social order. Peoples of the Book could submit to this order, as monotheists, but pagans could not.

IMAM MALIK, AL-SHAYBANI, AND AL-SHAFI'I: A UNIFIED ISLAMICATE WORLD

In the two centuries after the Prophet Muhammad's death, Islam became the dominant political and religious force across much of North Africa and Southwest Asia. The Umayyad caliphate stretched from southern Spain to Persia in the east. This strong polity was surprisingly unified, at least during the early period of conquest.[29] Although the Umayyads were overthrown in 750 CE, the Islamic world remained united under the new 'Abbasid caliphate until around 809 CE. The 'Abbasids shifted their capital from Damascus to Baghdad, but kept most of the administrative and bureaucratic structures of the state intact.[30] Internal stability resulted in a strong polity able to challenge its neighbors.

The works of these three scholars – Imam Malik, al-Shaybani, and al-Shafi'i – are remarkably similar, partly because of sharing virtually identical historical conditions and partly because of Islamic law's relative intransigence. Innovation was not encouraged, so "new" ideas had to be shown to have precedence in older scholarship, or better yet, in the life of the Prophet himself. Starting in this period, Quranic verses specifying nonaggression were reinterpreted in ways that made aggressive war

[28] Rahman, *Major Themes of the Qur'an*, 63.

[29] This is not to say that there were no tensions. The Ummayads, treating even political disobedience as "religious corruption" endangering the community, fought frequently to put down rebellions across their wide empire. Wadad al-Qadi, "The Religious Foundation of Late Umayyad Ideology and Practice," in Fred M. Donner, ed., *The Articulation of Early Islamic State Structures* (Burlington, VT: Ashgate, 2012), 37–79.

[30] Irit Bligh-Abramski, "Evolution versus Revolution: Umayyad Elements in the 'Abbasid Regime 133/750–320/932," in Donner, *The Articulation of Early Islamic State Structures*, 389–406.

permissible.[31] Without a doubt, this reflects the *realpolitik* of the time.[32] With no serious outside threats to consider, these writers' scholarship primarily handles questions of voluntary (offensive) *jihad* against unbelievers, especially pragmatic questions such as the treatment of prisoners of war and the division of spoils. They are also deeply concerned with internal dissension, especially as a result of theological divisions within the Islamic community. Each also offers increasingly detailed prescriptions for *in bello* conduct, working out more and more nuanced rules regarding civilian immunity. Such matters are handled with more depth than in the early Christian just war tradition, more closely resembling the early modern Christian thinkers than Augustine or Aquinas. Al-Shaybani goes the furthest, discussing responsibility for property damage and the rights of prisoners of war.

MALIK IBN ANAS

Little is known about the background of Malik ibn Anas (715–796). Malik came from a Yemeni family of early converts to Islam who had migrated to Medina some three generations before. His grandfather, too, was a legal scholar.[33] Malik studied at Medina, learning *hadith* from a scholar who had served one of the Prophet's Companions.[34] Malik wrote at the very beginning of the 'Abbasid caliphate, which had overthrown the Umayyads by 750. During the Umayyad period, many independent judges had flourished, using reasoned opinion (*ra'y*) to develop Islamic jurisprudence. But this practice led to "legal divergences through the empire," and "the product of this activity became rather chaotic," with each region developing different rules of law out of its own customary practices, or *sunnah*.[35] With the decline of Umayyad power, this

---

[31] Asma Afsaruddin, "The Siyar Laws of Aggression: Juridical Re-interpretations of Qur'anic Jihad and Their Contemporary Implications for International Law," in Maria-Luisa Frick and Andreas Th. Müller, *Islam and International Law: Engaging Self-Centrism from a Plurality of Perspectives* (Amsterdam: Brill, 2013), 45–63, 49. A reinterpretation of Qur'an 2:190, which permits believers to fight "those who fight you," is one of the key steps in this process.

[32] Ibid., 45.

[33] Malik ibn Anas, *Al-Muwatta of Imam Malik ibn Anas*, trans. and ed. Aisha Abdurrahman Bewley (New York: Routledge, Chapman and Hall, 1989), xxviii.

[34] Ahmed El Shamsy, *The Canonization of Islamic Law* (Cambridge: Cambridge University Press, 2013), 20.

[35] Muhammad Yusuf Guraya, "Historical Background of the Compilation of the Muwatta' of Malik b. Anas," *Islamic Studies* 7(4), 1968, 382.

decentralized legal system added fuel to the 'Abbasids' revolutionary fire. The 'Abbasids, after all, claimed that the Umayyads were "godless" and held up the lack of a single, authoritative Islamic law as proof.[36]

When the 'Abbasids came to power, then, the new regime was under pressure to standardize the law. A vigorous debate was swirling in legal circles at the time, between scholars who favored the use of reasoned opinion (*ra'y*) to determine cases and those who believed that judges should strictly follow the precedent established by the Prophet and his Companions, or the *hadith*. These reports of things said and done by the Prophet and his followers in the earliest years of Islam were initially an oral tradition. In a sense, *hadith* can be understood as a form of sacred history. In this scholarly debate between reasoned opinion and sacred history, Malik favored the use of the latter.[37] When a relevant *hadith* did not exist, Malik invoked Medinan traditions.[38] It's not that Malik was partial to his hometown for personal reasons. But Medina had, after all, developed a constitution under Muhammad's guidance. The continuity this legal framework provided meant that Medinan practices could "function as an independent carrier of cultural memory alongside the Qur'an and the body of Hadith."[39] Put simply, Malik preferred to rely on precedent rather than personal judgment.

The traditional stories, circulated by his disciples, claim that Malik's *al-Muwatta* played a key role not only in the *hadith* debate, but also in consolidating 'Abbasid power. The second 'Abbasid caliph, al-Mansur, apparently visited Medina on his pilgrimage to Mecca. According to tradition, al-Mansur inspired the text, asking Malik to write a book assuming a "mediatory position based on the straightforward middle course, and on what the leaders (of the Community) and the Companions have agreed upon."[40] In other tellings, al-Mansur praised Malik's book, called for it to be "kept in a prominent place in the Ka'bah, so that all the people should refer to it," and ordered copies of *al-Muwatta* to be "circulated in all parts of the Empire."[41]

---

[36] Ibid., 385.

[37] The view that Malik was entirely against *ra'y* is a later imposition; his own conclusions often concluded that the practice of Medina was superior to the practice suggested by specific *hadith*. See Knut S. Vikør, *Between God and Sultan* (Oxford: Oxford University Press, 2006), 89.

[38] John Esposito, *The Oxford History of Islam* (Oxford: Oxford University Press, 2000), 95.

[39] El Shamsy, *The Canonization of Islamic Law*, 21.

[40] Guraya, "Historical Background," 385.

[41] Malik ibn Anas, *Muwatta Imam Malik*, trans. Muhammad Rahimuddin (Lahore, Pakistan: Sh. Muhammad Ashraf, 1980), iv.

Why would a caliph intervene in an academic debate about the sources of law? The supporters of *hadith* promised a stable and consistent basis on which to develop a unified legal system, while the debating process of *ra'y* allowed individual jurists a great deal of leeway. For a caliph interested in centralizing authority, a legal system based on *hadith* seemed practical. As the story goes, al-Mansur met Imam Malik and declared himself to be "disgusted with the differences of the jurists on Islamic law in different regions of the Empire."[42] The use of *ra'y* or individual reasoning only accentuated these differences. *Ra'y* encouraged constant debate, leading to the impression that the law was constantly changing. As Malik put it, "whenever *ra'y* is followed, someone else who is stronger in *ra'y* comes along and then you follow him. So whenever someone comes who defeats you [in debate], you follow him. I see no end to this."[43] Regardless of al-Mansur's precise role, *al-Muwatta* was of great significance for the 'Abbasids. The fourth and fifth 'Abbasid caliphs consulted Malik personally on religious matters, the latter, Harun al-Rashid, even making the Maliki school of jurisprudence the caliphate's official school of law.[44]

The majority of the *hadith* collected in the *Muwatta'* address Islamic religious practice and civil law. Malik's followers transcribed several different versions of the *Muwatta'*. Two of the most important, by Yahya ibn Yahya al-Laithi al-Andalusi and Muhammad al-Shaybani, are used here. Additionally, I draw on the *Al-Musawwanna al-Kubra*, a collection of *fiqh* (jurisprudence) attributed to Malik and written down by one of his followers, Sahnun ibn Sa'id ibn Habib at-Tanukhi. During this early stage in the development of *fiqh* it was not common for scholars to write down their own decisions and arguments. A century earlier, students would have been expected to recall all these conversations from memory, but by Malik's time, students customarily took notes.

Malik describes war and other forms of violence as punishments incurred by peoples who turn away from God. Malik cites Muhammad's cousin Ibn 'Abbas as explaining that "if a people ever rule by anything other than the truth, then [the spilling of] blood becomes widespread among them. If a people are ever unfaithful to their contracts, then the

---

[42] Ibid.
[43] Ibn 'Abd al-Barr, *Jami'bayan al-'ilm*, ed. Abu al-Ashbal al-Zuhayri, 2 vols. (Dammam: Dar Ibn al-Jawzi, 1994), 2:1085–86, cited in El Shamsy, *The Canonization of Islamic Law*, 28.
[44] Vikør, *Between God and Sultan*, 98.

enemy is given power over them."[45] Conflict arises when people fail to submit to God. Likewise, Malik deploys another *hadith* that assures soldiers that they "are fighting in the cause of the Lord with people who have disbelieved and rejected the Lord."[46] War in this sense is a judgment on people who have turned their backs on God and justice. It is a punishment carried out by those who remain loyal to Him.

For Malik, the idea of *jihad* is wrapped up in the concept of order. Non-Muslims must be fought because their way of life is disordered by definition. Islamic law, in his view, offered the only rational and stable foundation for a just society. For this reason, Malik argued that non-believers – even invaders – should not be fought until they had been given the chance to accept Islamic law: "and irrespective of whether we invaded them or whether they advanced upon us as invaders and entered our lands, we do not fight them ... until we have invited them [to Islam.]"[47] Merely repelling unjust attackers would do nothing more than restore the prewar status quo. Expanding the Islamic order is so important that it takes precedent over traditional defense. Attackers who do not submit to Islam must not only be repelled, but conquered. Contrary to post-Westphalian conceptions of sovereignty, Malik claims that wrongdoing that crosses borders cannot simply be pushed back over the border. Its unjust roots at home must also be addressed.

The invitation to join the community of Islamic peace, however, did not need to be offered over and over. Thus, in the case of the Byzantines, the 'Abbasids' peer competitors, Malik declared that "the invitation is discarded, due to their familiarity with what they are being invited to, their state of contempt and enmity for the religion and its adherents, and their long-standing opposition to and fighting against the armies [of Islam]."[48] The recognition that the Byzantines were not likely to suddenly shift course and accept the invitation to Islam pragmatically benefited Muslim forces. While Malik disapproved of night ambushes

---

45 Muhammad ibn al-Hasan ash-Shaybani, *The Muwatta' of Imam Muhammad*, trans. Mohammed Abdurrahman and Abdassamad Clarke (London: Turath Publishing, 2004), 379, 17.0.861. "ash-Shaybani" reflects Iraqi and Syrian dialects of Arabic, but this is indeed the same al-Shaybani that we shall meet later in the chapter.

46 Malik ibn Anas, *Muwatta' Imam Malik*, 272.959, 201.

47 Malik ibn Anas, *Al-Mudawwanna al-Kubra li al-Imam Malik ibn Anas al-Ashabhi* (Beirut, Lebanon: Dar al-Kutub al-'Ilmiya, 1994), trans. Aziz el Kaissouni in Nesrine Badawi, "Sunni Islam, Part I: Classical Sources," in Greg Reichberg, Henrik Syse, and Nicole Hartwell, eds., *Religion, War and Ethics: A Sourcebook of Textual Traditions* (Cambridge: Cambridge University Press, 2014), 316.

48 Ibid., 316.

against disbelievers who had not been previously invited to Islam, he argued that it would be permissible to take the Byzantines "unawares; the invitation [to Islam] would serve them only as a warning, to prepare themselves to fight the Muslims and prevent the victory over them that the Muslims desire."[49]

Despite 'Abbasid claims to rule the entirety of the Islamic world, local centers of power, especially in the Maghreb and the Levant, challenged the empire's stability, as did minority sects, such as the Shi'a. Malik himself was caught up in at least one of these disputes. He was asked to rule on whether an oath taken by a Shi'a rebel to Caliph al-Mansur was binding. Malik was no sympathizer to the cause, but he argued that the oath had no legal standing as the man had taken it under duress. Al-Mansur was furious; Malik was flogged.

It is clear, nonetheless, that Malik shared al-Mansur's concern with the unity of the Islamic community. Factions are not to be tolerated. Malik refers to a *hadith*, for example, that declares "there is no good in departing from the obedience to the Amir and from the united body of the Muslims . . . one must simply hold firm to the united body."[50] However, because the unity of the community is the primary goal, Malik counsels that rebels ought to be given a "fair adjudication" before either side resorts to force.[51] This suggests not only a simple airing of the rebels' concerns, but a willingness to really hear them out. Even if the community judges the rebels to be in the wrong, the rebels should be given the chance to repent. If they are willing to rejoin the community, they should not be fought. (This distinguishes rebels from apostates, who can be executed as soon as their apostasy is revealed.) In other words, so long as the conflict remained *political* and nonviolent, the rebels should merely "be arrested, imprisoned, beaten, boycotted, and socially ostracized until they repent."[52]

Individuals who threaten the internal *political* unity of the Muslim community may be opposed violently, if they themselves use force. The dissenter's choice to take up arms invalidates the protection normally accorded to him as a Muslim "because he made his own blood permissible by advancing against people with his sword."[53] In other words,

---

[49] Ibid., 316–317.
[50] Ash-Shaybani, *The Muwatta of Imam Muhammad*, 17.2.864, 380.
[51] Malik ibn Anas, *Al-Mudawwanna*, 346. See also ash-Shaybani. *The Muwatta of Imam Muhammad*, 17.60.1002, 426.
[52] Khaled Abou El Fadl, *Rebellion and Violence* (Cambridge: Cambridge University Press, 2003), 137.
[53] Ash-Shaybani, *The Muwatta of Imam Muhammad*, 17.2.865, 371.

when rebels turn to violence they by default "[attack] the other unjustly," and so must be fought until they "revert to Allah's command."[54] Nonetheless, such political rebels retain certain rights. They were entitled to regain their full status as members of the Muslim community after the conflict ends.[55] Similarly, their property should be returned after the cessation of hostilities, and they are to be absolved from having shed the blood of their fellow Muslims.[56] The end goal of putting down a rebellion, therefore, is not simply victory, but the recovery of the social order.

In terms of *in bello* restrictions, Malik believed that Muslim armies' tactics should reflect the fact that they were fighting for God. Hence, they should fight in an orderly and restrained way. In an ideal *jihad*, "the best of property is expended and the companion is loved and the leader is obeyed and disturbance (riot) is avoided."[57] By contrast, if the forces disobey their leader, squabble among themselves, and avoid real sacrifice, the resulting *jihad* will, "instead of bringing any reward, [make] it difficult to return alive."[58] An orderly campaign is not only morally good, but pragmatically wise.

Among the specific rules of discipline Malik lays out are protections for noncombatants. He cites Abu Bakr, the first caliph to succeed Muhammad, in this regard:

"You will find some people who imagine they have devoted their lives to Allah (the hermits), leave them to their work ... I instruct you in ten matters: Do not kill women or children, nor the old and infirm; do not cut fruit-bearing trees; do not destroy any town; do not cut the gums of sheep or camels except for the purposes of eating; do not burn date-trees nor submerge them; do not steal from booty and do not be cowardly."[59]

These rules of engagement forbid targeting civilians who are, as the Christian tradition would have put it, *innocent*.[60] Women and children, the old and infirm, and religious monks and hermits are unlikely to be combatants. (Women who take up arms, however, may be targeted.)[61] The rules also forbid gratuitously damaging civilians' living environment – their homes should not be destroyed, nor their crops and livestock. Put differently, "enough of their wealth is to be left to them to allow

---

[54] Ash-Shaybani, *The Muwatta of Imam Muhammad*, 17.60.1002, 426.
[55] Ibid., 17.4.868, 382.   [56] Malik ibn Anas, *Al-Mudawwanna*, 346.
[57] Malik ibn Anas, *Muwatta Imam Malik*, 283.985, 211.   [58] Ibid.
[59] Ibid., 272.958, 200. See also Malik ibn Anas, *Al-Muwatta*, 21.3.10, 174.
[60] Malik ibn Anas, *Al-Mudawwanna*, 327.
[61] Ash Shaybani, *The Muwatta of Imam Muhammad*, 17.3.867, 381.

them to subsist. They should not take all their wealth and leave them with nothing to live off so that they would perish."[62] Destruction of the goods necessary for sustenance is effectively a death sentence. Furthermore, such violence would be, above all, unnecessary. To reinforce this point, Malik prohibits mutilation of enemy corpses.[63] Just as a dead soldier can do no further harm, and so should be left alone, so too civilians should be spared.

Although Malik seems aware that the principle of necessity might militate against strictly observing civilian immunity, he does not quite endorse double effect. When one of his students asks if Muslim forces can attack "infidels" holding Muslim captives in their fortress or on one of their ships at sea, Malik replied, "I am not of the opinion that fire should be hurled at them."[64] To explain his position, which seems to value individual Muslim lives more than victory, Malik points to a verse in the Qur'an, in which God explains that Muslims should not fight in the Ka'ba at Mecca because it was impossible to separate the believers from the disbelievers.[65] Malik's students also push him to weigh the lives of non-Muslim noncombatants against military victory, asking whether the same logic would hold if the fortress under siege housed the infidels' women and children, but no Muslims. Would it be possible to burn the fortress, or to destroy it by flooding it? Malik replies, "I know of nothing to recite in this regard, but I view that as reprehensible, and I do not like it."[66] Interestingly, although Malik clearly views such an indiscriminate action as morally dubious, he does not forbid it outright. Without a *hadith* to confirm his personal judgment, Malik can do no more. Still, this view represents a far narrower tolerance of the idea of double effect than we will find later.

AL-SHAYBANI

Born in Iraq in 750 CE, Muhammad ibn Hasan al-Shaybani began his studies in his hometown of Kufa. His family was fairly prosperous, and he began to study with Abu Hanifa around the age of fourteen, and later with Abu Yusuf.[67] Al-Shaybani's wealth permitted him to devote his life

---

[62] Ibid., 328.   [63] Malik ibn Anas, 21.3.11, 174. See also *Al-Mudawanna*, 328.
[64] Malik ibn Anas, *Al-Mudawwanna*, 333–334.   [65] Ibid., 334. See Qur'an 48:25.
[66] Ibid.
[67] Majid Khadduri, *The Islamic Law of Nations: Shaybani's Siyar* (Baltimore: Johns Hopkins University Press, 2001), 30.

to research and writing, freed from the "material temptations" of office, at least for some time.[68] Sometime after Abu Hanifa's death, while still a young man, al-Shaybani journeyed to Medina to study under Malik ibn Anas. On the way, he stopped off in Syria to study with Awza'i, author of a very early version of the *siyar*, or Islamic international law.[69] After the completion of his studies, he returned to Kufa, becoming a popular lecturer on the law. Despite his studies with Malik, al-Shaybani's thinking was primarily influenced by the Abu Hanifa. Like many Iraqi scholars of his time, al-Shaybani preferred *ra'y*, penning a blistering critique of Malik's Medinan doctrine.[70] Although the new *hadith* gathered in Malik's *Muwatta* could not be ignored entirely, al-Shaybani's solution (typical of the Hanafi position) was to prefer locally known *hadith* over "new" ones.[71]

Abu Yusuf's motives in recommending al-Shaybani for a position as a *qadi*, or judge, likely reflected a mixture of hearty respect for the young man's talents and mild jealousy of his popularity.[72] After all, scholars at the time looked down on public office, feeling that it entailed "the subordination of their consciences to official pressures."[73] Being offered such a position was no great honor. So when al-Shaybani was summoned to Baghdad, the seat of 'Abbasid power, he marched straight to Abu Yusuf to express his displeasure.[74] Under pressure from his old teacher and the caliph's first minister, al-Shaybani reluctantly accepted the office of *qadi* in Raqqa. However, his period of official service was short, as the result of a disagreement with Caliph Harun al-Rashid. The caliph had wanted to withdraw an *aman* he had extended to a political competitor who later engaged in the 'Alid rebellion. Shaybani, however, deemed that the promise of security was binding.[75] Al-Shaybani was by no means a sympathizer, but he was "a representative of the emerging conception of law and order."[76] In his view, the law was superior even to the will of the caliph. Al-Rashid, however, disagreed. The rebel was executed, and Shaybani – along with other scholars who had opposed the caliph – were dismissed.[77] Nonetheless, by the last year of al-Shaybani's life he was back in the caliph's good graces. He was appointed *qadi* of Rayy,

---

[68] Ibid., 32.   [69] This text is no longer extant.

[70] Vikør, *Between God and Sultan*, 25; El Shamsy, *The Canonization of Islamic Law*, 47. For an excellent discussion of Iraqi *ra'y* and al-Shaybani's role in it, see ibid., 22–22.

[71] El Shamsy, *The Canonization of Islamic Law*, 53. This rather scandalized al-Shafi'i.

[72] Khadduri, *The Islamic Law of Nations*, 31.   [73] Ibid., 32.   [74] Ibid., 31.

[75] Ibid., 33.   [76] Abou El Fadl, *Rebellion and Violence in Islamic Law*, 83.

[77] Ibid., 82.

in Khurasan (eastern Persia). He died on an expedition with the caliph to suppress a rebellion in Samarqand, in what is now Uzbekistan, in 804.[78]

Al-Shaybani is most famous for writing one of the first treatises on Islamic international law.[79] The term *siyar* itself means "movements," in this case, movements "between and within two broadly defined political-territorial associations, namely the 'territory of Islam" and the 'territory of war.'"[80] The *siyar* is a special branch of Islamic law, dealing with "relations with non-Islamic states as well as with the tolerated religious communities within its own territory."[81] A text primarily concerned with the technical aspects of how to fight, al-Shaybani's *siyar* is markedly different than Malik's work. First, much more of the text deals with war onset, tactics, and postwar resolution. Second, because its focus is practical, it does not engage in exhortation or encouragement to *jihad*, but instead presumes that Muslim forces will be engaged in fighting.

Al-Shaybani's *siyar* divides the world into two categories: the *dar al-harb*, or the world of war, and the *dar al-Islam*, the world of peace. The *dar al-harb* is that part of the world that is not under Islamic political control. Most (but not all) of its inhabitants are presumed to be non-believers. In fact, believers are expected to migrate to the *dar al-Islam*, particularly if the free exercise of their religion is impeded. By contrast, the *dar al-Islam* is the territory governed by Islamic law. Not all of its population is Muslim, but its minority religious communities submit to Islamic political authority. Separate rules apply in each context, affecting everything from general property rights to the rights of prisoners of war.

For al-Shaybani, the *dar al-Islam* constitutes a political entity, incorporating diverse populations. Non-Muslim "peoples of the book" who agree to make peace and to submit to Islamic political authority are permitted to maintain their traditional religious practices and family law, in exchange for paying a tax, called the *jizya*.[82] This tax stands in exchange for the mandatory military service required of Muslims to fulfill the requirements of both defense and *jihad*. As the tax was not meant to be punitive, al-Shaybani felt the *jizya* should be levied "according to their capacity to pay," and not at all on women,

---

[78] al-Shaybani, *The Islamic Law of Nations*. 34. See also Abou El Fadl, *Rebellion and Violence in Islamic Law*, 82.

[79] Bonner, Jihad in History, 99.

[80] John Kelsay. *Arguing the Just War in Islam* (Cambridge, MA: Harvard University Press, 2007), 99.

[81] Khadduri, *The Islamic Law of Nations*, 2.   [82] Ibid., V.480–529, 142–147.

children, "the blind, the old and very aged, the insane, the crippled, the helpless, and the poor."[83]

While non-Muslims could be incorporated into the political order of the *dar al-Islam*, the *dar al-harb*, on the other hand, remained disorderly. Hence, offensive wars to expand the territory are a duty. Citing the famous *hadith* of the Prophet, al-Shaybani declares that Muslims should

combat [only] those who disbelieve in God ... Whenever you meet your polytheist enemies, invite them [first] to adopt Islam. If they do, accept it and let them alone ... If they refuse ... then call upon them to pay the jizya (poll tax); if they do, accept it and leave them alone.[84]

Like Malik, Shaybani argues that the invitation to accept Islam need be made only once, although renewing the invitation would be commendable.[85]

The obligation to expand the *dar al-Islam* is incumbent on the entire community, rather than falling to any particular individual. Muslims are "obligated to provide a fighting force," and "those who stay behind [should] contribute to those who go."[86] Appropriate contributions include horses and military supplies, as well as payment for a substitute. Al-Shaybani also invokes a *hadith* that favored sending unmarried men to war, rather than married ones.[87] This suggests a practical approach. Offensive *jihad* should not overly strain the resources of the community, nor undermine its security.

One interesting feature of al-Shaybani's discussion is what *isn't* said. In an "interesting demonstration of confidence, al-Shaybani and his colleagues do not address the question of fighting defensively in response to an enemy invasion."[88] Al-Shaybani does, however, address the possibility that the Islamic state may not be powerful enough to successfully expand its boundaries. In cases where "the inhabitants of the territory of war are too strong for the Muslims to prevail against them," al-Shaybani recommended a conciliatory policy.[89] Such treaties were a pragmatic solution to a real-world problem, but inherently unideal. Under such a treaty, the non-Muslim neighbors had no obligation to reform their religious or political institutions to conform to the Islamic order. They would also not be subject to the *jizya*, because they would not be considered as part of the *dar al-Islam*."[90]

---

[83] Ibid., V.482–489, 163.   [84] Ibid., I.1, 76.   [85] Ibid., II.55. 95.   [86] Ibid., I.22. 85.
[87] Ibid., I.24. 85.   [88] Kelsay, *Arguing the Just War in Islam*, 104.
[89] al-Shaybani, *The Islamic Law of Nations*, V.603, 154.   [90] Ibid.

Any disorder within the *dar al-Islam* had to be combatted, with force if necessary. However, the *in bello* rules for fighting Muslim rebels are quite strict. After all, the primary goal of counterinsurgency is to restore the community's unity. Consequently, al-Shaybani recommends restrained force. Rebels do not completely lose their property rights even when they take up arms: "when the war comes to an end, everything should be returned to its [original] owners."[91] This contrasts starkly to the property of residents of the *dar al-harb*, which is to be distributed among the Muslim fighters as the spoils of war. Women rebel fighters, if captured, were not to be executed.[92] Like Malik, al-Shaybani waives the usual duty for atonement or to pay blood-money for killing Muslims – for both loyalists and rebels.[93] Al-Shaybani's commitment to maintaining the stability of the *dar al-Islam* is such that he even argued that loyalists must defend rebel-held territories against non-Muslim incursions.[94] As the *hadith* states, "Muslims should support one another against the outsider."[95]

A second, less restrictive, set of *in bello* regulations apply to wars with unbelievers in the *dar al-harb*. Many echo Malik's injunctions. In the very first section of the *Siyar*, al-Shaybani cites the Prophet: "Do not cheat or commit treachery, nor should you mutilate anyone or kill children."[96] Later, he repeats that "whenever the Apostle of God sent forth a detachment he said to it: 'Do not cheat or commit treachery. Nor should you mutilate or kill children, women or old men.'"[97] While innocent persons could not be harmed, their property could be destroyed. To do so would even be "commendable," because in the Qur'an it had been written, "Whatever palm trees you cut down or left standing upon their roots, has been by God's permission, in order that the ungodly ones might be humiliated."[98] Ambush was permissible, and a city could be flooded or burnt, the era's equivalent of mass destruction.[99]

Al-Shaybani believed that such indiscriminate force could be used even if there were slaves, women, old men, and children in a city, and even if there were Muslims among them.[100] Here al-Shaybani upholds a principle of double effect, going one step further than Malik. Noncombatants themselves are not legitimate targets – Muslims among them even

---

[91] Ibid., VIII.1376, 232. See also the return of weapons, 1388.
[92] Ibid., VIII.1379–1380, 233.   [93] Ibid., VIII.1395–1400, 1405–1410, 234–235.
[94] Ibid., VIII.1535–1536, 245–246.   [95] Ibid., I.50, 93. See also VI.641, 159
[96] Ibid., I.1, 76 See also I.30–31, 87.   [97] Ibid., II.47, 92. See also I.31, 87.
[98] Ibid., II.88–89, 99.   [99] Ibid., II.55, 95.   [100] Ibid., II.110, 114–115, 101, 102.

less so – but if they are only indirectly killed (in the process of attacking a walled city, for example), then the Muslim soldiers are not guilty of violating the principle of noncombatant immunity. Al-Shaybani relies on a *hadith* to explain that "if the Muslims stopped attacking the inhabitants of the territory of war for any of the reasons you have stated, they would be unable to go to war at all."[101] Thus, for prudential reasons, al-Shaybani permits the deaths of innocents, so long as those deaths are not intended. (The parallel with Vitoria, who developed the Christian principle of double effect seven hundred years later, is remarkable.)

Al-Shaybani's discussion of prisoners of war also reflects prudential concerns. Al-Shaybani cites two apparently contradictory *hadith*, one in which Abu Bakr declares that a prisoner of war "should either be killed or become a Muslim," and another that asserts that "the prisoner of war should not be killed, but he may be ransomed or set free by grace."[102] Al-Shaybani argues that the first *hadith* has more merit, holding that the Imam (in that case Abu Bakr) ought to be the one to decide the fate of prisoners based on the interests of the Muslim community as a whole.[103] Prisoners who could walk were to be brought back to the territory of Islam; those who could not could be killed.[104] In al-Shaybani's view, male prisoners of war presumably acted either as combatants or political leaders. Hence, they could be punished by death, as their refusal to submit was a serious disruption of order. However, recognizing the potential value of such prisoners, al-Shaybani ultimately leaves it up to the Imam to prudentially decide.

Women and children, even if unable to walk, were not to be killed – instead, transport should be arranged for them.[105] Likewise, "the blind, the crippled, the helpless insane," if taken prisoner, should never be killed.[106] Because these persons fit al-Shaybani's understanding of innocents, as prisoners they could never be killed, as they bear no responsibility for the conflict.

While al-Shaybani discusses protections for noncombatants and prisoners of war in greater detail than Malik, he is even more pragmatic. Protections are offered when it is militarily feasible to do so. Soldiers should avoid killing the innocent in war, but are not morally guilty if civilians die as an unintended consequence of their actions. Likewise, the fate of prisoners is determined largely by necessity.

---

[101] Ibid., II.117, 102.   [102] Ibid., I.43–44, 91.   [103] Ibid., II.94–101, 100.
[104] Ibid., II.79–81, 98.   [105] Ibid.   [106] Ibid., 110, 101.

AL-SHAFI'I

Muhammad ibn Idris al-Shafi'i (767–820 CE) was born in Gaza. Al-Shafi'i's father was from the same tribe as the Prophet, and they shared a distant ancestor; this noble lineage surely opened doors for the young boy who grew up a poor orphan in Mecca.[107] A star pupil, al-Shafi'i tutored younger students to pay his way.[108] Having memorized the Qur'an by age seven, he began to deliver *fatwas*, or legal judgments, somewhere between age fifteen and eighteen.[109] Before setting off to Medina to complete his education in law, al-Shafi'i spent some time among the Bedouins, following the tradition of noble Arabs of the time to "perfect their Arabic in the desert, free from the corrupting influences of foreign dialects that had infiltrated the language of cities and towns."[110] Upon his return home, al-Shafi'i asked for letters of introduction from the governor of Mecca to the Medinan authorities and to Malik ibn Anas himself.[111] Al-Shafi'i spent a decade studying under Malik. After the senior scholar's death, he continued on to Yemen and Iraq to study medicine, physiology, poetry, and more theology. In Iraq, he sought out al-Shaybani, who had also been Malik's student.[112]

Al-Shafi'i's work was clearly influenced by his mentors, Malik ibn Anas and al-Shaybani. His brief, albeit intense, period of employment in the government shaped his views on law, rebellion, and justice. Al-Shafi'i came to the attention of the governor of Yemen, who convinced him to enter the service of the state when he was about thirty years old.[113] Al-Shafi'i was an apt administrator, but he quickly became "entangled with local interests and factional jealousies," which cost him his job.[114] A local rebellion against the 'Abbasid caliphs erupted in the province where al-Shafi'i was posted. Like al-Shaybani, he never took up arms, but he used the law to defend a Yemeni rebel.[115] His mentor, Al-Shaybani,

---

[107] Kecia Ali, *Imam Shafi'i: Scholar and Saint* (Oxford: Oneworld Publications, 2011), location 177. See also Muhammad ibn Idris al-Shafi'i, *al-Shafi'i's Risala: Treastise on the Foundations of Islamic Jurisprudence*, trans. Majid Khadduri (Cambridge: Islamic Texts Society, 1997), 10.

[108] El Shamsy, *The Canonization of Islamic Law*, 18.

[109] Ali, *Imam Shafi'i*, location 206, 227.

[110] Ibid., location 238. See also Al-Shafi'i, *al-Shafi'i's Risala*, 11.

[111] Ali, *Imam Shafi'i*, location 269. See also El Shamsy, *Canonization of Islamic Law*, 19.

[112] Ali, *Imam Shafi'i*, location 538. See also Al-Shafi'i, *al-Shafi'i's Risala*, 12.

[113] Al-Shafi'i, *al-Shafi'i's Risala*, 11.

[114] Ibid. See also Hodgson, *The Venture of Islam*, vol. 1, 327.

[115] Ali, *Imam Shafi'i*, location 453. See also Abou El Fadl, *Rebellion and Violence in Islamic Law*, 80.

stood by as the leaders of the rebellion were sentenced to death, but intervened to prevent the execution of his fellow jurist.[116]

After this incident, al-Shafi'i returned briefly to Mecca to teach, where he counted ibn Hanbal, for whom the Hanbali school of *fiqh* took its name, among his students. Within five years, however, al-Shafi'i returned to Baghdad. This time when offered the position of a judge by Caliph al-Ma'mun, he declined.[117] Theologically, al-Shafi'i and al-Ma'mun were at odds. The caliph had declared in 827 that the Qur'an was created by God, and by 833 had decreed that no judge who held an alternate viewpoint could hold office. Al-Shafi'i held the traditional – and opposing view – that the Qur'an was co-eternal with God. So, at the age of fifty, al-Shafi'i left for Egypt, making his final choice "between his love for power and his love for the law."[118] The *Risala* was written during this period.[119] Already in frail health, al-Shafi'i died after being beat up by his rivals' students following a particularly heated scholarly debate.[120]

Recognizing both the merits and the limitations of both Malik's strict reliance on *hadith* and al-Shaybani's emphasis on *ra'y*, al-Shafi'i developed an innovative new methodological approach. This new approach deemphasized *hadith* and local practice, instead using the Qur'an and the *sunna* as the basis of the law.[121] This had obvious political benefits, as the Islamic world had extended far beyond the cultural community where it had begun. This multiculturalism created the need for a universal Islamic law. As a theoretician, Shafi'i proposes a methodology based on analogy (*qiyas*), meant to serve as a bridge between the supporters of *ra'y* and the advocates of the *hadith*.[122] This strategy calls for reliance upon the Qu'ran first, with precedent (as expressed in *hadith*) second. When the *hadith* are incomplete, absent, or contradictory, judges could exercise personal judgment through the careful use of analogy to reach a decision.[123] This approach treats the Qur'an and the *sunna* as canonical, almost constitutional, texts.

---

[116] Abou El Fadl, *Rebellion and Violence in Islamic Law*, 83.

[117] Al-Shafi'i, *Al-Shafi'i's Risala*, 14.   [118] Ibid.   [119] Ibid., 19.

[120] Ibid., 16. See also Ali, *Imam Shafi'i*, location 722.

[121] El Shamsy, *The Canonization of Islamic Law*, 69. See also Al-Shafi'i, *Al-Shafi'i's Risala*, 327.

[122] Vikør, *God and Sultan*, 28, 64. Al-Shafi'i's synthesis was not widely accepted for a half-century after his death. See Wael B. Hallaq. "Was al-Shafi'i the Master Architect of Islamic Jurisprudence?" *International Journal of Middle East Studies* 25(4), 1993, 587–605, 601.

[123] El Shamsy, *Canonization of Islamic Law*, 60.

Al-Shafi'i lived under two especially powerful, absolutist caliphs: al-Mahdi (775–785) and al-Rashid (786–809). Both were interested in pursuing an aggressively centralizing agenda, to further unify their vast empire.[124] Al-Mahdi actively asserted 'Abbasid power, waging raids on the Byzantine empire and internally persecuting minority religious groups, such as the Manicheans.[125] Al-Rashid ruled at the peak of the caliphates' power and luxury: "for a brief generation there was relatively unbroken peace and prosperity in the caliphal empire. The occasional rebellions and foreign wars were important only locally."[126] Al-Rashid seems to have "preferred to alternate between leading the caravan of the hajj to Mecca one year and the jihad army the next," although battle strategy was left up to the generals.[127]

The power and stability of the 'Abbasid empire, however, began to falter in the last decade of al-Shafi'i's life. Al-Rashid appointed his elder son, al-Amin, as his first successor, and his younger son, al-Ma'mun, as his second, in 809. But al-Ma'mun was not satisfied with governing only the province of Khurasan, and usurped the caliphate after his elder brother's assassination in 813.[128] The internal struggle for power that followed – not helped by al-Ma'mun's turn to Shi'ism – kept him from conquering the capital until 819. In Egypt, where al-Shafi'i had recently taken up residence, the commander of the 'Abbasid troops took advantage of the power vacuum to claim control of the south of the country for himself; the north came under the control of an Arab tribal alliance.[129] Al-Ma'mun's power grab not only upset the political order – it challenged the balance between political and religious authorities as well. Unlike his predecessors, al-Ma'mun attempted to claim for the caliph the right to determine "what was valid law in the eyes of *God*."[130] This put him in direct conflict with scholars like al-Shafi'i, who argued that only the consensus of the community (the *'umma*) had that power.

It was in this context – a period of both academic disputes and serious political turmoil – that al-Shafi'i wrote the *Risala*. Al-Shafi'i's discussion of war makes up only a very small proportion of the entire *Risala*, as his primary aim is to establish his legal method. In the text,

---

[124] Ibid., 103.   [125] Al-Shafi'i, *Al-Shafi'i's Risala*, 289.   [126] Ibid., 292.
[127] Ibid., 292.
[128] Philip K. Hitti, *History of the Arabs* (New York: Palgrave Macmillan, 2002), Kindle Version, location 7875.
[129] El Shamsy, *Canonization of Islamic Law*, 108–109.
[130] Patricia Crone and Martin Hinds, *God's Caliph: Religious Authority in the First Centuries of Islam* (Cambridge: Cambridge University Press, 2003), 93.

al-Shafi'i deals with only two issues: whether *jihad* is a collective or individual duty, and whether Muslim soldiers ought to uphold non-combatant immunity.

Like his predecessors, Al-Shafi'i writes that *jihad* is a duty laid down in the Qur'an itself. Providing what may be the first fully articulated definition of *fard kifaya* (collective duty) in the legal literature, al-Shafi'i argues that to struggle with arms against unbelievers is a communal duty, not an individual one, although individuals can certainly win merit by taking part: "the duty of [*jihad*] is a collective (*kifaya*) duty different from that of prayer: Those who perform it in the war against the polytheists will fulfill the duty and receive the supererogatory merit, thereby preventing those who have stayed behind from falling into error."[131] Those who do not go are not punished, so long as a sufficient number do perform the duty. But if Muslims as a group fail to carry out *jihad*, then all are guilty.

Al-Shafi'i also treats *jihad* as primarily an offensive venture. He argues that just as the Prophet "vanquished the unscriptured until they adopted Islam, voluntarily and coerced, and ... slew and enslaved the People of the Book until some of them adopted Islam, and some paid the *jizya*, humbled, and his command ... ruled them," so too should Muslim armies go forth and demand that the surrounding infidels either convert to Islam or pay the *jizya*.[132] And like Malik, al-Shafi'i takes the pragmatic view that there is likely "no one today whom the invitation to Islam has not reached, save that there be a nation of infidels behind our enemies who are fighting us," somewhere beyond the Byzantines, Turks, and the nomadic Khazars of the Caucasus.[133]

Treating *jihad* in this way as an "obligatory duty for all and as offensive combat" is an innovation that seems to "defer to Realpolitik," supporting the state's policies of territorial expansion.[134] Indeed, al-Shafi'i is not particularly interested in the role of individuals, but instead in "the role, in the allocation of resources, of something that we are tempted to identify as the state, an entity that al-Shafi'i calls the *sultan*."[135] That a legal scholar close to 'Abbasid authorities would frame *jihad* as a collective military duty suggests the interlocking of political and

---

[131] Al-Shafi'i, *Al-Shafi'i's Risala*, 42, 84. For an analysis of its uniqueness, see Bonner, *Jihad in History*, 107.

[132] Al-Shafi'i, *al-Umm*, vol. IV, trans. Aziz el-Kaissouni, in Badawi, "Sunni Islam, Part I: Classical Sources," 315, 317.

[133] Ibid., 317.   [134] Afsaruddin, *Striving in the Path of God*, 4.

[135] Bonner, *Jihad in History*, 107.

theological circles, especially since several other authorities of the era who were outside the political sphere endorsed only a defensive *jihad*.[136]

While Malik and al-Shaybani dealt with the subject of rebellion briefly, al-Shafi'i was the first to develop a "systematic exposition of the law."[137] Considering the fraught political conditions of his time, and the general classical Islamic preference for domestic order and unity, it is not terribly surprising that al-Shafi'i discussed the legitimacy of rebellion in rather roundabout terms that could be seen as legitimizing the current caliph's reign, rather than permitting rebellion more broadly. Al-Shafi'i, after all, believed that "it was legitimate to fight alongside and pray behind anyone who proclaimed himself caliph after attaining military victory and gaining the backing of the populace."[138] This pragmatic approach seems to be a judgment in favor of *order*. If the established authorities are unable to maintain order, then successful newcomers may be permitted to do so. Rather ironically, this is the very claim that the 'Abbasids themselves had made against the Umayyads, and which this particular caliph – Harun al-Rashid – had made against his predecessor.[139]

Although al-Shafi'i never specifically describes a just ruler, his definition of a *baghi* or a rebel as "one who refuses to obey the just ruler ... and intends to rebel by fighting him" opens up the possibility that resisting an unjust ruler may not be rebellion at all – and may, in fact, be justified.[140] Given the novelty of this move, it is telling that al-Shafi'i's writing on rebellion dates to *after* his move to Egypt, after he had stepped outside of the political circles of his day. In later centuries, Ibn Taymiyya singled al-Shafi'i out for criticism, accusing him of "opening the door for rebellion and civil discord, and encouraging chaos and anarchy."[141]

If opening the door, ever so slightly, to justified rebellion was radical, al-Shafi'i's understanding of why it was permissible to fight *against* rebels was politically conservative. Although "it is not proper to claim that a rebel's blood may be spilled without exception," al-Shafi'i wrote, until order was reestablished "we may fight him either to protect ourselves or

---

[136] Afsaruddin, *Striving in the Path of God*, 4. The outside authorities in question are Abu Salama bin 'Abd al-Rahman and Sufyan al-Thawri.
[137] Khaled Abou El Fadl, "The Rules of Killing at War: An Inquiry into Classical Sources." *Muslim World* 89(2), 1999, 147.
[138] Ali, *Imam Shafi'i*, location 443.
[139] Abou El Fadl, *Rebellion and Violence in Islamic Law*, 80.
[140] Abou El Fadl, "The Rules of Killing at War: An Inquiry into Classical Sources," 148.
[141] Ibid., 149.

to insure compliance with what is demanded of him."[142] The community itself is at stake. For this reason, rebels differ from apostates and criminal gangs. Rebels, unlike apostates, remain part of the Muslim community. But they are not mere criminals, because their violence carries a political meaning – it results from a difference of interpretation.[143] When it is not a single individual who disagrees, but an entire "rebelling faction," then the problem is not one of disobedience but of the health of the community.[144]

The community is supposed to be in agreement. When it is not, the proper response is to seek reconciliation first. This logic is reflected in al-Shafi'i's *in bello* counterinsurgency rules. Rebels must be "warned, debated, and given a full chance to repent before being fought."[145] Rebels can be fought only as long as they use arms against the state; when they cease fighting, their blood again becomes inviolable.[146] Indiscriminate weapons, such as mangonels or flame-throwers, cannot be used against rebels, except in "dire necessity ... [when] the rebels use these weapons first, or if the rebels occupy a fortress where it becomes difficult to defeat them otherwise."[147] Rebel property may not be taken as booty, and any goods that are confiscated during the battle for the sake of fighting must be returned afterwards, along with all captives. Taken altogether, these rules suggest that the rebel must be fought not as a "legal imperative," but rather as a "necessary evil," where the "necessity of maintaining order and stability" outweighs the unavoidable costs in terms of Muslim lives.[148]

Al-Shafi'i also sets out rules of engagement for Muslims participating in warfare against non-Muslims, upholding a pragmatic sort of civilian immunity. Only adult males should be fought.[149] Although monks should not be killed, al-Shafi'i does not offer similar protection to "cowards, freemen, slaves and craftsmen who do not fight."[150] Instead, al-Shafi'i argues that extending noncombatant protections to such persons relies on a mistaken analogy. While Abu Bakr did forbid killing monks, other *hadith* show that the Prophet did not denounce the slaying of an elderly, invalid man lying on a stretcher during the Battle of Husain.[151]

---

[142] Al-Shafi'i, *al-Umm*, IV.215–216, in Abou El Fadl, "The Rules of Killing at War," 150.
[143] Abou El Fadl, "The Rules of Killing at War," 151.
[144] Al-Shafi'i, *al-Umm*, in Badawi, "Sunni Islam, Part I: Classical Sources," 359.
[145] Abou El Fadl, "The Rules of Killing at War," 152.
[146] Ibid., 153. See also al-Shafi'i, *al-Umm*, in Badawi, "Sunni Islam, Part I: Classical Sources," 361.
[147] Abou El Fadl, "The Rules of Killing at War," 152.   [148] Ibid., 157–158.
[149] Al-Shafi'i, *al-Umm*, in Badawi, "Sunni Islam, Part I: Classical Sources," 329.
[150] Ibid., 330.   [151] Ibid.

From al-Shafi'i's point of view, the disabled man bears more in common with peasants and slaves – and the wounded and prisoners of war – than he does with the monks.[152] Although al-Shafi'i does not make his reasoning explicit here, it seems that the difference is that monks have chosen to eschew fighting *on a moral principle*, in service of God, while the other categories of men are simply out of the fight at the moment. They are *potential* fighters and *potential* leaders, even if they are not presently so engaged.

Al-Shafi'i's protection of women and children is a bit more robust. They should not be slain, unless they take up arms against the Muslims.[153] Although women and children should not be killed "deliberately," their deaths as the result of a legitimate raid against a non-Muslim fortress would require "neither blood money, nor retributive punishment, nor acts of expiation."[154] This concept of double effect, emerging out of al-Shafi'i's resolution of an apparent conflict between two *sunna*, appears both in *al-Umm* and in the *Risala*.[155] In both texts, al-Shafi'i is asked to reconcile the tension between one tradition in which the Prophet permits the killing of women and children during a night ambush on unbelievers, and another where Muhammad explicitly prohibits the killing of women and children. Considering the specific circumstances surrounding each, al-Shafi'i explains that understood together, they mean that women and children should be excluded "from the order of killing whenever they could be distinguished from others."[156]

Non-Muslim women and children living in the *dar al-harb*, after all, were not immune from killing based on the law that prohibits shedding Muslim blood, nor immune from ambush based on the rule prohibiting ambush in the *dar al-Islam*.[157] Thus, legally, one who kills women and children, even in a night ambush, would not be guilty of violating the law, since none was applicable. Compensation and atonement would not be necessary.[158] Nonetheless, al-Shafi'i reasserts the claim that "whoever kills women and children should not do so intentionally, if they are recognizable and distinguishable. He [the Prophet] prohibited the killing of children because they do not comprehend disbelief sufficiently to be able to practice it, and the women, because they do not fight."[159]

---

[152] Ibid.   [153] Ibid., 332.   [154] Ibid., 335.
[155] Ibid., 336. See also al-Shafi'i, *Al-Shafi'i's Risala*, 312, 220–221.
[156] al-Shafi'i, *Al-Shafi'i's Risala*, 312, 220.   [157] Ibid.   [158] Ibid., 316, 222.
[159] Ibid., 312, 221.

While Malik had been hesitant to endorse the idea of double effect, al-Shafi'i, like al-Shaybani, clearly accepts it as a legal principle.

Likewise, al-Shafi'i does not share Malik's qualms about targeting nonbelievers' fortresses and ships in attacks that could endanger Muslims. Al-Shafi'i asserts that "it is not established that a habitation that is otherwise permissible to attack becomes forbidden due to the presence of a Muslim, whose blood is inviolable, within it."[160] It would be permissible to attack such a target, al-Shafi'i argues, although it would be "reprehensible" to attack such a site as a mere "precaution."[161] If the forces are not already engaged, al-Shafi'i would prefer that "[the infidels] be left alone until it is possible to fight them without their human shields."[162] Once the battle has begun, al-Shafi'i permits "targeting the [infidel] warriors, but not the Muslims," nor any children who might be used as shields.[163] Still, al-Shafi'i emphasizes that it would be best to use methods "other than those which [inflict] widespread damage from burning and drowning."[164] Al-Shafi'i's advice here is quite pragmatic. Discrimination between combatants and noncombatants, and especially between Muslims and non-Muslims, is a key principle for a just war. Al-Shafi'i makes it clear that it is desirable – although not required – to use the most discriminate tactics available, perhaps even considering alternate targets.

AL-MAWARDI: AN ISLAMICATE WORLD DIVIDED – AND UNDER SIEGE?

By the second decade of the tenth century, however, this unified Islamic world had come to an end. By the time al-Mawardi was born three rulers simultaneously claimed the title of caliph, ruling from Cordoba, Cairo, and Baghdad. Cordoba was the capital of the Umayyad caliphate, which in the tenth century was at the pinnacle of its power, having conquered nearly all of Spain and part of Morocco. The succession of a ten-year-old boy to the throne in 972, the year of al-Mawardi's birth, marked the beginning of the end, and by 1031 the caliphate had crumbled into more than a dozen independent emirates. These weak states were vulnerable to attack from the Christian principalities in the north.

Cairo was the capital of the Fatimid caliphate, which at its greatest extent stretched from Morocco to Syria. Political power shifted from Baghdad to Cairo, and religious dominance from Sunni Islam to Shiite

---

[160] Al-Shafi'i, *al-Umm*, 337.　[161] Ibid.　[162] Ibid.　[163] Ibid.　[164] Ibid.

Islam. The Fatimid caliph claimed to be an *imam*, the spiritual head of the Ismaili Shi'a community.[165] The Fatimids sent out missionaries, not only to preach the Shi'a message, but also to subvert Sunni authority abroad. The Fatimids peaked in 1057, when Buyid general al-Basasiri changed sides and proclaimed the Fatimid caliphate in Mosul and later Baghdad. The Fatimids, however, could provide no real support. Ethnic strife within the Fatimid military, coupled with a severe drought, had led to serious civil unrest in Egypt. The Seljuk Turks put an end to Fatimid expansion in Mesopotamia, reconquering Baghdad in 1059. The Christian Byzantines also took advantage of the Fatimids' internal collapse. Aleppo fell to crusaders in 962; Antioch, Damascus, Beirut, and Acre soon followed.

In Baghdad, a strange hybrid government ruled. The 'Abbasid caliph still claimed nominal authority. But since 945, the Persian Buyids held the political reins. The Buyids were Shi'a, and "militantly so, which caused sparks to fly when dealing with their Sunni Abbasid puppets."[166] Recognizing that the caliph was the key to legitimacy in the eyes of their Sunni followers, the Buyids permitted the caliph to maintain a palace in Baghdad. *De jure* sovereignty belonged to the 'Abbasids, but in practice the Shi'a Buyids governed.[167] The Buyid dynasty, however, was short lived and collapsed at the end of al-Mawardi's life. The Sunni Seljuks, Turkic warriors from central Asia, fought the Buyids for control of the 'Abbasid caliphate, founding their own sultanate based in Baghdad in 1055. Like their predecessors, the Seljuks maintained the 'Abbasid caliph.

Abu al-Hasan al-Mawardi (972–1058) was born in Basra, in southern Iraq. A Sunni legal scholar of the Shafi'i school, Al-Mawardi was fortunate to enjoy the favor of both the 'Abbasid caliphs and the Buyid sultans.[168] He served as a judge, and as an ambassador of the 'Abbasid caliph to other Muslim polities, especially the Buyids.[169] The 'Abbasid caliph even raised him to the second highest judicial post.

---

[165] Hourani, *A History of the Arab Peoples*, 40.

[166] Stephen O'Shea, *Sea of Faith: Islam and Christianity in the Medieval Mediterranean World* (New York,: Walker Publishing Company, 2009), 107. See also Hourani, *A History of the Arab Peoples*, 38–39.

[167] Qumar-ud-Din Khan, *Al-Mawardi's Theory of the State* (Lahore, Pakistan: Islamic Book Foundation, 1983), vii. See also Hanna Mikhail, *Politics and Revelation: Mawardi and After* (Edinburgh: Edinburgh University Press, 1995), 27.

[168] Khan, *Al-Mawardi's Theory of the State*, 21.

[169] Anthony Black, *The History of Islamic Political Thought: From the Prophet to the Present* (New York: Routledge, 2001), 85.

The Buyids, too, found in al-Mawardi a helpful mediator, as his legal judgments tended to favor their *de facto* authority in secular matters.[170]

Al-Mawardi's work was significant in that he "rethought the operations of the caliphate in the light of 'Abbasid experience."[171] He wrote *Al-Ahkam As-Sultaniyyah* (On the Principles of Power) between 1045 and 1058, as the Seljuks were coming to power in the 'Abbasid heartland.[172] Both external and internal threats increasingly threaten his world. The authority of the caliph was at an all-time low. Al-Mawardi tried to find within the tradition "conditions under which caliphal authority could be delegated to subordinates, and tried to bring order and legal legitimacy into such delegation – which seemed likely to prove continuingly necessary."[173] Thus, *Al-Ahkam As-Sultaniyyah* represents the first attempt at a Muslim theory of government and politics.[174] Unlike texts of jurisprudence that focus on elucidating civil law, al-Mawardi's book attempts to reason through what we might today consider to be constitutional questions. In particular, he was deeply concerned with the "superstructure of right authority," reflective, no doubt, of the disintegration of authority so evident in his time.[175]

Al-Mawardi legitimated a system of divided authority "between the caliph on one hand and the sultan and amirs on the other."[176] Pragmatically admitting "the inferior power of the caliphate," he nonetheless argued that the caliph had "the right to influence the superior power of worldly princes."[177] The caliph retained this right because he remained important as the symbolic head both of the *'ulama,* the learned elite, and of the *'umma,* the Muslim community at large. Al-Mawardi's theory tries to save what is left of the caliph's prestige by granting him a universal spiritual role, while abdicating practical governance to local authorities.[178] Thus, the caliph was involved only in affairs that affected the Muslim community as a whole. For example, he was responsible for rallying the learned elite to combat "subversive heresies" and for providing "moral

[170] Ibid., 24.
[171] Marshall G. S. Hodgson, *The Venture of Islam: Conscience and History in a World Civilization, Vol. 2: The Expansion of Islam in the Middle Periods* (Chicago: University of Chicago Press, 1974), 55.
[172] Black, *The History of Islamic Political Thought,* 86.
[173] Hodgson, *The Venture of Islam,* vol. 2, 55.   [174] Mikhail, *Politics and Revelation,* 19.
[175] Kelsay, *Arguing the Just War in Islam,* 110.
[176] Black, *The History of Islamic Political Thought,* 56.
[177] Mikhail, *Politics and Revelation,* 43.
[178] Khan, Al-Mawardi's Theory of the State, 25.

support, at least, to anyone engaged in defending the frontiers of the *dar al-Islam* (but not the frontiers of any given ruler's domain, which were a matter of purely local interest."[179] In the end, the weakness of the caliph resulted in the development of a Muslim "international order in a society rapidly growing too large to be held together by a political organism of the usual kind," in which the "precarious position of any individual government in point of political ideals ... contributed to ... recurrent social destruction on a vast scale in unchecked warfare."[180]

Al-Mawardi treated political and religious power as interdependent. While reason and revelation can enable man to understand what he *ought* to do, these guides cannot sufficiently restrain his actions.[181] Political power is needed to establish order. Political authorities are responsible for "the guardianship and protection of religion, refutation of false beliefs, guarding against any change in religion ... and chiding those who stubbornly persist in their error or act perversely."[182] Conversely, "any power that is not based on religion which creates a consensus so that people will consider obedience a duty and cooperation an obligation ... is an oppressive and corrupting power."[183]

In this context, al-Mawardi devotes considerable attention to the problem of the use of force against fellow Muslims. Wars fought against Muslim "renegades, rebels or bandits" are all legitimate.[184] All three groups reject Islam in some sense.[185] Renegades are groups of apostates who "withdraw into an area away from the Muslims;" al-Mawardi argues that they "must be fought ... but only after having expounded Islam to them."[186] After all, apostasy shatters the Islamic community. Yet al-Mawardi does not quite relegate renegades to the *dar al-harb*. It may still be possible to reintegrate them into the community. Consequently, the applicable *in bello* rules represent a compromise between the relatively lax rules for fighting non-Muslims and the more restrictive rules for fighting Muslim political rebels. Renegades taken as prisoners may be executed as apostates, but unlike people of the *dar al-harb*, they cannot be enslaved.[187] However, Islamic blood-money laws

---

[179] Hodgson, *The Venture of Islam*, vol. 2, 56.   [180] Ibid., 57.
[181] Mikhail, *Politics and Revelation*, 20.
[182] Al-Mawardi, *Adab al-dunya wa al-din*, edited by Mustafa al-Saqqa (Cairo, Egypt: Mustafa Babi al-Halabi and Sons, 1955), 121–122, cited in Mikhail, *Politics and Revelation*, 20.
[183] Ibid., 122, in Mikhail, *Politics and Revelation*, 21.
[184] Al-Mawardi, *Al-Ahkam as-Sultaniyyah*, 83.   [185] Ibid., 83.   [186] Ibid., 85.
[187] Ibid.

do not apply, nor do laws relating to property damage. If the renegades return to Islam after the fighting, their property should be returned to them; otherwise it becomes the property of the Islamic community as a whole.[188] But the only possible end to the conflict is the defeat of the renegades: they must submit or be killed. While peace treaties can be signed with polities in the *dar al-harb*, renegades cannot be offered peace treaties or the payment of the *jizya*.[189]

Bandits maintain the Islamic faith, but reject the community by spreading terror and disorder. Because they flagrantly disobey the law, they can be killed wherever they are found. Rebels pose a more interesting problem. Like al-Shaybani and al-Shafi'i, al-Mawardi does not see rebels as apostates, although they may have a political difference with the sultan or a heretical understanding of Islam. If the rebels do not "make a show of deviating from obedience to the Imam, and do not occupy a particular territory nor isolate themselves in it, and as long as they are dispersed individuals susceptible to the power of authority and the rule of law, then they are left alone."[190] Such individuals are inconvenient to civil political authorities, but are not significant threats to order. If the rebels do flaunt their mistaken beliefs, then the Imam "may reprimand and make discretionary punishments," but he may not impose the death penalty.[191] Instead, he should expose the wrongheadedness of their beliefs and try to convince them to rejoin the right path.

Rebels who try to establish territorial control, however, are a different matter. Their effort to opt out of the community poses a serious political threat. So long as they "do not refuse an obligation" – such as paying taxes or serving in the military – peace should be maintained with them.[192] But if they "refuse to obey the Imam, or to fulfill the obligations incumbent on them, and if they collect taxes and execute the laws independently," or if they set up an Imam for themselves, then they must be "fought to bring an end to the schism and to bring them to obedience."[193] Such actions amount to usurping the state or to secession, both of which violate the principle of the unity of the community.

Because the king is justified in fighting against such rebels only for the sake of reuniting the community, the *in bello* rules are quite restrictive, with the aim of making post-conflict reconciliation more possible. Al-Mawardi thus asserts that the "aim of the amir in fighting them is to dissuade them but not to kill them, whereas he may have the intention of

[188] Ibid.   [189] Ibid., 86–87.   [190] Ibid., 88.   [191] Ibid., 89.   [192] Ibid.
[193] Ibid.

killing the [unbelievers] or renegades."[194] Al-Mawardi's *in bello* restrictions follow those of al-Shafi'i. Ambushes are impermissible, and prisoners are not to be killed.[195] Because they are in the *dar al-Islam*, booty cannot be seized, nor can their homes or date palms be destroyed.[196] For the same reason, indiscriminate weapons such as ballistas or mangonels cannot generally be used. Nonetheless, the principle of necessity moderates these generous protections. If the state's forces (in Mawardi's terms the "people of justice") are themselves surrounded, they "may defend themselves in any way they are able," including by using indiscriminate weapons.[197]

As a further reminder that the purpose of fighting the rebels is to reestablish order, al-Mawardi argues that after the fighting ends, any property that has been taken from the rebels must be returned.[198] Restitution for goods destroyed during the "heat of the battle" is not required, but should be paid for goods destroyed or lost outside of the fighting.[199] Rebels who have been killed deserve the funeral prayers. Once the rebels have stopped fighting, they are to be reabsorbed into full membership in the community.

Internal conflict is not al-Mawardi's sole concern. Reinterpreting the Quranic approach to the use of force, al-Mawardi argues that after the Battle of Badr in 624 *jihad* became obligatory.[200] Unlike early Quranic scholars who argued that only defense was permissible, al-Mawardi claimed that it was equally permissible to fight "those who fight and those who desist from fighting."[201] In this vein, al-Mawardi identifies two groups of non-Muslims against whom war is permissible. First are those who have heard the message of Islam, but who have "refused it and taken up arms."[202] As these are aggressors, fighting them would have been permissible even interpreting the Qur'an as the earliest exegetes did. Because aggressors pose a material threat to the Islamic polity, they may be even using what we today call unconventional warfare. The generals can decide which will be most effective: "the first, to harry them from the houses and to inflict damage on them day and night, by fighting and burning, or else to declare war and combat them in ranks."[203] The nonconventional tactics al-Mawardi describes are quite different from the sorts of war implied in the eighth-century texts we examined earlier.

---

[194] Ibid., 90.   [195] Ibid.   [196] Ibid., 91.   [197] Ibid.   [198] Ibid., 91–92.
[199] Ibid., 92.   [200] Afsaruddin, "Siyar Laws of Aggression," 52.
[201] Ibid., 53. In particular, al-Mawardi pointed to Qur'an 2:193, 9:5, and 2:191.
[202] Al-Mawardi, *Adab al-dunya wa al-din*, 60.   [203] Ibid.

Malik, al-Shaybani, and al-Shafi'i took for granted that war against unbelievers would occur primarily on the battlefield. Thus, the idea of attacking the enemy's fortresses is employed as a device for thinking about the problem of double effect and noncombatant immunity. By contrast, al-Mawardi's description of war suggests that it is permissible to fight in the nonbelievers' towns, destroying the homes of noncombatants as a deliberate tactic. This harsher approach may reflect shifting power relations. The Islamic caliphate is no longer the predominant power in the region; European empires have become peer competitors. This makes winning more of a challenge, and may have made protecting noncombatants seem like more of a luxury.

The second category of peoples who may be fought are those who have not yet heard about Islam. Al-Mawardi claims that such groups "of whom we have no knowledge" must be far to the east or west, "beyond the Turks and Romans we are fighting."[204] Such groups cannot be attacked until the message has first been brought to them; if they reject the offer of Islam, then they become legitimate targets. Al-Mawardi's reference to these theoretically "innocent" unbelievers is interesting. True, earlier authors did argue that the message of Islam first needed to be proclaimed before the non-Muslim group could be attacked, an apparent presumption of innocence. Al-Mawardi presumes that the non-Muslims have rejected Islam specifically. This, too, suggests that the changing geopolitical environment led to a hardening of attitudes and a correlated slackening of the *in bello* rules.

Increasingly clear distinctions between protections for Muslims and non-Muslims have emerged by this point, the former enjoying weightier protections than the latter. Though this distinction can be explained theologically with reference to the Qur'an, it also reflects a political reality – Muslim armies were no longer perceived as having the upper hand. In terms of *in bello* restrictions, two broad differences emerge between al-Mawardi and the scholars of the previous generation. Al-Mawardi, like al-Shaybani, devotes significant attention to *in bello* regulations, and his colorful language gives us a better image of how wars were fought. This suggests that these questions were of greater interest to him than they had been to previous generations, reflecting the intensified conflict between the 'Abbasid caliphate and various European powers, as well as the growing internal conflict between various Islamicate powers.

[204] Ibid.

Al-Mawardi first declares that "a Muslim may put to death any ...
combatant he seizes, whether or not he is involved in the fighting."[205]
However, he admits that there is a "difference of opinion" about whether
killing noncombatant males, such as old men and monks, is acceptable.
Some argue that if they do not fight, they are immune; others that they
may be killed nonetheless because "their opinions will cause more harm
to the Muslims than fighting."[206] Women and children are not to be
killed. The assumption is that such persons are noncombatants and thus
not threats. But if such individuals take up arms, "then they are fought
and killed, but only face to face, not from behind while fleeing."[207]

Like his predecessors, al-Mawardi develops a principle of double
effect. He explains that "if they use their women and children as shields
in battle, then one must avoid killing them and aim only at killing the
men; if, however, it is impossible to kill them except by killing the women
and children, then it is permitted."[208] Likewise, a city's water supply may
be cut off, "even if there are women and children amongst them, as it is
one of the most potent means of weakening them and gaining victory over
them, either by force or through a treaty."[209] But if the human shields are
Muslims, such actions are impermissible: "if it is not possible to kill them
except by killing these captives, it is not permitted to kill them."[210]
In short, double effect excuses the unintentional, but foreseeable, killing
of non-Muslims, but not Muslims.

Cities may be besieged by any means necessary; surrounding vineyards
and palm trees can be destroyed.[211] However, this should not be done out
of bitterness. Such valuable property should be destroyed only if the
general "reckons that by cutting their date-palms and their trees down it
will serve to weaken them, such that they are overcome by force or are
compelled to make a peace agreement ... he should not, however, act in
this way if he does not see any benefit in it."[212] Here the principle of
necessity acts as a restraint. When necessary, indiscriminate weapons can
be used and civilian property can be destroyed. But such tactics are
justified only if they lead toward victory. Destruction for destruction's
sake – or out of frustration or anger – is not permissible.

As for prisoners of war, al-Mawardi declares that the amir may decide
what to do with them, depending on the circumstances. He offers four
possible outcomes: the prisoners of war could be executed, enslaved,

---

[205] Ibid., 64.   [206] Ibid.   [207] Ibid., 65.   [208] Ibid.   [209] Ibid., 80.
[210] Ibid., 65.   [211] Ibid., 79.   [212] Ibid.

ransomed, or pardoned.[213] The amir is expected to choose based on what is most expedient at the time.

IBN TAYMIYYA: COUPS, CONQUERORS AND THE COLLAPSE OF THE CALIPHATE

If al-Mawardi's times were troubled, Ibn Taymiyya's were nearly apocalyptic. In 1174, the vizier of Fatimid Egypt – the famous Saladin – proclaimed himself sultan, launching the Ayyubid dynasty. But the Ayyubids' rule was to be short; the dynasty fractured after Saladin's death. While his heirs squabbled over their inheritance, many of his conquests – including Jerusalem, fell to the Franks.[214] In 1249, the widow of the Egyptian Ayyubid sultan (a former slave girl) took power for herself. While her rule lasted only eighty days, she succeeded in establishing a new dynasty: the Mamluks, a class of mostly Turkic slave soldiers who had served the Ayyubids.

The Mamluks quickly established control over much of Saladin's former lands, but domestically things were a mess.[215] As newcomers – and non-Arab ones to boot – the Mamluks faced a domestic crisis of legitimacy from the very start. In 1261, they appointed an 'Abbasid as caliph, to serve as a figurehead and also to cast an aura of religious legitimacy over their enterprise.[216] Sultans could not expect to hold their office long, nor to be removed from office peaceably. One historian has described the early decades of the regime as "remarkably fragile."[217] Within Ibn Taymiyya's lifetime, not only did Syria attempt to revolt, but a series of coups shook the center of power in Cairo. Fundamentally, the problem had to do with succession to the position of sultan. Because the position was not hereditary, there was constant jockeying among the elite. Ibn Taymiyya's patron, al-Nasir Muhammad, for example, had his reign interrupted by coups three times from 1293 to 1340. On top of it all, newcomers from all over the Islamic world flooded to Cairo, the seat of the Mamluk government, seeking their fortune or fleeing the Mongols, or both. These stressful demographic changes were coupled with exceedingly

---

[213] Ibid., 76.   [214] Hitti, *History of the Arabs*, location 16477.

[215] The era embodied "social disharmony and disorder." Abdul Hakim ibn al-Matroudi, *The Hanbali School of Law and Ibn Taymiyyah* (New York: Routledge, 2006), 15.

[216] Ibid., 14.

[217] Peter Jackson, "The Crisis in the Holy Land in 1260," *English Historical Review* 95 (376), 1980, 500.

high taxes – "primarily due to a state of perpetual war."[218] This, in turn, fed more political discontent.

The internal instability plaguing the Mamluk state made it susceptible to external threats. Mongols pushed in from the east, Crusaders from the west. In 1258, with the sack of Baghdad by the Mongols, the last of the 'Abbasid caliphate collapsed entirely, an event seen by contemporaries "as the greatest disaster ever sustained by the Islamic world."[219] Just one year later in 1259, the remaining stronghold of the Ayyubid dynasty in Syria fell to the Mongols. In 1260, the Mamluks would turn the tide, repulsing the Mongols from Egypt, but they would spend the next sixty years struggling against repeated Mongol incursions. The contemporary historian Ibn al-Athir "referred to these tragic events as the worst disaster in the history of the Islamic world, in which men, women and children … faced the same fate."[220] The Mamluks' domestic political situation hindered their ability to resist the Mongols. In 1260, the Mamluks were victorious, having just emerged from a "decade of political disarray," but twenty years later the Mamluks were again deeply divided by "political troubles and instability" when the Mongols again took Aleppo in 1281.[221]

The last of the crusader incursions, under Louis IX of France, has already been discussed, in reference to Aquinas. From the Islamic point of view, the threats posed by Mongols and Crusaders were linked. After all, in 1280, the Mongols allied with various Christian groups, including the Armenians and Hospitallers, during their invasion of Syria. Although the invasion was largely successful, the Mongols retreated, for reasons of their own. Furthermore, Argun, Mongol Khan in Persia, made offers of cooperation to European princes four times between 1285 and 1290.

The Europeans, however, did not respond (although urged to by Popes John XXI and Nicholas V). This left the Christian city-states of the Middle East vulnerable to attack by the Mamluk rulers of Egypt. Eventually, the Mamluks were able to reunite the Egyptian and Syrian provinces, and turned their attention to the remaining Frankish enclaves in the Levant. Tripoli fell to the Mamluks in 1289; Acre, the last crusader stronghold, in 1291. Despite surviving the Crusader threat, the Mamluks remained extremely vulnerable to the Mongol empire. Although the

---

[218] Al-Matroudi, *The Hanbali School of Law*, 15.
[219] Jackson, "The Crisis in the Holy Land," 481.
[220] al-Matroudi, *The Hanbali School of Law*, 14.
[221] Reuven Amitai, "The Logistics of the Mongol-Mamluk War, with Special Reference to the Battle of Wadi 'l-Khaznadar, 1299 C.E.," in John H. Pryor, ed., *Logistics of Warfare in the Age of the Crusades* (Aldershot, UK: Ashcroft, 2006), 31.

Mongol invasion of 1280 was relatively brief, the third time the Mongols returned to the Middle East they were not pushed back so easily. In 1299, the Mongols invaded Syria again and were not successfully pushed back until 1304.[222] In 1300, the Mongols penetrated as far as Damascus in the south, besieging and then sacking the city.

Ibn Taymiyya knew first hand about the Mongol threat. Born in Harran, Syria in 1263, Ibn Taymiyya's family fled the invading Mongols for Damascus when he was just seven years old. Legend has it that they "abandoned all their property except their books."[223] His hometown was razed. In Damascus, Ibn Taymiyya's father established himself as a teacher in the city's central mosque. Although Ibn Taymiyya studied Hanbali law, his focus was theology. In 1283 he succeeded his father as the chair of *hadith* scholarship in several leading Damascus madrassas, and began to preach in the central mosque, attracting large audiences. During this period, Ibn Taymiyya became something of a political pundit, calling for unity in the Muslim community and for a strong, but just, government to resist outside opponents.[224] Nonetheless, initially he enjoyed a privileged relationship with the Mamluk leadership. He had close links first with the Mamluk sultan Qala'un, and then his son al-Nasir Muhammad, who remained in power – on and off – for forty-four years.

Ibn Taymiyya was directly involved in the effort to repel the Mongol attackers, even meeting the Mongol emperor, Ilkhan Mahmud Gazhan, and fighting on the frontlines at the Battle of Shaqab in 1304. These bold actions won Ibn Taymiyya popular support, but his strict theological interpretations earned him powerful enemies. In 1306, he was brought before three councils of Qadis, but each time the courts upheld him as orthodox. The third time, he was ordered to proceed to Cairo, the seat of Mamluk power, to face a council of Qadis. He infuriated the chief justice – a member of an opposing legal school – and was summarily sentenced to

[222] Interestingly, Ilkhan Ghazan had converted to Islam by this time. The irony is that just as the Mamluks deemed the Mongols to be a disorderly force, the Mongols disdained the internal disorder of the Mamluk regime. Upon taking the city of Damascus, the Ilkhan ordered a letter to be read in the Umayyad Mosque that declared that the "sovereigns of Egypt and Syria have left the way of the religion, that they no longer follow the prescriptions of Islam ... that each of their sovereigns, when he comes to power, takes it upon himself to bring unhappiness to the land ... [but] Allah does not love disorder." See Ibn Taymiyya, *Lettre à un roi croisé*, trans. Jean R. Michot (Lyon: Tawhid, 1995), 32–33. Translation mine.

[223] Al-Matroudi, *The Hanbali School of Law*, 16.   [224] Ibid., 17.

prison, where he stayed for seventeen months.[225] In 1308 he was yet again put on trial and forced to stay in exile in Alexandria. In 1310, when his protector, the Mamluk sultan al-Nasir Muhammad, returned to power, Ibn Taymiyya was released. He spent the next three years in Cairo, retuning to Damascus in 1313. In 1326, he was again put on trial and imprisoned in the citadel of Damascus, where he died in 1328. For most of this stay was comfortable. The government permitted his followers to visit (no doubt bringing food and books), so his prison life was characterized by "ease and calm," which provided "the leisure to engage even more assiduously in his polemical activity."[226]

The tumultuous historical milieu in which Ibn Taymiyya lived left him longing for unity and security. Within the Islamic world, the unity of the early, unified caliphate had long since disintegrated. The period of the early caliphs has often been idealized, and even at the time of Ibn Taymiyya, scholars wrote wistfully of a return to a politically unified Islam, where the entire *umma* (community) would be under the same rule. In response to these threats, Ibn Taymiyya proposed not only fighting non-Islamic outsiders, but also proposed uniting the *umma* by purifying the practice of Islam. If the *umma* was divided politically, it was even more fractured religiously. Both Sufism and Shi'ism had grown in their popular influence. In Ibn Taymiyya's view the popularity of such heterodox practices fractured the *umma* as much as any political or military conflict.

This longing for a stable political order is reflected in his discussion of the human need for society. Sounding very Aristotelian, Ibn Taymiyya asserts that man is "civil by nature," and the nature of group living is that they need someone to direct them, to coordinate their actions.[227] Thus, the ruler and his government held the sacred responsibility of "ordaining what is proper and forbidding the improper."[228] For Ibn Taymiyya, while the Qur'an serves as the basis for distinguishing between the proper and improper, human law must fill in for matters not

---

[225] Muhammad Umar Memon, *Ibn Taymiya's Struggle against Popular Religion, With an Annotated Translation of His Kitab iqtida' as-sirat al-mustaqim mukhalafat ashab al-jahim* (The Hague: Mouton & Co., 1976), 53.

[226] Ibid., 83.

[227] Ahmad ibn 'Abd al-Halim Ibn Taymiya, *Public Duties in Islam: The Institution of the Hisba*, trans. Muhatar Holland (Leicester: Islamic Foundation, 1985), 20. His uncited reference to Aristotle is a bit ironic, given that he wrote a treatise against the Greek logicians.

[228] Ibid., 23, 38.

specifically addressed in the holy text: "The ordaining of what is fitting and the proscription of the improper is completed only by means of the legal penalties, for God curbs through ruling power (*sultan*) what He does not curb through the Qur'an."[229]

Although Ibn Taymiyya admits that even non-Muslim peoples look to their leaders for such guidance,[230] he makes it clear that this burden lies especially strongly upon Muslim leaders. In that case, the duty to "enjoin what is good and forbid what is evil" is the responsibility of the king not only as a political leader, but as a Muslim – just as it is the responsibility of each and every Muslim to do so, as much as he or she is able.[231]

As such, enjoining the good and forbidding evil is an act of worship in itself.[232] This duty is "incumbent on every able Muslim," although the "responsibility is collective."[233] Admittedly, some Muslims are more able than others to enforce the good: "ability is power and authority, for those who have power are more able than others and so come under obligations which others do not bear."[234] The "most complete expression" of this duty to command the proper and forbid the improper is *jihad*.[235]

But which *jihad* does Ibn Taymiyya mean? As Ibn Taymiyya points out, *jihad* is "achieved sometimes by the heart, sometimes by the tongue, and sometimes by the hand."[236] The struggle (jihad) to conquer one's heart – one's own willfulness and sinfulness – is a duty present "in every case, since its action cannot be detrimental, and he who shirks it is no believer."[237] Thus, the *jihad* of the heart is an *individual* duty. But in the section of the *Hisba* where Ibn Taymiyya upholds *jihad* as the greatest expression of this duty, he refers to it as a *collective* duty, for when it "is not performed by those whose duty it is, the sin lies with every able person in accordance with his capacity, for it is a duty incumbent upon every human being according to his capacity."[238] Because *jihad* of the heart is by definition individual, the *jihad* he is praising here must be the *jihad* of the tongue and/or hand.

This interpretation is further strengthened by examining his later discussion of military *jihad*. Just before discussing the status of professional soldiers, Ibn Taymiyya reiterates the point that *jihad* is "incumbent on the

---

[229] Ibid., 60.   [230] Ibid., 20.

[231] Ahmad ibn 'Abd al-Halim Ibn Taymiyah, *Al-'Ubudiyyah: Being a True Slave of Allah*, trans. Nasiruddin al-Khattab (London: Ta-Ha Publishers, 1999), 33.

[232] Ibid., 36. See also Ibn Taymiyya, *Lettre à un roi croisé*, 167.

[233] Ibn Taymiya, *Public Duties in Islam*, 23.   [234] Ibid.   [235] Ibid., 77.

[236] Ibid., 78.   [237] Ibid.   [238] Ibid., 77.

Muslims in general and on a sufficient number of them at any time."[239] He explains that soldiers who give booty or funds for *jihad* are bound to it, for it then becomes "a duty for particular individuals," in this case "imposed on them by the Sacred Law and the contract they entered into when they contracted with those in authority to serve in the *Jihad*."[240]

But why does Ibn Tamiyya see the *jihad* of the sword as so important for Muslims of his time? The internal religious and political troubles may have contributed to his strong condemnation of minority Islamic groups, and his lack of toleration for non-Muslims living in Islamic lands. First and foremost, such groups challenged the ideal of a unified *umma*. The "greatest ordeals" borne by the community of believers are "sectarianism within it and the differences in matters of doctrine and worship."[241] Group solidarity is of fundamental importance. Appealing to one's clan or ethnicity was "objectionable;" indeed, one should avoid "man's absolute fanaticism for his party after the fashion of the pagans."[242]

Second, Ibn Taymiyya understood both Shi'a and Sufis to be guilty of *shirk* or polytheism, for practices such as participating in festivals not explicitly enjoined by the Qur'an, visiting saints' graves and other pilgrimage places, and other "innovations."[243] Certainly, for a theologian as committed to purifying practice as Ibn Taymiyya, declaiming such beliefs as unorthodox and attempting to sway simple people away from such mistaken (though popular) practices would have indeed been important. It must be acknowledged that Ibn Taymiyya did devote much of his career to sorting through the thousands of *hadith* on which the law was based to confirm their accuracy and legitimacy.

Third, Ibn Taymiyya seems to have seen the Shi'a and the Sufis as a potential fifth column. After all, the Mongols allied with both groups against the Mamluks. The Mongols in Iran were converted to Islam by Sufis.[244] Later, the Ilkhan Kudabanda made Shi'ism the state religion of the Mongols.[245] Furthermore, the Shi'a in Kasrawan (near Beirut) were

---

[239] Ibid., 129.   [240] Ibid., 129–130.   [241] Ibn Taymiya, *Public Duties in Islam*, 99.

[242] Memon, *Ibn Taymiyya's Struggle against Popular Religion*, II.72–73, 141.

[243] See Memon, *Ibn Taymiyya's Struggle against Popular Religion*, 11, 46. See also Ahmad ibn 'Abd al-Halim ibn Taymiyah, *A Muslim Theologian's Response to Christianity: Ibn Taymiyya's Al-Jawab Al-Sahih*, trans. Thomas F. Michel, S.J. (Delmar, NY: Caravan Books, 1984), 15, 56.

[244] Reuven Amitai-Preiss, "Sufis and Shamans: Some Remarks on the Islamization of Mongols in the Ilkhanate," *Journal of the Economic and Social History of the Orient* 42(1), 1999, 27.

[245] Ibn Taymiyah, *A Muslim Theologian's Response to Christianity*, 61.

"accused of assisting the Mongols, and in response, Ibn Taymiyya wrote a lengthy *fatwa* to show the permissibility of *jihad* against them."[246] In a letter to his patron, the Mamluk sultan al-Nasir Qala'un, Taymiyya called for *jihad* against the Shiites, on the grounds that their unorthodox Islamic beliefs led them to prefer "the Franks and the Tatars [Mongols] over the people of the Qur'an and the faith."[247] Ibn Taymiyya didn't just write against the Shi'a – he took part in two separate military campaigns against them, in Kasrawan, in 1300 and 1305.[248]

In this context, Ibn Taymiyya lays out his condemnation of civil war. The difference between true Muslims and those sectarians who only claim to be following Islam, he argues, is that true Muslims uphold "adherence to the community and renunciation of armed struggle against the leaders, as well as renunciation of civil war."[249] Because the unity of the community is so essential, when individuals or groups of Muslims threaten the community, the community as a whole may use force against them. To this end, Ibn Taymiyya draws on earlier legal scholars to categorizes three types of Muslims who must be fought: those who "renounce authority," those who "fight out of partisanship for a group or town," and "those who set out against the Muslim community," including highwaymen, revels and dissenters.[250]

So concerned is Ibn Taymiyya with order that even the existence of unjust leaders could not justify revolt. Tyrants might perpetrate "injustice and oppression," and might even attempt to justify that behavior based on invalid legal interpretations, but nonetheless "it is not permissible to remove them, on account of the further injustice and oppression involved. For the usual psychological tendency is to remove one evil with another that is even worse ... Coming out in revolt against them results in injustice and corruption worse than their injustice, so it must be suffered with patience."[251] Like Luther, he takes a dim view of rebellion – even an unjust ruler is better than the chaos of war.

---

[246] Ibid., 57.

[247] Ibid., 58. The words are Taymiyya's own, from the "Risala ila al-Sultan al-Malik al-Nasir," cited in Muhammad ibn 'Abn al-Hadi, *Al-'Uqud al-Durriya*.

[248] Tariq al-Jamil, "Ibn Taymiyya and Ibn al-Mutahhar al-Hilli: Shi'i Polemics and the Struggle for Religious Authority in Medieval Islam," in Yossef Rapoport and Shahab Ahmed, eds., *Ibn Taymiyya and His Times* (Oxford: Oxford University Press, 2010), 229–241, 233.

[249] Ibn Taymiyya, *Public Duties in Islam*, 79.

[250] Ibn Taymiyya, *Ibn Taymiya's Struggle against Popular Religion*, II.74–75, 243.

[251] Ibn Taymiyya, *Public Duties in Islam*, 126.

Another of Ibn Taymiyya's innovations (perhaps not surprisingly given the weakness of the Mamluk state) is to identify defensive *jihad* as an individual duty. Following his predecessors, Ibn Taymiyya considered offensive *jihad* to be a "duty of collective action: part of the Muslims assure its execution while the others find themselves free," although the "moral merit comes only to those who do it."[252] Defensive *jihad*, on the other hand, is "a duty of individual obligation for all the believers, even if they are not personally attacked. It is considered like a duty of solidarity and cooperative help."[253] Defensive *jihad* is fought "out of necessity," while offensive *jihad* is "voluntary."[254]

In addition to wars of self-defense (defensive *jihad*), Ibn Taymiyya legitimized wars fought to punish wrongdoing. He criticizes the people of ancient Israel for "only" defending themselves, and for not "[summoning] their opponents and [enjoining] upon them what is proper... They justified fighting on the grounds that they and their children had been expelled from their homes. Even then, they were reluctant to fight."[255] He also described "the killing of infidels plus the seizure of their property" as a "composite" punishment, involving both physical and financial punishment for wrongdoing.[256]

In terms of *in bello* principles, Ibn Taymiyya is quite similar to al-Mawardi. He too upholds a principle of noncombatant immunity, albeit tempered with double effect. Still, he more clearly establishes that some civilian groups are immune:

Those who, like women, children, priests, old people, the bind, the invalid, etc., are not able to be considered as "resistants" or "combatants," will not be killed ... at least when they have not effectively fought by their words or by their acts ... We must fight only those who fight us, since we want to make the religion

---

[252] Ahmad ibn 'Abd al-Halim Ibn Taimiya, *Le Traité de droit public d'ibn Taimiya: Traduction annoté de la Siyasa sariya*, trans. Henri Laoust (Beirut: Institut Français de Damas, 1948), 133. For an alternate translation directly into English, see Rudolph Peters, *Jihad in Classical and Modern Islam* (Princeton: Markus Wiener Publishers, 1996), 53: "If we take the initiative, it is a collective duty [which means that] if it is fulfilled by a sufficient number [of Muslims], the obligation lapses for all others and the merit goes to those who have fulfilled it." Rudolph is drawing on the edition by Muhammad Ibrahim al-Banna and Muhammad Ahmad 'Ashur, published in Cairo by Dar al-Sha'b in 1971.

[253] Ibn Taymiya, *Le Traité de droit*, 133. Peters, *Jihad in Classical and Modern Islam*, 53: "But if the enemy wants to attack the Muslims, then repelling him becomes a duty for all those under attack and for the others in order to help them."

[254] Ibn Taymiya, *Le Traité de droit*, 134. Peters, *Jihad in Classical and Modern Islam*, 53–54.

[255] Taymiya, *Public Duties in Islam*, 75.   [256] Ibid., 64.

of God triumph. God said: "Fight for the cause of God against those who make war against you. But don't commit any injustice in attacking them first, since God doesn't like aggressors at all."[257]

Likewise, in regard to non-Muslim prisoners of war, he urges mercy: "The law imposes the duty of fighting infidels, but not that of killing them when one has seized them."[258]

Elsewhere, although he urges Muslim soldiers to show bravery in battle, he also makes it clear that they must also show restraint. Courage is not the same as rashness or anger; moderation must be observed on the battlefield as well.[259] Soldiers must not be iniquitous, unjust, or immoral.[260] And they must be gracious in both victory and defeat, so their spirit will impress their enemies.[261] War, after all, is meant to build an Islamic order, not create disorder.

AL-MUHAQQIQ: SHI'I CHALLENGES TO AUTHORITY AND OFFENSIVE WAR

Abu al-Qasim Ja'far al-Hasan al-Muhaqqiq al-Hilli was born in 1205 or 1206 in Hilli in Iraq. A scholar in the *Imami* tradition, he was part of the *Usuli* movement, which emphasized the importance of using logic to interpret the traditions of the imams.[262] This movement encouraged Shi'i scholars to study broadly, even from Sunni schools, in order to improve their understanding of the principles of judicial reasoning. Interestingly, al-Muhaqqiq's student – his nephew 'Allama al-Hilli – came to Ibn Taymiyya's attention after publishing a defense of the imamate under the aegis of the Ilhan Öljeitü.[263]

The fundamental point of departure between the Sunni and Shi'i communities in their thinking about governance is the absence of the true imam. For the Sunni, the successors to the Prophet – the caliphs – are political figures, chosen by the community. They serve a practical function, but they have not inherited the Prophet's special connection to God. For the Shi'a, by contrast, some of the Prophet's successors were – like Muhammad himself – true imams, combining political and religious authority. While the major Shi'i sects disagree about the number and

[257] Ibn Taimiya, *Le Traité de droit public d'ibn Taimiya*, 128.   [258] Ibid., 129.

[259] Taymiya, *Public Duties in Islam*, 106.   [260] Ibid., 133.   [261] Ibid., 208.

[262] Albert Hourani, "From Jabal 'Amil to Persia," *Bulletin of the School of Oriental and African Studies* 49(1), 1986, 135.

[263] Ibid., 135. See also al-Jamil, "Ibn Taymiyya and Ibn al-Mutahhar al-Hilli," 235.

identity of the true imams, most agree that the imam ceased to be apparent by the eleventh century.[264] This posed a theological and political problem, as the Shi'i doctrine of the imamate decreed that only the imam possessed the legitimate authority to carry out certain key functions for the Islamic community, including calls to Friday prayers and to *jihad*. In the absence of a living imam, the Shi'i emphasis on "pietistic religiosity" led to a "de-emphasis on the Islamic 'political ethic.'"[265] Shi'i doctrine came to emphasize personal faith and the willingness to become a martyr by sacrificing one's self for one's belief, rather than through dying in combat.[266] This religious doctrine dovetailed nicely with the political realities faced by the Shi'i community, which more often than not was outside the circles of power.

Like Ibn Taymiyya, al-Muhaqqiq lived during an era of upheaval. Baghdad was invaded by the Mongols in 1258, who burned libraries and massacred civilians. Al-Muhaqqiq had achieved such prominence, however, that the Persian scholar Nasir al-Din Tusi came to hear him lecture when he arrived in Baghdad with his patron, Hulegu Khan. The region was ruled by Mongol Ilkhans for the rest of his life, until his death from an accidental fall in 1277. Hulegu and his descendants were tolerant of Islam – as they were of Christianity, Judaism, and Buddhism. Some even adopted Islam personally, but they did not adopt Islam as a state religion or enforce Islamic law until some twenty years after al-Muhaqqiq's death.

The quietist tendencies of Shi'i thinking are evident in al-Muhaqqiq's discussion of the obligation to take part in *jihad*. On the one hand, al-Muhaqqiq asserts that all free, male, adult Muslims are obliged to take part in *jihad*.[267] *Jihad* is treated as a collective duty, which "so long as it is fulfilled by a sufficient number of persons, ceases [to be binding] for the

---

[264] Two small sects maintained a continuous line of Imams to the modern era. The Nizari Ismailis are the only Shi'i community led today by a living Imam; the civil war in Yemen ended the Zaidi line of Imams in 1962.

[265] Said Amir Arjomand, "Religion, Political Action and Legitimate Domination in Shi'ite Iran: Fourteenth to Eighteenth Centuries AD," *European Journal of Sociology* 20(1), 1979, 67.

[266] Etan Kohlberg, "The Development of the Imam Shi'i Doctrine of *jihad*," *Zeitschrift der Deutschen Morgenländsichen Gesellschaft* 126(1), 1976, 78.

[267] Ja'far ibn al-Hasan al-Muhaqqiq al-Hilli, *Droit Musulman: Recueil de lois concernant les Musulmans Schyites*, trans. Amédée Querry (Paris: L'Imprimérie Nationale, 1871), I.9.1.1.1, 321. For an English translation, see Ja'far ibn al-Hasan Abu al-Qasim Najm al-Din al-Muhawwiw al-Hilli, *Sharai'i' al-Islam: Fi Masa'il al-Halal wal-Haram*, trans. Hasan M. Najafi, 3 vols. (Qum, Iran: Ansariyan, 2009).

other members of the community."[268] Like his Sunni counterparts, al-Muhaqqiq then identifies three groups of people against whom *jihad* should be undertaken: nonbelievers who do not pay the *jizya*, nonbelievers who do pay the *jizya* but are in violation of the treaty, and "Muslims who rise up against the authority of the legitimate Imam."[269]

Al-Muhaqqiq also offers practical advice, suggesting that *jihad* should first be carried out against the nearest peoples, unless a people "farther away inspires greater fears."[270] Likewise, although Muslims are not supposed to flee a battle once it has begun, if their number is inferior to that of the enemy al-Muhaqqiq deems it permissible to wait for reinforcements to arrive.[271] And, like his Sunni counterparts, he asserts that the invitation to Islam does not have to be renewed more than once.

Al-Muhaqqiq's next move definitively changes the meaning of the obligation to conduct *jihad*. He asserts plainly that "jihad is not obligatory unless the Imam manifests his presence, or in the presence of an agent delegated by [the Imam]" for this purpose.[272] Effectively, this shuts down the obligation to conduct an offensive *jihad* in the absence of the Imam. The right to launch *jihad* is reserved to the imam or a deputy specifically appointed by him for the purposes of *jihad*.[273] Other earthly rulers may use force only in defense, not to expand the *dar al-Islam*.

Defensive war, however, remains an obligation for Muslims. The *dar al-Islam* must be defended against outside incursions. Even in the absence of the true imam, defense of the borders is "commendable."[274] To some extent, this follows naturally for al-Muhaqqiq from individuals' right to self-defense, which pertains both to the *dar al-Islam* and in the *dar al-harb*.[275] Consequently, "it is permitted for any Muslim finding himself in the *dar al-harb* to help the inhabitants to repulse assailants, when the Muslim fears for his personal safety."[276] In fact, even if the attackers themselves are Muslims, Muslim inhabitants of the *dar al-Islam* may respond with force.[277] This is significant, because with the arrival of the Mongols, al-Muhaqqiq's own homeland was no longer governed by *shari'a*, and thus did not pertain to the *dar-al-Islam*. But given al-Muhaqqiq's construction of legitimate defense, the Shi'a subjects of the Ilkhan could rightfully fight to defend the empire against incursions – even, for example, against armies led by other Muslims. Al-Muhaqqiq

[268] Ibid., I.9.1.1.3, 321. [269] Ibid., I.9.2.3.25–28, 324. [270] Ibid., I.9.2.2.33, 325.
[271] Ibid., I.9.2.2.34, 325. [272] Ibid., I.9.1.1.4, 321. [273] Ibid., I.9.2.3.32, 325.
[274] Ibid., I.9.1.2.20, 323. [275] Ibid., I.9.1.1.6–7 and 323, I.9.1.2.20, 322.
[276] Ibid., I.9.1.1.6, 321–322. [277] Ibid., I.9.1.1.6, 322.

emphasizes, however, that neither case constitutes *jihad*, and he also reminds his readers that defense of the borders may not necessarily even constitute war, as "precautionary and demonstrative" measures may be sufficient.[278] Nonetheless, if those against whom *jihad* should (theoretically) be undertaken launch an offensive war against Muslims, "defensive war becomes obligatory."[279]

Al-Muhaqqiq also develops a set of *in bello* restrictions designed to maintain order even in war. Some of these are virtually identical to what we have seen so far in the Sunni tradition. For example, al-Muhaqqiq acknowledges the principle of noncombatant immunity. It is "forbidden to kill women, children and the insane ... unless they take part in the defense or the attack."[280] Prisoners cannot be mutilated, and perfidy is forbidden. Indeed, "one should avoid assailing the enemy during the night or before noon if it isn't necessary."[281] Al-Muhaqqiq also recommends against cutting down trees, or using incendiary projectiles or cutting off the flow of water to cities, "except in cases of absolute necessity."[282]

Necessity also figures into al-Muhaqqiq's version of double effect. He argues that it is permitted to put the enemy under siege, to prevent all trade or communication with him, to use siege weapons, and to destroy the walls of the fortresses and houses, "in a word, to make use of all the appropriate means to assure victory."[283] Nonetheless, if the enemy uses women or children as human shields, one should avoid attacking them "as much as is possible, at least as long as the combat has not begun."[284] This remains true even if the enemy uses Muslim prisoners. Likewise, if the circumstances do not make it possible to avoid killing such prisoners, the Muslim forces nonetheless are not responsible for paying blood money to the prisoners' families.[285]

The absence of the imam affects al-Muhaqqiq's rules for the treatment of prisoners of war. "After the war is over," he writes, "prisoners should not be put to death, but the Imam has the right to send them back, to exchange them for Muslim prisoners or for a ransom, or to enslave them."[286] The imam has the right to order prisoners to be killed – if, for example, they cannot walk – but if the Muslim combatants are not specifically aware of such an order, they may not kill incapacitated prisoners.[287] Given the occultation of the imam, this rule effectively rules

---

[278] Ibid., I.9.1.1.6. and 323, I.9.1.2.20, 322.   [279] Ibid.,.9.1.3.29, 324.
[280] Ibid., I.9.2.2.45, 326.   [281] Ibid., I.9.2.2.48, 326.   [282] Ibid., I.9.2.2.40, 326.
[283] Ibid., I.9.2.2.39, 326.   [284] Ibid., I.9.2.2.42, 326.   [285] Ibid., I.9.2.2.43, 326.
[286] Ibid., I.9.3.1.92, 332.   [287] Ibid., I.9.3.1.94, 332.

out the massacre of prisoners. Furthermore, al-Muhaqqiq lists rules for protecting prisoners of war that presage the Geneva Conventions. It is "recommended" not to torture them, and "obligatory" to provide food and drink.[288]

Put altogether, the protections offered noncombatants – whether civilians or prisoners – in al-Muhaqqiq's work are more expansive than those we have seen in the Sunni texts. Two aspects of al-Muhaqqiq's political context may account for this. First, al-Muhaqqiq likely witnessed first hand the terrible fury of the invading Mongol hoards. Their willingness to spill blood indiscriminately may have made a great impression. Second, al-Muhaqqiq's work is, despite being a legal text, largely theoretical. Although he earned the respect of other scholars and was tolerated by Hulegu Khan, he was not in a position to offer policy advice to anyone. Indeed, the Shi'i community had been outside the circle of power for nearly two hundred years before al-Muhaqqiq, after the fall of the Buyid dynasty. As a result al-Muhaqqiq's advice did not need to reflect the interests and concerns of the ruling powers to the same extent.

AL-MISRI: REASSERTING CENTRAL AUTHORITY

Ahmad ibn Naqib al-Misri (1302–1367) was a Shafi'i scholar. He was the son of an Antioch Christian captive who converted to Islam, and then served his Muslim master as a captain in Cairo. Obviously, his early life was lived in the same tumultuous times as Ibn Taymiyya, under the threat of Mongol invasion. But by 1313, when he was just a boy, the Mongols had already adopted Islam; by 1323, the Mamluk kingdom in which he lived had made peace with them. A little more than a decade later, in 1335, the Ilkhanate itself had disintegrated into warring states. The new rising power were the Ottoman Turks, established Muslims, who had begun to expand into Europe from the 1360s onward. In this period, the Islamic world can be seen as reemerging as a powerful force, reuniting under stable Ottoman rule. The issue of cause is downplayed further, with less emphasis on defensive *jihad* than in the more tumultuous times of Ibn Taymiyya.

Al-Misri lays out his rules for warfare within the *Reliance of the Traveler* (*'Umdat al-Salik*), a general manual of Islamic law. Jihad against non-Muslims is seen as a communal obligation; so long as "enough people perform it to successfully accomplish it, it is no longer obligatory

[288] Ibid., I.9.3.1.97, 332.

upon others."[289] Al-Misri explains that this collective obligation falls upon "every able-bodied man who has reached puberty and is sane," so long as he is not in debt and has his parent's permission.[290] It becomes a personal obligation to anyone present on the battle lines.[291] This includes not only soldiers who volunteer, but also "everyone when the enemy has surrounded the Muslims."[292] Indeed, if the Muslims are surrounded, then even debtors and young men without their parents' permission may fight.[293]

Just as Christian authors from Aquinas onward sought to encourage domestic order by limiting the right to wage war to the highest sovereign authority, al-Misri argues that "it is offensive to conduct a military expedition against hostile non-Muslims without the caliph's permission."[294] Here he is building on the hierarchical chain of command between amirs and caliphs developed by al-Mawardi previously. It is, after all, the caliph's responsibility to carry out *jihad* against "Jews, Christians and Zoroastrians ... until they become Muslim or else pay the non-Muslim poll tax."[295] All other peoples too must be fought until they become Muslim or agree pay the *jizya*, except for apostates or Arab idol worshipers, who have no choice but to convert to Islam.[296] This duty is passed on to rulers ranking below the caliph "if the area has a border adjacent to enemy lands," in which case the lesser leader also has an obligation to undertake *jihad* against enemies.[297]

Just like his predecessors, al-Misri sees the unity of the Islamic community as essential. For this reason, "when a group of Muslims rebel against the caliph ... and want to overthrow him, or refuse to fulfill an obligation imposed by Sacred Law ... and rise in armed insurrection," the caliph's first response ought to be to send "someone to them and [redress] their grievances if possible."[298] A peaceful reconciliation would be ideal. If negotiations prove unfruitful, the caliph must fight against them, although with "weaponry that does not cause general destruction, as do fire and mangonel."[299] The point is to correct them, or at least suppress their insurrection, not to destroy them. Likewise, the caliph's army should not "pursue those who retreat, or kill the wounded."[300] Still, neither side is liable for property damage pursuant to the conflict. Interestingly,

---

[289] Ahmad ibn Naqib al-Misri, *Reliance of the Traveler: A Classic Manual of Islamic Sacred Law*, trans. Nuh Hah Mim Keller (Beltsville, MD: Amana Publications, 1994), o9.1, 600.
[290] Ibid., o9.4, o9.5, 601–602.   [291] Ibid., o9.2, 601.   [292] Ibid., o9.3, 601.
[293] Ibid., o9.5, 602.   [294] Ibid., o9.6, 602.   [295] Ibid., o9.8, 602.
[296] Ibid., o9.9, 603.   [297] Ibid., o25.9, 647.   [298] Ibid., o6.1, 593–594.
[299] Ibid., o6.1, 594.   [300] Ibid., o6.2, 594.

al-Misri explicitly notes that if these Muslims "do not rebel by war, the caliph may not fight them."[301] This reflects even greater tolerance for dissension than seen in any of the previous scholars.[302]

Al-Misri's understanding of noncombatant immunity is similar to that of earlier scholars. He insists that "it is not permissible to kill women or children unless they are fighting against the Muslims," although it "is permissible to kill old men."[303] Anyone who accepts Islam before being captured "may not be killed, or his property confiscated, or his young children taken captive."[304] Women or children taken captive "become slaves."[305] Male captives are subject to the same four options offered by al-Mawardi: death, slavery, manumission, or ransom, unless they convert to Islam, in which case they cannot be killed.[306] Taken altogether, al-Misri's emphasis on *ad bellum* authority, coupled with his limitations on *in bello* conduct, reflect his concern with maintaining order in a society that was religiously unified, and yet politically fractured.

CONCLUSION

This altogether too brief foray into the Islamic tradition of just war thinking makes it clear that, just as in the Christian tradition, ideas about the ethics of war are interwoven with pragmatic considerations about how to win wars. This linkage occurs on two levels. First, each of the jurists we have explored – and indeed the Qur'an itself – shares several key assumptions with classical realists. Human nature is corrupt and combatative, and although humans have had a better path revealed to them through the Prophet, it is difficult for them to submit. War – both within and between states – is tragically inevitable.

Just as in the Christian tradition, changes in the political environment are correlated with changes in just war thinking. The emigration of the Prophet and his followers from Mecca to Medina, and his rise to political power there, is correlated with a shift from an essentially quietist position on the use of force to one which permits defensive war. Likewise, after the Prophet's death, the reality of (highly successful) military expansionism during the Golden Age is correlated with a shift in thinking about just

---

[301] Ibid., 06.4, 594.
[302] Ibid., 08.0–08.4, 595. It should be noted that these rebels are *not* apostates; apostasy remains a crime punishable by death.
[303] Ibid., 09.10, 603.   [304] Ibid., 09.12, 604.   [305] Ibid., 09.13, 604.
[306] Ibid., 09.15, 604.

cause in Sunni Islam. The legal scholars examined here, themselves closely tied to political power, thus came to permit offensive war for the sake of world order. The requirement to offer terms of peace along with missionary message of Islam comes to be treated as pure formality, as the enemy's refusal is assumed. Effectively, this expands the permissibility of offensive war.

The most compelling evidence connecting the political context and the development of specific just war principles dates to the cataclysmic Crusader and Mongol invasions in the twelfth century. Ibn Taymiyya, with his Mamluk patron, advances the idea of defensive *jihad*. By making this duty incumbent on individuals – rather than diffusing it through the community – he reveals the intensity of his security concerns. Conversely, his contemporary al-Muhaqqiq takes a quietist approach that privileges defensive, rather than offensive war. Tellingly, this position reflects the relatively weaker position of the Shi'i community (and the Mongol occupation of his homeland) – not to mention Al-Muhaqqiq's own distance from the inner circles of power. Al-Muhaqqiq also afforded civilians and prisoners of war more *in bello* protections. All this suggests that it bears remembering that what seems just and necessary in war depends on who (and where) one is.

6

Balancing the Mandala

The Hindu Just War Tradition

The Christian and Islamic just war traditions, as we have seen, have many commonalities. Sharing assumptions about human nature, the two Abrahamic religions draw similar conclusions about the importance of earthly governance. Drawing from their own source texts and their own internal debates, both traditions raise similar questions about the ethical dilemmas war poses. The long history of (often conflictual) inter-action between these two traditions is outside the scope of this book, but it is important to note that this shared history reinforced these similarities, as ideas about just conduct and soldierly virtue evolved on the battlefield.[1]

The Hindu way of thinking about war, by contrast, evolved from a very different set of religious assumptions and a very different set of historical conditions. To make matters even more complicated, it is difficult even to speak of *a* Hindu way of thinking about war. While Christianity and Islam are scriptural traditions, built around a core text that limits the range of possible beliefs and practices, Hinduism as a practice is decidedly *not* textual. Furthermore, both Christianity and Islam self-consciously evolved just war canons, sets of texts seen as iconic crystallizations of important sets of just war ideas. But one would be hard put to identify a Hindu religious canon in general, not to mention one specific to just war.[2]

This is not to say that Hinduism as a tradition has not considered the ethical problems of war. Instead, I simply wish to call attention to the fact

---

[1] Marcel A. Boisard, "On the Probable Influence of Islam on Western Public and International Law," *International Journal of Middle East Studies* 11(4), 1980, 429–450.

[2] Wendy Doniger, *The Hindus: An Alternative History* (New York: Penguin Books, 2009), 25.

that I have had to draw out what I term the Hindu just war tradition from a variety of types of sources. I am not alone in this project, by any means. Starting in the early post-colonial period, Indian scholars have scoured Hindu texts, seeking to produce an authentically Indian theory of international relations, and within that, an Indian approach to international law and just war theory.[3] This process continues to this day, and my choices of sources reflect this developing tradition. Additionally, the key Hindu sources are considerably more ancient than their Christian and Islamic counterparts. Identifying the historical contexts of such texts is a challenge when it is difficult to establish dates of composition or writing with any degree of certainty.

Methodological challenges aside, in this chapter I sketch the development of just war principles on the subcontinent from ancient times through the tenth century, when invading Muslim forces began to occupy northern India. In broad terms, on the subcontinent the rules of warfare were most clearly articulated during the post-Vedic period, before the onslaught of foreign invaders. This was a time characterized by relatively strong states, fighting enemies who shared similar cultural and religious traditions. In the periods both before and after, the rules of conduct were considerably less restrictive.

To trace this history, we will look at several types of texts. On the one hand, *sruti* works (literally, "what is heard") are considered to be revealed texts. These include the Vedic texts themselves, and their commentaries, including the Upanishads, which are discussed in the first section of this chapter. By contrast, *smriti* works ("what is remembered") include multiple genres. The great epic histories, such as the Mahabharata and the Ramayana, fall into this category, as do the *dharmasutras* (codes of law) and books of advice for kings, including Kautilya's *Arthasastra*, Kamandaka's *Nitisara*, and Narayana's *Hitopadesa*.

VEDIC AGE: INDIVIDUAL GLORY AND FEW RESTRAINTS

The Vedic age spans nearly one thousand years, from roughly 1500 BCE to 500 BCE. The history of the earliest centuries is virtually impossible to

---

[3] Consider, for example, H. S. Bhatia, ed., *International Law and Practice in Ancient India* (New Delhi: Deep and Deep Publications, 1977); K. K. Bhattacharya, *Public International Law* (Allahabad, India: Central Law Agency, 1982); Buch, The Principles of Hindu Ethics; Jagat J. Ghosh, *Indian Thesis on War and Peace* (Raniganj, India: Mahima Ranjan Sarkar (Rajashree Press), June 1972); and most recently Kaushik Roy, *Hinduism and the Ethics of Warfare in South Asia* (Cambridge: Cambridge University Press, 2012).

clearly articulate. Most of the evidence comes from archeology; the textual accounts of this era were written down long after they were first orally composed. Vedic society was arranged around lineage, or clan, groupings. Within this system, there were multiple nodes of leadership. Each village had a headsman; each clan a chief; and each tribe a ruler.[4] The *raja*, or tribal leader, is sometimes described in the Vedas as an elected king.[5] The ideal structure of society at this time discouraged certain conflicts (namely between the members of particular clans or tribes), while effectively encouraging conflict with members of outside groups. However, the brutal reality of intense intratribal conflict drove the formation of the caste system in an attempt to pacify internal factions for the sake of strengthening the tribe vis-à-vis outsiders.[6]

To a certain extent, the tension between religion and politics that we have seen in Christianity and Islam arises from the fact that there have been periods in both traditions where the two spheres overlapped. This inevitably led to tension between the spheres, which competed for authority. Arguably, this tension inspires serious debate over just war principles. The establishment of the caste system reduced this tension by clearly separating the priestly (*brhamin*) and kingly (*ksatriya*) castes.[7] Each had its own unique duties. The earliest intimations of this caste separation date to the Vedic period, when "rituals originally designed to guarantee success in war evolved into a division between warrior and priest classes, with an emphasis upon asceticism as the means for an elite few to obtain ultimate peace."[8]

The Vedas and the Upanishads were composed by *brahmins*, and naturally reflect their beliefs about a rightly ordered society. The ideology of this Vedic society and its supporting rituals "were designed, on the one hand, to enhance *Ksatriya* power, and on the other, to ensure the recognition by the *Ksatriyas* that the source of their power was the Brahmin."[9] This mutually supporting relationship between kings and priests is revealed in the *Aitareya Brhamana*, where the gods themselves – in the midst of a struggle with malevolent demigods – exclaim, "Through our lack of a king

---

[4] Roy, *Hinduism and the Ethics of Warfare in South Asia*, 16.   [5] Ibid.

[6] See Ram Sharan Sharma, *Aspects of Political Ideas and Institutions in Ancient India*, 4th ed. (Delhi: Motilal Banarsidass Publishers, 1996), 174–176.

[7] The term *ksatriya* is derived from *ksatra*, meaning "authority or power." Ibid., 171.

[8] William J. Frost, *A History of Christian, Jewish, Hindu, Buddhist and Muslim Perspectives on War and Peace, vol. 1: The Bible to 1914* (Lampeter, Wales: Edwin Mellen Press, 2004), 140.

[9] Patrick Olivelle, trans., *Upanishads* (Oxford: Oxford University Press, 1996), xxxv.

they conquer us; let us make a king."[10] The spiritual elite thus ceded political life to the kings, except insofar as they had ritual duties to perform to support the political sphere.[11]

War falls to the duties ascribed to the kingly caste, to be regulated in the political sphere. Nineteenth-century European scholars described this period in terms of an Aryan invasion of the subcontinent, a view reflecting their racial ideology more than reality.[12] It is more likely that the Aryans referred to in the Vedas were not a racial group, or even a single people, but instead a diverse group of Aryan speakers slowly migrating into the Indus Valley during this period.[13] Conflicts broke out both among the various groups of Aryan speakers and between the newly arrived Aryans and the Dravidian speakers who were already there.

War seems to have been frequent. Raids sought to capture women and cattle, while larger battles were fought to capture new territory.[14] Fortifications were raised for defense as urban centers began to emerge.[15] In contrast to the Christian tradition, where military service was initially viewed skeptically, "war as an instrument of state policy was never rejected" in ancient India.[16] Because a separate class existed for fighting, conscription was not typical, and given the social and economic costs of perpetually maintaining a standing army, in time of war little changed.[17]

Despite the frequency of resource wars, war was not considered to be without spiritual motives or consequences. Indeed, in Vedic society, "militarism was a philosophy holiest of holy,"[18] in which ritual violence supported and even demanded social violence.[19] For example, the *Vedas*, ancient Aryan texts that contain the earliest formulations of Hinduism, "regarded wars as instrument of progress," making it possible for the emerging proto-states to consolidate themselves and become economically and militarily more secure.[20] In this context, rather than being a

---

[10] *Aitareya Brahmana*, I. 14, in Arthur Berriedale Keith, trans., *Rigveda Brhamanas: The Aitareya and Kausitaki Brhamanas of the Rigveda* (Cambridge, MA: Harvard University Press, 1920), 114.

[11] *Aitareya Brahmana*, VIII.3 and VIII.5, 321, 322.

[12] Doniger, *The Hindus*, 89–95.

[13] Roy, *Hinduism and the Ethics of Warfare in South Asia*, 16.

[14] Ibid., 21. See also "Hymn to Arms," *Rig Veda Samhita* 6.75, in Wendy Doniger, *The Rig Veda* (London: Penguin Classics, 1981), 236.

[15] Roy, *Hinduism and the Ethics of Warfare in South Asia*, 25.

[16] S. K. Bhakari, *Indian Warfare: An Appraisal of Strategy and Tactics of War in Early Medieval Period* (New Delhi: Munshiram Manoharlal Publishers Pvt. Ltd., 1980), 16.

[17] Ibid., 17.   [18] Ibid.   [19] Doniger, *The Hindus*, 104.

[20] Bhakari, *Indian Warfare*, 15.

regrettable phenomenon, war was "sacrialized and considered a religious ritual."[21] To this end, the brahmins were consulted to "appease the gods and end the fault ... [and conduct] the sacrifices to bring military success and legitimate the power of the various kings and warriors."[22] War was so central to the identity of the *ksatriya*s that they came to regard dying outside of battle as a disgrace.[23] This Vedic belief that death in battle is a *ksatriya*'s highest calling recurs periodically in Hindu texts. Later texts, however, take a more pragmatic view of warfare, cautioning kings to consider the costs and benefits not only for themselves, but for society.

The *Rig-Veda* gives us some idea of the importance of war in ancient India. Warriors were revered, and those who died in battle, "who [sacrificed] their bodies," could hope to go straight to heaven.[24] There were few rules regarding just conduct. Indeed, during the Vedic age, it seems that the "Indo-Aryans had no scruples in battle; their aim was victory and all means to achieve it were considered fair."[25] Even poisoned weapons and indiscrimInate targeting of the enemy's forces seem to have been permitted. For example, a benediction recited on the eve of military expeditions declares that "the bow ruins the enemy's pleasure; with the bow let us conquer all the corners of the world."[26] Describing an arrow "smeared with poison," it then expresses the hope that the arrow will "go straight to our foes, and ... not leave a single one of them there."[27] Ultimately, it concludes "whoever would harm us, whether it be one of our own people, or a stranger ... let all the gods ruin him."[28]

POST-VEDIC PERIOD: RESTRAINT AND REALISM

Although the Vedic period was characterized by no-holds-barred warfare, a chivalric code began to develop later, when the Indo-Aryans fought wars of domination among themselves. Similar to the more restrictive rules that the Islamic tradition developed for fighting against Muslim rebels, the existence of strict *in bello* restrictions in this era reinforces my theoretical claim that humanitarian rules are emphasized more when the likely targets of violence are "one's own," as opposed to externalized others. The literature dealing with the ethics of war in the post-Vedic

---

[21] Katherine K. Young, "Hinduism and the Ethics of Weapons of Mass Destruction," in Sohail H. Hashmi and Stephen Lee, eds., *Ethics and Weapons of Mass Destruction: Religious and Secular Perspectives* (Cambridge: Cambridge University Press, 2004), 283

[22] Ibid., 147.   [23] Frost, *A History*, 146.   [24] *The Rig Veda*, 10.154.3. 54.

[25] Gurcharn Singh Sandhu, *A Military History of Ancient India* (New Delhi: Vision Books, 2000), 116.

[26] *The Rig Veda*, 6.75.2, 236.   [27] Ibid., 6.75.16, 238.   [28] Ibid., 6.75.19, 238.

period falls into three types: epic poems or mythological histories, codes of law, and advice to kings. While the latter two categories include some discussion of the ethical limits on warfare, their focus is strategic: concerns with winning trump questions of how to win ethically. The epic poems, however, reveal an elaborate set of principles governing just conduct. In the sections that follow, I first analyze the two most famous epic histories, the *Mahabharata* and the *Ramayana*. Next, I examine the *Code of Manu* as an example of the legal writing of the age. Finally, I survey Kautilya's *Arthasastra*, as well as two texts it inspired – the *Nitisara* and the *Hitopadesa* – to explore the interweaving of ethical principles and pragmatic approaches to politics.

The Mahabharata

The *Mahabharata* recounts the Kurukshetra war between the Kauravas and the Pandavas. The conflict occurred sometime between 5561 BCE and 3183 BCE, sparked by a dispute over the secession to the throne. According to the story, the Pandavas are the rightful heirs – in terms of both descent and dessert. But they are cheated out of their kingdom after a night of dubious gambling. The Pandava brothers and their wife are then condemned to spend the next thirteen years in exile, occasionally harried by their Kaurava cousins. The *Mahabharata* is extremely useful for our purposes because the story clearly references the chivalric code, thus "reflecting as well as creating practices of war."[29]

The *Mahabharata* as a text is much more recent than the events it narrates, dating to somewhere between 500 and 50 BCE. The famous *Bhagavad Gita* chapter is an even newer addition, dating to approximately 200 BCE.[30] Tradition identifies Vyasa as the author who rendered the oral tradition into a literary form.[31] During the period of its composition and revision, there were numerous clashes between *ksatriyas* and kings (*rajanyas*) as the latter grew in power and developed more centralized kingdoms, first under the short-lived Nanda empire and then under the

---

[29] Frost, *A History*, 151.

[30] The *Baghavad Gita* has not only inspired generations on the subcontinent – including both Mohandas Gandhi and Jawaharlal Nehru – but has also had a significant impact on many Western thinkers, including transcendentalists Hendry David Thoreau and Ralph Waldo Emerson, authors Auldus Huxley and Herman Hesse, and even J. Robert Oppenheimer, the director of the Manhattan Project.

[31] Frost, *A History*, 164.

rule of the Mauryas.[32] Eventually, the epic was cemented in its present form during the Gupta era (320–550 CE), a period of stability and increasing prosperity, sometimes called India's Golden Age.

The *Mahabharata* was written down just as Indian warfare was undergoing a great transition, away from heroic, individualized warfare to warfare between massive state armies.[33] We can see evidence of this shift in the text's valuation of set battles, rather than ingenious tactics. At this time, battles were seen as falling into two general types: *dharmayuddha* and *kutayuddha*.[34] The former were fought according to *dharma* or law, and were seen as righteous. The rules for *dharmayuddha* derive from those earlier days of heroic warfare, and require that the two parties declare war, establish a set time and place for the battle, and fight fairly. *Kutayuddha* was considered unjust and was theoretically shunned. The word "kuta" means "crookedness," even "evil genius," and so refers to a realpolitik strategy, that assumes "in war everything is free and fair."[35] Such tactics were reserved for a "last resort," out of desperation and necessity.[36] *Kutayuddha* is inherently pragmatic, permitting the use of deceptive stratagems, ambushes, assassinations, biological warfare, and what we might consider today to be psychological warfare.

By and large, in the *Mahabharata* the Pandavas fight according to *dharmayuddha*, as do some of the more heroic characters on the Kaurava side. The last man to serve as general for the Kauravas, however, before their defeat, risks *kutayuddha* to accomplish his goal, believing that "through stealth could come success," while he would "throw away [his] life if [he] fought them lawfully."[37] Although he knows that his plan "might be culpable, reprehensible, or scorned by the world," he nonetheless slaughters the Pandava camp as they sleep following the final pitched battle.[38]

---

[32] Ibid., 169. During the Vedic period, the terms *ksatriya* and *rajanya* were used interchangeably, although *rajanya* technically refers to the ruler's close kinsmen. See Sharma, *Aspects of Political Ideas and Institutions in Ancient India*, 171.

[33] Kaushik Roy, *From Hydaspes to Kargil: A History of Warfare in India from 326 BCE to CE 1999* (New Delhi: Manohar, 2004), 36–37.

[34] *Yuddha* is generally translated as "war," but the description of tactics used to differentiate *dharmayuddha* and *kutayuddha* suggests that "battle" might be a more apt term for our purposes.

[35] Roy, *Hinduism and the Ethics of Warfare in South Asia*, xv.

[36] V. R. Ramachandra Dikshitar, *War in Ancient India* (Delhi: Motilal Banarsidass, 1987), 274.

[37] *Mahbharata, Book Ten, Dead of Night and Book Eleven, The Women*, trans. Kate Crosby (New York: New York University Press, 2009), 10.1.45, 15.

[38] Ibid., 10.1.50, 15.

The *Mahabharata* imagines war as part of an inescapable cycle of international relations. War consistently recurs, unless a single ruler emerges to unify the entire system. After all, "quarrels which have seethed for a long time do not just die down," nor can they be easily extinguished, for over time a "quarrel only becomes stronger, just as a fire grows greater still with the oblation ... So peace can never exist in any way other than total annihilation, for there is always a weakness in the end which one or the other side can exploit."[39] Put differently, even victory is ephemeral: "The consequences are evil for the surviving victors ... In an attempt to put an end to the entire dispute, people try to annihilate everyone. Victory brews hatred, for the defeated man lives miserably."[40] Thus, war is a cyclical, "eternal problem," inescapable in this world.[41]

War may be cyclical, but specific conflicts arise from kings' unvirtuous impulses. On the one hand, good kings should embody "patience, self-restraint, truth, and non-violence."[42] Such virtuous leaders "should provide protection or the citizens, act with virtue, be conscientiously generous," and uphold the religious laws and traditions.[43] Developing the right virtues leads to prosperity and security. "Resolve, peace, self-control, purity, compassion, gentle speech, and faithfulness to friends are, together, the kindling sticks of fortune."[44] The Pandava brothers are described as living "always bent solely upon the Law, faithful in their promises, arising with alertness, forbearing, and punishing their ill-wishers ... Thus they conquered this earth entire."[45] It is their virtue that will enable their dynasty to "[prosper] perfectly," conferring protection upon it.[46]

And yet, for most of the epic (thirteen years in real time), the Pandava brothers are out in the wilderness, cheated out of their birth right. So the *Mahabharata* must address the difficult question of why bad things happen to good people who so clearly embody kingly virtue. The answer is essentially that life isn't fair, especially when your kinsmen are less than virtuous. The Kauravas, after all, "do not understand morality and pay no heed to virtue."[47] And "when a king becomes malicious, takes on

---

[39] *Mahabharata, Book Five, Preparations for War, Part I*, trans. Kathleen Garbutt (New York: New York University Press, 2008), 72.60, 603.

[40] Ibid., 72.55, 603.   [41] Ibid., 72.65, 603.

[42] Mahabharata, *Book Five, Preparations for War, Part I*, 8.35, 47.

[43] Ibid., 29.25, 195.   [44] Ibid., 38.35, 339. See also 34.10, 265.

[45] *The Mahabharata, Volume 1: The Book of the Beginning*, trans J. A. B. van Buitenen (Chicago: University of Chicago Press, 1973), 1(6)55.25-30, 128.

[46] Ibid., 1(7)103.1, 329.

[47] *Mahabharata, Book Five, Preparations for War, Part I*, 29.30, 197.

power, and is greedy for someone else's property, he is open to destiny's fury," and "the result is war between kings."[48]

Greed is the underlying cause of war in the *Mahabharata*, reflecting a critique of human nature anyone familiar with Hobbes would recognize. At the heart of greed is the lust for power. Someone thus "led by his senses . . . abandons law, wishing to attain his desire and profit by wicked means."[49] But the result of being "robbed of sense by . . . greed" is inevitably an "awesomely terrible catastrophe."[50] For example, the Kaurava brother who challenges his cousin to a game of dice for the kingdom sinned "in his greed, [lusting] for power."[51] By cheating to gain what was not his by rights, he set in motion the events that lead to the destruction of his entire family. Filled with wickedness, he believed that he deserved "dominion."[52] "Impatient, full of fury, hateful of what is good," he becomes "drunk with power," incapable of reversing course for the sake of his kingdom.[53] Put concisely:

When a man born and raised in a noble family covets other people's possessions, his greed destroys his wisdom, and once his wisdom is destroyed then it ruins his shame. When shame is dead it puts an end to morality, and once morality is dead it kills one's good fortune. When good fortune is dead it kills the man, for poverty is a man's downfall.[54]

In these circumstances, even though virtuous kings "strive in every way for peace [and] do not desire war," the circumstances make "war . . . inevitable."[55] War may be unavoidable, but it is not desirable. The *Mahabharata* emphasizes that neither side really benefits. There is always regret in killing, even enemies.[56] The "evil duty of a warrior" is that he is obliged to kill, but on some level, killing remains wicked.[57] The law requires that "warrior kill warrior," but yet "war is entirely disastrous, for which killer is not killed? Victory and defeat are the same to a dead man."[58] What is at stake is not a *moral* wrong per se, for "no law can be found against killing enemies."[59] Even if *ksatriya* kill in pursuit of their duty, "they incur no evil."[60]

[48] Ibid., 29.30, 197.
[49] *Mahabharata, Book Five, Preparations for War, Part II*, trans. Kathleen Garbutt (New York: New York University Press, 2008), 124.35, 223.
[50] Ibid., 95.10, 77.
[51] *Mahabharata, Book Five, Preparations for War, Part I*, 51.55, 491.
[52] Ibid., 72.15, 595.   [53] Ibid., 73.40, 617.   [54] Ibid., 72.15, 595.
[55] *Mahabharata, Book Five, Preparations for War, Part I*, 72.70, 605.
[56] Ibid., 72.55, 603.   [57] Ibid., 72.45, 601.   [58] Ibid., 72.45, 72.50, 601.
[59] Ibid., 3.15, 21.
[60] *Mahabharata, Book Six, Bhisma, Volume One*, trans. Alex Cherniak (New York: New York University Press, 2008), 14.65, 121.

How can a king kill without sin, if killing is morally questionable? The answer hinges on the duties assigned to each caste. The primary duty of the king is to preserve order. To protect his citizens, he must be willing to use force to uphold the law domestically and internationally. "A king should carefully protect all of these castes, and assign them to their respective duties," making sure that a proper order is maintained within society.[61] Likewise, "just as much effort should be put into protecting one's own kingdom as is put into laying waste to one's enemy's kingdom," for if "one obtains a kingdom through righteousness, and defends it with righteousness, then one will [not] lose the good fortune rooted in morality that one has gained."[62] There can be no sin in doing one's duty – so long as one does it for duty's sake and not (for example) out of lust or greed. Intent matters.

The *Bhagavad Gita* chapter as a whole makes the case for the importance of practicing one's kingly duty. On the eve of the final battle between the Pandavas and the Kurus, the warrior Arjuna looks out at the assembled armies and completely loses his nerve. Even though his cause is just, how can he kill his kinsmen, his teachers, the people with whom he spent his youth? How can this possibly be right? Just at this moment, his charioteer reveals himself to be the god Krishna. He explains his miraculous appearance by informing Arjuna that if men fail to perform their sacred duty and do not act to preserve order when "chaos prevails," then he must make himself known to inspire men of virtue to their duty, and to protect them while destroying men who do evil.[63] Krishna exhorts Arjuna to "look to [his] own duty; do not tremble before it; nothing is better for a warrior than a battle of sacred duty."[64] Classifying the battle ahead as a "sacred duty," Krishna warns that abandoning such a duty would not only lead to shame and slander among men, but would also be in itself a morally evil act. The conversation is meant to encourage Arjuna to do his duty and to fight the battle without fear or guilt.

---

[61] *Mahabharata, Book Five, Preparations for War, Part I*, 29.25, 195.

[62] Ibid., 34.30, 269.

[63] *The Bhagavad Gita: Krishna's Council in Time of War*, trans. Barbara Stoler Miller (New York: Bantam Books, 1986), IV.7–8, 50.

[64] Ibid., II. 31, 34. Consider also Krishna's argument: "Your own duty done imperfectly is better than another man's done well. It is better to die in one's own duty; another man's duty is perilous" (III.35, 46). This concept is repeated again later for emphasis: "Better to do one's own duty imperfectly than to do another man's well; doing action intrinsic to his being, a man avoids guilt" (XVIII.47, 149).

Nonetheless, while a king is duty bound to fight when *compelled* to do so, peace should always be sought first. The epic makes it clear that war should be the last resort, for both prudential and moral reasons. The heroic Pandavas, who wait thirteen years before seeking justice through force, are praised because "they desire peace ... [and] do not want war."[65] War, after all, is a risky and disastrous enterprise. The text asks three times, in almost identical language, why anyone would voluntarily *choose* to go to war. Yudhishthira wonders, "Peace is preferable to war ... Who would fight if he had achieved peace ... Who but a man whose fate is cursed would choose war?"[66] A wise man advises the Kurus not to fight the Pandavas, asking "What man is so cursed by Fate that he would undertake with war what can be accomplished by conciliation?"[67] The narrator later repeats, "what is more frivolous than going to war? Why would a man knowingly go to war? Who cursed by his fate would choose war?"[68] This deliberate repetition reinforces the message that war should not reflect choice, but necessity.

Before resorting to war, peaceful means of conflict resolution should be sought. The text carefully explores these alternatives. Several sages advise one of the characters that "peace between the good should be sought at least once" and that the good should attempt to form alliances with each other.[69] Even Dhritarashtra, the father of the Kauravas, hopes that his sons will try to make peace before the battle, as "men do not praise war in any circumstance ... Indeed, all the Kurus think it conforms with moral duty that you consider peace with the high-souled Pandavas."[70] Indeed, most of Book 5 is taken up with various entreaties for peace made by elderly sages, brahmins, and former kings, and repeated attempts at negotiation between the two parties. Recognizing the horrors war would unleash, Samjaya Vasudeva, the envoy, declares, "If without hurting the Pandavas' cause, I succeed in bringing peace to the Kurus, It will be a deed of high merit and import and they will be saved from the noose of death."[71] When negotiation fails, the use of means short of war is the next best way to accomplish one's political objectives: "Victory gained by means of conciliation is said to be the best. When it is won by sowing dissension in the enemy ranks, it is intermediate, whereas victory won in a

---

[65] *The Mahabharata*, vol. 2, 5(49)21.1, 221.   [66] Ibid., 1.165–167, 26.
[67] *The Mahabharata*, vol. 1, 1(14)107.25, 386.
[68] *The Mahabharata*, vol. 2, 5(50)26.1, 233.   [69] Ibid., 10.20, 71.
[70] Ibid., 58.1, 531.   [71] *The Mahabharata*, vol. 2, 5(50)29.40, 244.

war is the worst kind ... Battle is a source of great evils, foremost of which is slaughter."[72]

If war is meant to restore order, then the way it is fought should reflect that aim. The kingly code of conduct invoked in the *Mahabharata* serves to limit the scope of violence. These rules fall into two general types. Some rules are meant to protect innocent bystanders, a sort of civilian immunity. Others are aimed at making sure warriors fight fairly. Together, these limitations aim at warding off the most disastrous effects of war.

Many types of individuals have protected status in the text: "aged men, women, children, the retreating, or one who ... [shows] a sign of unconditional surrender, should not be killed."[73] Variations of this list appear at several points. The most powerful fighter on the Kaurava side, Bhisma declares:

I do not like to fight with one who has cast aside his arms, who is fallen, whose armor and banner are shattered, who is fleeing, who is frightened, who says, "I am yours," who is female, who bears a female name, who is disabled, who has only one son, or who is vile.[74]

Another Kaurava admits that "to cow, Brahmin, king, friend, mother and teacher, to the impaired, idiots, the blind, the sleeping, the terrified or one getting up from sleep, to the drunk, deranged or unconscious, one should never raise a weapon."[75] Furthermore, "surrendering one who has come to your house or who has sought refuge, or killing a supplicant, is reckoned the greatest cruelty."[76]

At first, such long lists of protected individuals seem somewhat cluttered and overly specific. Yet these diverse groups of people share a single characteristic: they're all helpless. Some of these individuals fall squarely into categories that the Christian and Islamic traditions would recognize as noncombatants: women, children, old men, the sick and insane. Others are combatants in name only. Unable to participate in the battle at hand, whether because they are too hurt, or too scared, or because they have been disarmed, they no longer pose a threat. A broad cross section of nonthreatening persons are thus ruled out as targets.

---

[72] *Mahabharata, Book Six, Bhisma, Volume One,* 3.80, 39.
[73] Dikshitar, *Ramachandra,* 69. Paraphrase of *Santi,* 97.74.
[74] *Mahabharata, Book Six, Bhisma, Volume Two,* trans. Alex Cherniak (New York: New York University Press, 2009), 107.75, 369.
[75] *Mahbharata, Book Ten, Dead of Night and Book Eleven, The Women,* 10.6.20, 51–53.
[76] *The Mahabharata, vol.* 1, 1(19)149.10, 309.

The immunity of women and brahmin is especially emphasized. For example, when he raises his arm to kill the sister of a horrifying demon, Bhima is chided: "Even in anger ... never kill a woman! Preserve the law, Pandava, before you preserve your life."[77] In another scene, the wife of a brahmin agrees to be surrendered to a demon, in the hope that her gender will protect her: "Those wise in the Law declare in the decisions on the Law that women may not be killed. They say that the Raksanas know the Law – perhaps he won't kill me. Men are sure to be killed, but that women are is open to doubt."[78] Her husband, a brahmin, also offers himself, arguing that killing a brahmin is such "a vile and cruel deed" that it could never be atoned.[79] And undefeatable Bhisma is finally killed when he secretly alerts the Pandavas to his unwavering commitment to the law: because he refuses to fight a woman, even a woman who has become a man, the Pandavas can use such a person to serve as a shield for Arjuna in the final battle.[80]

Just as the failure to act virtuously can cause war in the first place, failure to fight according to the rules leads to disaster. For example, warriors are blinded in punishment for a war crime involving the merciless slaughter of an entire race "down to the children in the womb."[81] And even as he stealthily enters the Pandavas's camp to kill them in their sleep, Drona's son recognizes that his act will undo him:

Whoever disregards the injunctions found in the law books and sets out to kill in violation of them has fallen from the path of good and is driven onto the path of evil ... Now that I've lost my way by trying to do such a thing, I have brought a terrible disaster upon myself.[82]

The Kauravas, in the end, get their due – they are utterly defeated. Clearly, acting against *dharma* risks serious consequences, whether in peacetime or war.

The second set of *in bello* rules described in the *Mahabharata* are meant to ensure that the fight is "fair." Before the battle, the Kauravas and the Pandavas agree on a specific set of rules. The first set of these principles demands that soldiers should fight each other with equally matched weapons. "A charioteer should fight against another charioteer," a horseman, a horseman; a foot soldier, a foot soldier; and so on.[83]

---

[77] Ibid., 1(9)143.1, 300. [78] Ibid., 1(10)146.30, 306. [79] Ibid., 1(19)149.10, 309.

[80] *Mahabharata, Book Six, Bhisma, Volume Two*, 107.80, 369.

[81] Ibid., 1(11)169.20, 339.

[82] *Mahbharata, Book Ten, Dead of Night and Book Eleven, The Women*, 10.6.20, 51–53.

[83] *Mahabharata, Book Six, Bhisma, Volume One*, 1.30, 13.

This principle suggests that no one should have an unfair advantage due to possessing a superior weapon. The battle is imagined as a series of duels, in which adversaries should first declare their intention to fight.[84] This means that combatants should "never strike anyone who is unsuspecting or in distress ... [or] someone already engaged in combat with another, or someone who has surrendered, or someone who has his back turned."[85] Soldiers who are not yet ready to fight because they are still "unarmed or unarmored" are also considered *hors de combat,* as are those individuals – such as charioteers and drummers – who support the soldiers, but who do not bear arms.[86] These rules suggest that battles themselves were understood to have a ritual aspect, and as such, had to be carried out in an orderly way.

The Ramayana

Like the *Mahabharata,* the epic tale of Rama found in the *Ramayana* emphasizes kingly duty and virtue. This handsome and virtuous eldest son of King Dasaratha, Rama, rules from Kosala's capital at Ayodhya, on the Ganges plain in northern India.[87] Rama wins Sita's hand in marriage by demonstrating his remarkable talents as an archer. But Rama's stepmother jealously prods her husband to banish Rama so that her own son can rule. Reluctantly, Rama's father complies. At first, true love transforms exile in the wilderness into a honeymoon of sorts for the newlyweds. But then Sita is abruptly kidnapped by Ravana, a fierce (and ugly) *raksasa* . The demon sweeps her off to his fort on the island of Lanka. And so, the main thrust of the story deals with Rama's efforts to recover the lovely Sita, aided by his brother Laksmana and his monkey ally Hanuman.

The exact historical reference for the story – if there ever was one – is unclear. But the text certainly reveals the tension between two competing polities, one with a clear concept of kingship, the other a clan-based system.[88] The *Ramayana* emphasizes its distaste for the latter, where the lack of a central authority means no one to enforce law, no justice, no security, and no real wealth.[89] By contrast, the kingdom of Kosala, Rama's home, is consistently portrayed in a positive light.

---

[84] Ibid.   [85] Ibid.   [86] Ibid.   [87] Ibid., 222.
[88] Romila Thapar, The Past before Us: Historical Traditions of Early North *India* (Cambridge, MA: Harvard University Press, 2013), 211.
[89] Ibid., 240.

The Hindu variant of the Ramayana is the dominant version today, although Buddhist and Jain versions also exist. Tradition names Valmiki as the author, but very little is known about him. The text describes him as a *rishi*, an inspired poet of Vedic hymns, who lived as an ascetic on the banks of the Tamasa River. Valmiki is also mentioned in the *Mahabharata*, where he is described as the son of Garuda.[90] The story of the *Ramayana* predates Valmiki, and indeed, there was at least one written version that likely preceded Valmiki's work.[91] As he wrote, he compiled several oral versions into a single tale, sometime between 400 BCE and 400 CE.[92]

Like the *Mahabharata*, the *Ramayana* reveals a set of assumptions about what constitutes just authority in general, and a *ksatriya's* duties in particular. Rama himself is the exemplar of ideal kingship. In the happy ever after, the story tells us, Rama rules Kosala with Sita as his queen, and "the world was free from thieves, and misfortune afflicted no one ... Everyone was content. Everyone was devoted to righteousness. Looking constantly to Rama alone, people did not harm one another ... While Rama ruled, his subjects adhered to their own proper occupations and were satisfied with their own duties."[93] As in many Hindu texts, the king's foremost duty is the maintenance of order. This requires action, and a good king must not allow himself to despair or to become passive.

Just kings prosper, but the unvirtuous reap what they sow. Ravana's uncle thus criticizes his decision to fight to keep Sita, arguing that "in rampaging through the worlds, you trampled glorious righteousness and embraced unrighteousness instead. It is for this reason that your enemies have grown more powerful than we."[94] Likewise, one of Rama's envoys informs Ravana that his lack of virtue (demonstrated by the kidnapping of Sita) has cost him his legitimate authority: "You have lost your royal majesty, your lordship is at an end. You have lost your wits and doomed yourself."[95] Indeed, "since you are unrighteous, unrestrained, wicked, and surround yourself with fools, you cannot possibly continue to enjoy your kingship for even another moment."[96]

---

[90] Ibid., 226.

[91] Ibid., 209. The earlier volume is the Buddhist *Dasaratha Jataka*, which dates to the second century BCE.

[92] Ibid., 220, 209. It is likely that the final written version did not take form until between 400 and 1200 CE.

[93] *The Ramayana of Valmiki, Volume VI: Yuddhakanda*, trans. Robert Goldman, Sally J. Sutherland Goldman, and Barend A. can Nooten (Princeton: Princeton University Press, 2009), VI.2.18, 123.

[94] Ibid., VI.6.14., 186.   [95] Ibid., VI.31.51–53, 200.   [96] Ibid., VI.31.58, 201.

Ravana's defeat at the hands of Rama and his monkey army is understood to be the natural result of his own misdeeds:

You are suffering the immediate consequences of your wicked deed, just as evildoers suffer an instant descent into their respective hells ... In the sheer arrogance of your strength, you did not consider the consequences ... [You have] no comprehension of the distinction between sound and unsound policy.[97]

Later, Ravana's wife cuts to the chase, reminding him that she herself had urged him to make peace with Rama. "You would not listen," she chides him, "it was your sensual appetites alone that vanquished you."[98] In her eyes, Ravana sealed his fate by assaulting Sita, "which has only led to the loss of your sovereignty, your kinsmen, and your life."[99]

While the virtuous prevail in the end, and the loving couple Rama and Sita are reunited, the *Ramayana* must, like the *Mahabharata*, deal with the question of why such horrors befell good people in the first place. At a low point, Rama's brother, Laksmana, cries out:

since the practice of righteousness has been unable to protect you, noble brother – you who have always trodden the path of virtue and controlled your senses – from calamities, it is truly pointless ... If the force of unrighteousness were real, Ravana would go to hell, while you, sir, who are devoted to righteousness, would not thus suffer calamity.[100]

Laksmana's questions are never answered directly, but in the next scene, one of Rama's generals arrives to tell Rama to compose himself and return to the fight. The implication is clear. Evil befalls good people because wicked people exist. It is inevitable. But good people must not cease struggling against evil. Put into the context of international relations – and indeed, for all its fantastical aspects, the *Ramayana* is essentially the tale of a clash between two kingdoms, like that between the Greeks and the Trojans – the message seems to be that war is inevitable, but necessary.

War on the international level is parallel to criminality in the domestic context. Thus, Rama asserts that he will use his "rod of punishment" to defeat Ravana, the same rod that would be used to discipline domestic lawbreakers.[101] But force is a tool that can backfire when used inappropriately. The king must understand his position in the mandala. A wise king "who acts with sound policy will long exercise sovereignty and bring his foes under his power," if "he makes peace or war with his enemies at the appropriate times and strengthens his own side."[102] Weaker kings, or

---

[97] Ibid., VI.51.3–5, 274. [98] Ibid., VI.99.9, 13, 442. [99] Ibid., VI.99.14, 17, 443.
[100] Ibid., VI.70.14–17, 358. [101] Ibid., VI.731.53, 200. [102] Ibid., VI.26.7, 186.

those whose forces are merely equal, should sue for peace: "only one who is stronger should make war, but even then he must never underestimate his enemy."[103]

While force is sometimes necessary, it should only be used when truly needed. "The learned have prescribed as appropriate the use of force," Ravana's brother advises him, "only on those occasions where one's object cannot be achieved by means of the other three stratagems."[104] Peaceful means should be explored first, as such means provide a safer way of securing one's ends. War, then, is a last resort – undertaken only when necessary and when there is a chance of victory.

Little is said in the *Ramayana* about *in bello* concerns. The virtuous warrior should behave virtuously in war, exercising compassion. Evil cannot be met with evil.[105] Instead, "a noble person must act compassionately whether people are wicked, virtuous, or even if deserving of death. For ... no one is entirely innocent."[106] Consequently, acts of mass destruction are impermissible. Laksmana, Rama's brother, is not permitted to use a weapon of mass destruction against Lanka, even though the enemy was "fighting an unjust war with an unjust objective."[107] Likewise, when Hanuman destroys the entire city of Lanka by fire, he surveys the women, children, and other civilians fleeing the flames and cries out "woe is me, whom wrath could lead to do this shameless deed."[108] In that moment, he recognizes that his own lack of virtue will lead to his destruction.

The only individuals identified as immune in the *Ramayana* are ambassadors and persons seeking refuge. Thus, Ravana is warned that it would be against the moral law to kill Hanuman, who was acting as Rama's ambassador.[109] Likewise, individuals – even enemies – who come seeking refuge are not legitimate targets. Rama thus cautions his monkey general, "one ought never slay a poor wretch who has come for refuge, begging for protection with is hands cupped in reverence, even should he be one's enemy."[110] Necessity does not mitigate this duty, for "even at the cost of

---

[103] Ibid., VI.26.6–8, 186.   [104] Ibid., VI.10.9, 140.   [105] Ibid., VI.102.35, 450.

[106] Ibid., VI.102.36, 450.

[107] Manoj Jumar Sinha, "Hinduism and International Humanitarian Law," *International Review of the Red Cross* 87(858), June 2005, 292.

[108] *Ramayan of Valmiki*, trans. Ralph T. H. Griffith (London: Trübner and Co.), V.55. Available online at www.sacred-texts.com/hin/rama/index.htm. The scene of the destruction is repeated, but without Hanuman's commentary, a book later. *The Ramayana of Valmiki*, VI.62.6–24, 333–334.

[109] Sinha, "Hinduism and International Humanitarian Law," 292.

[110] *The Ramayana of Valmiki, Volume VI: Yuddhakanda*, VI.12.14, 149.

his own life, a magnanimous person should save an enemy who has come for refuge from his enemies."[111] Failure to "offer this protection to the best of one's ability and the limits of one's strength, whether through fear, confusion, or greed, that would be a sin condemned by all the world."[112]

Although the issue of fighting one's kin is not as acute in the *Ramayana* as in the *Mahabharata*, the point is nonetheless repeated that kinsmen should not war among themselves. When Ravana's younger brother warns Laksmana of an impending ambush by Ravana's son, the latter bitterly chides his uncle saying, "even if one's enemy is virtuous and one's kinfolk devoid of every virtue, still, one's kinfolk, devoid of virtue though they be, are to be preferred. An enemy is always an enemy."[113] Later, Ravana's brother tells Rama that although he knows that he has duties toward his brother – in this case, carrying out his funeral rites – he cannot fulfill them, for "although he should be respected because of the deference one owes to one's elders, still Ravana does not merit respect."[114] Rama, however, does not accept this excuse. "Hostilities cease with death," he declares, and despite Ravana's wickedness, he fought heroically. Thus, he is due the brotherly respect a funeral would entail.

Finally, fighting fair is a key theme of the *in bello* ethics embedded in the *Ramayana*. Open warfare is to be preferred to concealed tactics, for moral reasons. Laksmana decries the behavior of Ravana's son, saying "what you accomplished in battle on that other occasion by making yourself invisible, that is the way of thieves. It is not to be followed by heroes."[115] Likewise, the text implies that combatants should only fight with similar weapons, even if a superior weapon would turn the tide of battle. Rama fights the final battle on foot, while Ravana remains mounted in his chariot. The gods interrupt in Rama's favor on the grounds that this is an unfair match.[116] As in the *Mahabharata*, order is valued in fighting as much as it is in politics.

LAWS OF MANU

The Code of Manu is one of the oldest Hindu *smriti* or sacred texts, dealing with *dharmasastra* or legal and religious codes. Although it was

---

[111] Ibid., VI.12.15, 149.   [112] Ibid., VI.12.16, 149.   [113] Ibid., VI.74.15, 370.
[114] Ibid., VI.100.33, 444.   [115] Ibid., VI.75.11, 373.
[116] Torkel Brekke, "The Ethics of War and the Concept of War in India and Europe," *Numen* 52, 2005, 100. See *The Ramayana of Valmiki, Volume VI: Yuddhakanda*, sarga 96, 434–437.

written sometime between 200 BCE and 200 CE, its material dates back to 500 BCE or even 1500 BCE. It became a written text during the age of the great Indian empires, when large parts of the Indian subcontinent were unified under a centralized regime. By the early centuries of the Common Era the Code of Manu had become "the standard source of authority in the orthodox tradition" of Hinduism.[117] By the middle of the fifth century CE, Manu had achieved "the preeminent position ... among legal authorities."[118]

The Code of Manu discusses war in terms of the rights and duties of kings. The responsibilities of a good king include "not turning away from battle, protecting subjects, and obedience to priests."[119] Protecting his subjects is a particularly urgent duty. If "bandits abduct from his realm subjects screaming for help, while he and men in his service stand by – he is surely dead, he is not alive."[120] Such a king has forgotten that "for a *ksatriya*, the protection of his subjects is the highest Law," and that one who fails to respect the law cannot hope to succeed.[121] Kings who uphold their duty will be rewarded, in this life and the next. As in the earlier Vedic tradition, kings who die in battle are guaranteed heaven.[122] Protection of the people requires the use of punishment, both domestically and internationally. Without punishment, chaos would ensue. Punishment disciplines and protects the subjects, from each other and from outsiders.[123]

In contrast to the Christian and Islamic traditions, the Code of Manu does not explicitly evaluate the justness of various causes of war. The Code simply divides wars into two types. While some wars are "waged of one's own accord and for (one's own) purpose," others are fought "to avenge an ally."[124] Given that protecting the people is the king's primary duty, defensive wars must be just. But what of offensive wars? A good king, the Code of Manu states, "should seek to acquire what he has not acquired ... What he has not acquired, he should seek to acquire with military force."[125]

---

[117] *The Laws of Manu*, trans. Wendy Doniger (London: Penguin Books, 1991), xviii.

[118] *The Law Code of Manu*, trans. Patrick Olivelle (Oxford: Oxford University Press, 2004), xvii.

[119] *The Laws of Manu*, 7.88, 137. See also Patrick Olivelle, ed. and trans. *Dharmasutras: The Law Codes of Apastamba, Gautama, Baudhyana and Vasistha* (Oxford: Oxford University Press, 1999), 113.

[120] *The Law Code of Manu*, 7.143, 116–117.   [121] Ibid., 7.144, 117.

[122] *The Laws of Manu*, 7.88, 137.   [123] Ibid., 7.16–18, 107.

[124] Ibid., 7.164, 145. See also Olivelle, *Dharmasutras*, 118.

[125] *The Law Code of Manu*, 7.99–101, 113.

The acquisition of new territories and resources, too, can be understood as a way of protecting one's people. A larger empire may provide more security and economic benefits. Augustine recognized this in remembering Rome's illustrious history. And yet, he worried about the dangers of overextension. The Code of Manu offers a "six-fold strategy" of international relations in response to such concerns.[126] Kings' foreign policy choices include forming alliances, going to war, and pretending to do one while really doing the other. Choosing comes down to a judgment about the king's relative power versus other actors in the system. "When he believes that all his subjects are in exceedingly high spirit and that he himself is overwhelmingly powerful, then he should consider waging war," but if victory is doubtful, he should look for other solutions to the problem.[127] The good ruler must also be the wise ruler, making pragmatic choices that reflect political realities.

Although war is treated as an acceptable tool of politics, the Code of Manu cautions that war should be an act of last resort. Whenever possible, a king should bring his adversaries under control "by the use of the strategies beginning with conciliation," employing military force only if "they still do not submit."[128] This point is driven home later, as the code repeats that the king should try to conquer his enemies "by conciliation, bribery, and dissension ... but never by fighting. For since it can be observed that neither victory nor defeat belongs permanently to either of two powers who fight in battle, therefore he should avoid fighting."[129] The second text suggests that avoiding conflict is not merely a moral consideration, but also a pragmatic one as well.

The Code of Manu does spell out specific *in bello* rules. There are various categories of nonthreatening individuals who are not to be harmed in battle, as well as some general rules for fighting fairly. Individuals who should not be killed in battle include

anyone who has climbed on a mound, or an impotent man, or a man who folds his hands in supplication, or whose hair is unbound, or anyone who is seated or who says "I am yours;" nor anyone asleep, without armour, naked, without, a weapon, not fighting, looking on, or engaged with someone else; nor anyone whose weapons have been broken, or who is in pain, badly wounded, terrified, or fleeing.[130]

---

[126] *The Laws of Manu*, 7.160, 118.   [127] Ibid., 7.170, 119.

[128] *The Law Code of Manu*, 7.107–108, 114. See also Doniger, *The Hindus*, 139.

[129] *The Laws of Manu*, 7.198–199, 148–148. See also Olivelle, *Dharmasutras*, 120–121.

[130] *The Laws of Manu*, 7.91–93, 137–139.

These individuals are linked by the fact that – for the moment at least – they pose no threat. What is interesting is that unlike the *Mahabharata* lists, which include what we today call civilians, the entire list in the Code of Manu comprises combatants who are at least temporarily out of service. There are also weapons that are not to be used, such as those which are "concealed, barbed, or smeared with poison or whose points blaze with fire."[131] Altogether, the *in bello* regulations of the Code of Manu seem more concerned with the rights of combatants than with noncombatants.

KAUTILYA'S ARTHASASTRA

In comparison to the texts discussed so far, more is known about the origins and historical context of the *Arthasastra*. Its author, Kautilya (350–283 BCE), a brahmin otherwise known as Chanakya, was the advisor to the first of the Maurava emperors, Chandragupta.[132] Chandragupta founded the Maurya empire around 322 BCE. When Alexander the Great withdrew from the Sindhu valley, Chandragupta made use of the opportunity and over the course of almost a decade defeated the remnants of the Greek and Indo-Greek armies across northern India. In 305 BCE, the young Maurya empire would again be invaded by the Greeks under Seleucus, but the latter would be defeated and even driven out of Afghanistan.[133] After defeating the Greeks, Chandragupta focused on his next biggest competitor, the Nanda empire. Ultimately, Chandragupta conquered all but the southernmost states of India. This huge empire would last – almost unthreatened – through to the reign of his grandson Ashoka.[134]

The *Arthasastra* is a text of advice for kings. The word *artha* refers to wealth, in the broadest sense, and so one way of translating its title would be as the "Rules of Political Economy."[135] Kautilya's *Arthasastra* clearly

---

[131] Ibid., 7.90, 137.
[132] Herbert H. Gowen, "'The Indian Machiavelli' or Political Theory in India Two Thousand Years Ago," *Political Science Quarterly* 44(2), June 1929, 176.
[133] Sandhu, *A Military History of Ancient India*, 213.
[134] Interestingly, Ashoka adopted Buddhism (and financed its missionary spread through South and East Asia) and pacifism early in his career. Arguably, the military successes of his grandfather and father, who conquered the majority of India and established a stable regime, made Ashoka's pacifism possible, by eliminating many sources of external and internal dissent. See Roger Boesche, "Kautilya's 'Arthasastra' on War and Diplomacy in Ancient India," *Journal of Military History* 67(1), 2003, 12–13.
[135] Kautilya, *The Arthashastra*, ed. and trans. L. N. Rangarajan (New York: Penguin Books, 1992), 1–2.

reflects the warring times in which he lived. The Maurya empire faced primarily external threats: the Greek and Nanda empires. Not only is state violence treated largely as a practical, amoral question, but the text as a whole deals more specifically than does the *Bhagavad Gita* with warfare between great armies (rather than heroic individuals), reflecting the outcome of the changes in the ways wars were fought on the subcontinent.

Kautilya reads very much like a modern offensive realist. Expanding the state's territory – through war, if necessary – is the first priority of foreign policy; ensuring that other states do not do the same is the second.[136] Territory is power, and power is security. A wise king should seek to "add to his own power and increase his own happiness," while simultaneously "[endeavouring] to reduce the power of [his] traitors and enemies."[137]

War is one tool that the king can use to expand his power, particularly by gaining productive new territory. As in the Code of Manu, Kautilya argues that kings have six policy options. They can make peace, stay quiet, seek allies, prepare for war, wage war, or follow a dual policy of helping one king while warring with another.[138] Wise kings, in consultation with their advisors, should follow the strategy that best fits their political circumstances. The key to choosing the right strategy is accurately assessing one's position in the world. To this end, Kautilya imagines the international system as a mandala. This view portrays the universe as a series of concentric rings of friendly and unfriendly kings, of enemies and allies. Kautilya explains that "the Conqueror shall think of the circle of states as a wheel – himself as the hub and his allies, drawn to him by the spokes though separated by intervening territory, as its rim."[139] The king should identify the strongest power in the system. Put simply, Kautilya's policy advice amounts to this: "he shall make peace with an equally powerful or stronger king; he shall wage war against a weaker king."[140]

Most of Kautilya's work focuses on the practicalities of military operations: how to structure the army, how to prepare for battle, how to use technologies and tactics to the best effect. Kautilya envisions three types of battles, each with their own set of rules. *Prakasayuddha* are open battles, *kutayuddha* are concealed battles, relying on the element of surprise, and *tsuniyuddha* are silent battles, something akin to

---

[136] Sandhu, *A Military History*, 237.
[137] Kautilya, *The Arthashastra*, 6.2.30–34 and 6.2.35–37, 505.
[138] Ibid., 7.1.2–5 and 7.1.6–19, 528.   [139] Ibid., 6.2.39, 505.   [140] Ibid., 7.3.1–5, 530.

contemporary guerrilla warfare. Thus, wars are subdivided based not on their causes, but rather on the tactics used. The most honorable of the three are *prakasayuddha*, open battles whose place and time are agreed upon in advance. These "righteous" wars are to be fought according to all the rules of warfare set down in the *dharmasutras*.[141] Such wars should be openly declared and fought between evenly matched militaries.[142] Kautilya, however, is skeptical about the effectiveness of open battles. Only kings whose power is superior to their opponents should fight using such tactics.[143] Kings who are weaker than their opponents, or who are not sure about their relative power, should use *kutayuddha* or *tsuniyuddha*. Which tactics are considered legitimate are contingent on the state's relative power capability.[144]

Interestingly, Kautilya devotes more space to the discussion of *kutayuddha* tactics. Working backward from these, we can reconstruct his rules of *dharmayuddha*. While *kutayuddha's foundations are* deception and ambush, *dharmayuddha* does not permit such tactics. *Kutayuddha*, in Kautilya's account, permits keeping the enemy's warriors awake by night, so that they can be "attacked during the day when they are drowsy or sleep."[145] Likewise, when using *kutayuddha*, "the enemy's sleeping warriors can also be attacked with elephants, whose feet have been covered in leather" to silence their footsteps.[146] Presumably, therefore, Kautilya believed that *dharmayuddha* forbade attacking sleeping or otherwise unprepared soldiers, just as in the other Hindu texts we have examined.

Clearly, certain aspects of this tactical discussion imply moral standards. War for Kautilya is a "means to an end," the end being peace, prosperity, and stability.[147] Other means, however, are preferable as long as they are effective. Consequently, "for Kautilya, diplomacy, palace intrigues and counter-intrigues were more important" than set-piece battles and decisive encounters with the enemy; "as a result, India's grand strategy ... was always passive and concerned with internal affairs."[148] If all-out war could be avoided through other means (never mind that

---

[141] Sandhu, *A Military History*, 23.   [142] *The Arthashastra*, 10.3.26, 670.

[143] Jagadish Narayan Sarkar, *The Art of War in Medieval India* (Delhi: Munshiram Manoharlal Publishers, 1984), 275. See also *The Arthashastra*, 10.3.1, 670.

[144] Interestingly, this idea has recently been discussed within Western just war discourse, largely as a result of the vast asymmetry in power between Western militaries and the groups they fight. See, for example, Michael L. Gross, *The Ethics of Insurgency: A Critical Guide to Just Guerilla Warfare* (Cambridge: Cambridge University Press, 2015).

[145] *The Arthashastra*, 10.3.14–23, 671.   [146] Ibid.

[147] Brekke, "The Ethics of War," 49.   [148] Roy, *From Hydaspes to Kargil*, 215.

those means had been judged dishonorable in earlier periods), the subtler path should be chosen. This suggests a sort of proportionality, and a moderating impulse to an otherwise harsh realism: "war is a dangerous undertaking and the king should only use military means when he knows he can achieve something substantial by it."[149]

A hasty reading of Kautilya might suggest that he is uninterested in just cause. While Kautilya does not advance a positive theory about what constitutes just cause, he does argue that the king should fight only for the sake of the state, and not for personal reasons. Aggressive war can be just, *if* it is for the good of the state – and perhaps also for the good of the world. This emphasis on the motivation behind conquest led one Indian scholar to defend Kautilya against Machiavelli on the grounds that unlike his European counterpart, Kautilya does not "disregard all of morality," for "conquest is not an end in itself; victory is counter-balanced by responsibilities, and acquisitions by the necessity of having to provide for safeguarding them."[150] Once the king had "conquered the world," his responsibility was to establish a just government, implying that "for Kautilya, a world conquest is the true foundation for world peace."[151]

The moral connection between world conquest and world peace hinges on Kautilya's belief that only a truly virtuous king would be able to achieve conquest on such a scale. A king "who carries out his duties, rules according to law, metes out only just punishment, applies the law equally 'to his son and to his enemy,' and protects his subjects" would be rewarded with heaven.[152] Such virtuousness benefits the soul – and one's political career. "When a just king is attacked," writes Kautilya, "even if he suffers from a serious calamity, his subjects will help him."[153] With their backing, he can defeat his enemies. But the people will abandon an unjust king. At best, they will be "indifferent" to his troubles; at worst, "they can bring down even a strong king."[154] A virtuous king – one who is truly just, who truly looks out for his people's interests – is a force multiplier. His people will help him at every turn, ensuring his success.

Kautilya, like other Hindu authors we have explored, lists individuals who should be spared during battle. These include "anyone falling down in the fight; those turning their backs; anyone surrendering; anyone who unties his hair ... or throws his weapons down; anyone contorted by fear;

---

[149] Brekke, "Wielding the Rod of Punishment," 47.   [150] Dikshitar, *Ramachandra*, 309.
[151] Narsingha Prosad Sil, "Political Morality vs. Political Necessity: Kautilya and Machiavelli Revisited," *Journal of Asian History* 19(2), 1985, 123. Cited in Boesche, "Kautilya's 'Arthasastra'," 17.
[152] Boesche, "Kautilya's 'Arthasastra'," 16.
[153] Kautilya, *The Arthashastra*, 7.5.9–11, 536.   [154] Ibid.

or anyone who does not fight."[155] As we have seen elsewhere, this list seems to deal primarily with identifying which combatants should be considered *hors de combat*. But some of these rules would seem to apply to noncombatants as well.

Kautilya elaborates specific protections for noncombatants in the context of siege warfare. On the one hand, the fort's drinking water can be cut off along with the supply lines.[156] Any crops sown in the fort "shall be destroyed."[157] On the other hand, Kautilya recommends against completely razing a resistant stronghold, arguing that if "a fort can be captured by fighting, fire shall not be used at all."[158] Fire is seen as a "divine calamity whose effects are unpredictable."[159] It destroys not only property, but also animals and people, and is unnecessarily destructive. Furthermore, even as the siege is underway, the attacking military should ensure that "the countryside around the fort shall be protected from fear."[160] The people should be encouraged to move away from the battlefield, and if they do leave, they should be given favors. Because fighting is reserved to the *ksatriya*, people from other social groups – in this case, farmers – should not be treated as legitimate targets.

Beyond this normative concern, Kautilya's overall recommendation for kings to seek wealth suggests that these rules also serve a pragmatic purpose. The point of capturing new territory is to exploit it economically. If it is destroyed in the process, the conqueror wins nothing. This practical concern is most evident in Kautilya's discussion of the appropriate treatment of conquered peoples. Deposed kings should be treated with honor.[161] They can even be restored, to rule as provincial governors. Above all, the conqueror ought to "substitute his virtues for the enemy's vices, and where the enemy was good, he shall be twice as good."[162] The conquered territory becomes fully his own – and hence, it becomes the king's duty to care for it and its people. Hence, the conqueror must act according to the interests of the people he has conquered. In order to get to know his new subjects, Kautilya advises the conqueror to "adopt the way of life, dress, language and customs of the people," and to show devotion to their gods, and to participate in their festivals.[163] He should protect "the ill, the helpless and the distressed," and punish wrongdoers.[164]

---

[155] Ibid., 13.4.50–53, 697–698.   [156] Ibid., 13.4.9–13, 694.   [157] Ibid., 693.
[158] Ibid., 694.   [159] Ibid.   [160] Ibid., 13.4.1–7, 693.
[161] Sandhu, *A Military History of Ancient India*, 238.   [162] Ibid., 13.5.3–21, 699.
[163] Ibid., 700. Machiavelli makes a similar point, suggesting that conquerors should live in the territories they conquer, to learn about them and to earn the locals' respect.
[164] Ibid., 700.

Put simply, *post bellum* the conqueror should establish a just order. Kautilya's realism in the *Arthasastra* is imbued with normative concerns. Powerful kings should fight to expand their empires – but out of a sense of what we might call *noblesse oblige*, rather than greed. Because power accrues to the virtuous, using that power to extend the just ruler's realm only increases the net prosperity and happiness of the region. Newly conquered territories, in Kautilya's imagination, are not to be exploited for the conqueror's ends, but rather to be developed for their own benefit. A concern with order, both normatively and pragmatically, informs Kautilya's understanding of what constitutes appropriate policies before, during, and even after war.

Kamandaka's Nitisara

Although Kamandaka is widely believed to be the author of the *Nitisara*, there is some debate as to exactly who he was and when he lived. Whoever he was, Kamandaka was highly influenced by Kautilya's *Arthasastra*, and indeed many passages in the *Nitisara* reflect that earlier work.[165] Some traditions even describe Kamandaka as a disciple of Kautilya.[166] But this cannot be taken literally, as evidence within the text places it late in the Gupta period (300–550 CE), at least six hundred years after Kautilya's time.[167] While the Mauryas of Kautilya's day were a stable – even ascendant – power, the Guptas were in decline by the end of the fifth century.[168] Political fragmentation increased, and the urban economy declined steadily.[169] During the sixth century, parts of the empire were overrun by invaders from Central Asia.

Kamandaka treats security as the essential good kings provide. "A sovereign should protect his subjects," he writes, for "preservation of good order is preferable to a seeming increase of prosperity, for when

[165] Thapar, *The Past before Us*, 524.
[166] Kamandaki, *The Nitisara or The Elements of Polity*, trans. Sisr Kumar Mitra, ed. Rajendralala Mitra (Kolkata, India: Asiatic Society, 2008), i.
[167] Charles Drekmeier, *Kingship and Community in Early India* (Stanford, CA: Stanford University Press, 1962), 216. See also Kaushik Roy, "Hinduism," in Gregory Reichberg, Henrik Syse, and Nicole M. Hartwell, eds., *Religion, War, and Ethics* (Cambridge: Cambridge University Press, 2014).
[168] Drekmeier, *Kingship and Community in Early India*, 216.
[169] Upinder Singh, *A History of Ancient and Early Medieval India* (Chennai, India: Pearson, 2016), 473.

all order is lost, then prosperity, though present, is of no use."[170] Thus, the "highest duty of a king is to protect his subjects."[171] Without security, there can be no other goods, including material prosperity.

As we have seen before, virtuous behavior is materially rewarded. A king who protects his subjects will find that his kingdom – and his own treasury – will prosper.[172] "A flourishing sovereignty cannot well be obtained by the worthless; he only, who has qualified himself, is fit to wield the sceptre."[173] A "king of righteous conduct, who governs the state justly and properly," is beloved by his subjects and able to conquer others.[174] Kamandaka writes that "it is advisable therefore for a king to show due regard in righteousness even in matters of acquisition of wealth," because a kingdom only truly flourishes when it is righteously governed.[175] While the unvirtuous may seem to prosper temporarily, they will inevitably meet "with destruction even during ... (apparently) sunny days."[176] Greed, of course, undermines a king's rule. The wise king will avoid passions such as "lust, anger, avarice, fiendish delight in doing injury, morbid desire for honor, and arrogance," which will only lead to his downfall.[177]

The king's primary responsibility is to maintain order, of course, and this can only be done through the proper use of punishment (*danda*). Without punishment, disorder ensues. "In this world, where beings are related to one another as food and consumer, when proper chastisements are withheld, the exertions of a king to keep his subjects under control become as futile as those of an angler trying to catch fish without the help of a rod."[178] Unfortunately, human nature is such that few people discipline themselves. "Upright conduct is scarce in this slavish world of ours," Kamandaka writes, and "men only attend to their prescribed duties through fear of punishments."[179] Luther would have agreed.

But punishment must be carried out correctly. Too strict, too lenient, or obviously partial punishments undermine the king's rule.[180] Overly harsh punishments, like the unjust seizure of property, is a sign of weakness arising out of anger.[181] Although a king must punish wrongdoers, he must also be generous toward his subjects. He should "wipe away the tears of the oppressed and the helpless."[182] Consequently, he should not

---

[170] *Kamandakiya Nitisara: or, The Elements of Polity*, trans. Manmatha Nath Dutt (Varanasi, India: Chowkhamba Sanskrit Series Office, 1979), I.12, 4. See also *The Nitisara*, 7.

[171] Ibid., VI.4, 64.   [172] *Kamandakiya Nitisara*, IV.21, 33; I.14, 8.

[173] Ibid., IV.4, 30.   [174] Kamandaki, *The Nitisara*, I.11, 7.   [175] Ibid., I.17, 9.

[176] Ibid., V.5, 45.   [177] *Kamandakiya Nitisara*, I.55, 12.

[178] *Kamandakiya Nitisara or, The Elements of Polity*, II.40, 24.   [179] Ibid., II.43, 34.

[180] Ibid., II.36–37, 23.   [181] Ibid., XIV.6, 207.   [182] Ibid., III.5, 25.

"persecute a poor and helpless person," but instead should protect him.[183] He should "cherish every one of his subjects," even those who are poor, if he wishes his kingdom to enjoy flourishing prosperity.[184] When a king is cruel, his subjects will seek "the protection of the enemy," whose power will grow.[185] Proper imposition of punishments not only preserves justice, but also increases the wealth of the kingdom.[186]

Interestingly, Kamandaka introduces a moral principle similar to double effect when discussing punishment. The idea of double effect does not seem to appear elsewhere in the Hindu texts under examination here. Instead of simply asserting the proper use of *danda* as the duty of kings, Kamandaka asserts that "monarchs can inflict tortures for the purposes of justice ... therefore kings are not tainted with sin when they put impious wretches to death."[187] The fact that Kamandaka feels the need to explicitly assert that torture and killing do not taint kings suggests that attitudes toward the use of force may have shifted somewhat from the time of the earlier texts. It is no longer enough, for Kamandaka's audience, to assert that kings have a duty to use violence in particular ways – they seem to also want to be reassured that carrying out this duty will not cause them moral harm.

The just king's obligation to use punishment for the sake of order does not end at the border. The disorderliness of human nature also fuels international conflicts. "People proceed to fight with one another," Kamandaka declares, "possessed by thoughts of revenge, and with hearts burning with anger engendered by the infliction of mutual wrongs."[188] The sorts of wrongs likely to lead to war, in Kamandaka's view, include:

Usurpation of the kingdom, abduction of females, seizure of provinces and portions of territory, carrying away of vehicles and treasures, arrogance, morbid sense of honor, molestation of dominions ... destruction of property, violation of laws, prostration of the regal powers, influence of evil destiny, the necessity of helping friends and allies, disrespectful demeanor, the destruction of friends, the want of compassion on creatures, disaffection of the *Prakriti Mandala*, and common eagerness for possessing the same object.[189]

All these various disasters can be rectified by restoring order. Stolen territory and women can be returned, insults can be "extinguished" by offering honor instead, and minor concerns can simply be overlooked.[190]

---

[183] Ibid., III.6–7, 26.   [184] Ibid., VIII.53, 95.   [185] Ibid., XIV.13, 208.
[186] Ibid., VVI.6, 64.   [187] Ibid., VI.5, 64.   [188] Ibid., X.1, 136.
[189] Ibid., X.3–5, 136–137.   [190] Ibid., X.6–13, 137–139.

Ultimately, if the problem is minor, Kamandaka suggests that the wronged king should avoid prosecuting the war because in war "a man may lose all his treasure."[191] Above all, the king should try to win over his enemies, whether domestic or international.[192] Before choosing any course of action, especially a warlike one, the king should seek the counsel of wise men, for the "power of counsel is of greater importance than that of the arms."[193]

As the wise leader contemplates whether or not war is the right tool to address a particular problem of disorder, he or she must consider the relative balance of power. Like Kautilya, Kamandaka imagines the international system as a mandala, and asserts that kings must accurately plot their position in order to properly chart their course. A king should be ready to attack, however, when he is the more powerful than his foes, if the time is right. If "the three policies of conciliation, gift and alienation" have failed, the stronger king "should lead his army against those who deserve punishment."[194] War, therefore, can be used as a last resort for the restoration of order.

However, if a conflict arises with a more powerful king, "having no other remedy, [one] should seek peace."[195] If attacked by a stronger party, the wise king should bend and seek conciliation.[196] Likewise, in wars against equals, "victory is doubtful," so peace is preferred.[197] After all, two equally matched kings both "reap destruction" if they clash, and neither side is guaranteed a victory.[198] Although Kamandaka pragmatically recommends pursuing peace in these cases, peace as a strategy does not necessarily mean abandoning the conflict. Instead, he counsels that the "end should be reached by sowing dissension in the enemy's camp, by gift, bribery, reconciliation, tempting offers," and other nonviolent means.[199]

Kamandaka writes less about *in bello* regulations than Kautilya. In an era of increasing insecurity, he seems more concerned with winning than with winning well. However, his emphasis on the importance of order does resurface in his discussion of the treatment of defeated enemies. Thus, "a foe whose possessions have been snatched away, gets back his territory if he serves the victory faithfully."[200] In other words, a defeated enemy who accepts the terms of peace and submits to the authority of the victorious

[191] Ibid., X.13, 140. [192] Ibid., XI.49, 53–55, 223–224. [193] Ibid., XI.57, 225.
[194] Ibid., XVIII.1, 240. [195] Ibid., IX.1, 105. [196] Ibid., X. 33, 146.
[197] Ibid., IX.59, 127. See also X.32, 146. [198] Ibid., IX.60–61, 127.
[199] Ibid., X.14, 140. [200] Ibid., XI.61, 225.

king can maintain some of his power. Thus, a powerful king expands his sovereignty over more territory, but retains the local systems of governance for the sake of continuity and order. In this light, conquest is not an end in itself. Instead, it is a means by which to establish just order.

Narayana's Hitopadesa

Hitopadesa, or "Friendly Advice," is also a *niti* text, which aims to establish principles of right conduct and politics just as the *Arthasastra* and *Nitisara* that we have already examined. The style, however, differs. While Kautilya and Kamandaka write in a decidedly textbook style, the *Hitopadesa* is told through a series of stories. The frame plot involves a king who worries that his sons do not know how to live well or how to govern justly. He calls upon a wise man, Vishnu-sharman, to educate them. In the body of the text, the young men ask Vishnu-sharman a series of questions, and he replies with a mixture of fables and straightforward advice. The tales related by Vishnu-sharman are primarily drawn from the *Panchatantra*, an earlier collection of Sanskrit fables.

We know very little about the text, its author, and its time. The concluding verses of the book identify Narayana as the author, and a local king by the name of Dhavala-chandra as the patron.[201] The text cites two known works, including Kamandaka's *Nitisara*, thus placing its composition sometime between 800 and 950 CE.[202] Some internal evidence suggests it was written in the Pala empire of eastern India (and today's Bangladesh). The Pala empire expanded rapidly at the start of the ninth century, before entering into a period of decline in the middle of the century. This led to conflict with the neighboring Rashtrakuta and Assamese kingdoms. If the *Hitopadesa* does indeed date to this era, it was written at a time of greater strife and insecurity than its predecessors. This may explain its emphasis on seeking peace whenever possible, despite relying on the same logic of the mandala system of international affairs as the *Arthasastra* and the *Nitisara*.

Narayana uses a debate between several animals to explore the differences between a realist and an idealist approach to governance. In the chapter "On How to Win Friends," Golden, the king of mice, plays the role of the skeptical realist. He counsels against risking too much to help

---

[201] *"Friendly Advice" by Narayana and King Vikrama's Adventures*, trans. Judit Törzsök (New York: New York University Press, 2007).
[202] Roy, *Hinduism and the Ethics of Warfare in South Asia*, 151.

others, explaining that "experts in statecraft do not approve of sacrificing oneself to protect one's dependents."[203] Like a good realist, he places survival above all other values: "It is life that is the fundamental basis of duty, wealth, desire and liberation. If you destroy life, the rest is destroyed, and if you protect it, all is protected."[204] Elsewhere, another king is advised that "If your subjects have no king, they cannot survive, wealthy though they may ben ... Subjects prosper or perish with the king."[205]

Golden, unlike many of the creatures in the tales, distrusts everyone. He hesitates to make friends or – in the language of statecraft – form alliances with others. Thus, he counsels against making "peace with the enemy," even "with a well-defined peace treaty."[206] While even the *Arthasastra* and the *Nitisara* recommend buying off enemies with payments, Golden argues that "if you trust your enemy ... only because you have given them money – even if you have given them a lot – that's the end of your life."[207] Payments do not alter others' underlying interests, even if they may temporarily shift their preferences.

Golden's realist perspective is contrasted with the idealist views taken by the bird Speckled-Neck. The small bird values self-sacrifice for the sake of others on the basis that one ought not cling too much to this life, which is, after all, only transitory.[208] These views are treated as naïve and dangerous within the text. Thus, the cat tricks the vulture into trusting him by declaring *ahimsa*, or nonviolence, to be the ultimate moral obligation.[209] By putting the language of idealism into the mouths of foolish birds and cunning cats (who use it to trick their naïve victims), Narayana suggests that this worldview is risky.

The *Hitopadesa* emphasizes the importance of order for achieving all other goods. For this reason, a strong central authority is absolutely essential. Thus, "people should first have a king, then a wife and then wealth. Without a king protecting the land, where can you find your wife and wealth?"[210] In this vein, Narayana cites the *Nitisara*, asserting that "people generally control themselves because they fear punishment."[211] Likewise, "a king protects his subjects, who make their ruler prosperous; but protection is more important than prosperity – without it, we lose even what we have."[212] The king's primary role is to protect his subjects,

---

[203] *"Friendly Advice,"* I.95, 101. [204] Ibid. [205] Ibid., 3.400, 437.
[206] Ibid., I.215, 131. [207] Ibid., I.220, 131. [208] Ibid., I.100–105, 103.
[209] Ibid., I.160, 117. [210] Ibid., I.455, 195. [211] Ibid., I.460, 197.
[212] Ibid., 3.5, 337.

"from robbers, officers and enemies, from the king's favorites and from his own greed."[213]

As we have seen elsewhere, good kings prosper, while unvirtuous ones bring about their own destruction. "One should never behave improperly just because one has a kingdom," warns a king; "insolence destroys wealth."[214] A just king, however, wins allies and friends naturally to his cause. Such a person is "difficult to uproot," because "everybody will fight for him, for he loves his people and performs his duties."[215] By contrast, "he who is unpopular with his subjects will be abandoned by them in war; and he who is given to the pleasure of the senses is easy to conquer."[216]

Peace is to be aimed for when it can guarantee real security. But when it cannot, "when a wise man sees no advantage in not fighting," he must fight to defeat his enemies.[217] Because fighting to defend order is a king's duty, he should not be swayed by a false sense of compassion. When killing his enemy moves a lion to tears, his counselor Damanaka asks, "what is this new principle which makes you regret killing your enemy?"[218] Answering his own query, he replies

a king who desires his own welfare should kill those who threaten his life, whether it is his father, brother, son or his friend ... If you know the real nature of duty ... then you should never be too compassionate. He who takes pity on others cannot safeguard anything ... Forgiveness towards a friend or an enemy is beautiful in a hermit; but forgiving those who have committed an offence is a fault for a king.[219]

This sounds very much like the counsel Krishna offered Arjuna, which places the duty of upholding order above all sorts of other human concerns and ties. Put simply, a king needs "to follow the duty of a warrior – so [he] must fight."[220] It sounds at first rather harsh for a king to show no mercy to anyone threatening his life. But keeping in mind that a strong king is essential to order, and order is necessary for all other pursuits, Damanaka is essentially reminding the lion of the importance of the state itself.

Nonetheless, despite the counsel against trusting in a false sense of peace and security, Narayana argues that means short of war should always be explored first. In the chapter, "War," the king of the birds is counseled by his prime minister, a sheldrake, that "it's not right to march to war immediately," because one "should always try to defeat your

---

[213] Ibid., 2.250, 275.   [214] Ibid., 3.315, 419.   [215] Ibid., 4.115, 475.
[216] Ibid., 4.135, 481.   [217] Ibid., 2.440, 327.   [218] Ibid., 2.455, 331.
[219] Ibid., 2.460, 331.   [220] Ibid., 4.105, 473.

enemy without making war, for victory cannot be guaranteed on either side of the battle."[221] Vishnu-sharman, the teacher in the frame story, thus concludes the chapter on war by hoping for peace. "Then listen to one more verse," he says. "May no king ever need to wage war with his elephants, horses and infantry. May the enemy, swept away by the storms of statecraft and counsel, merely flee to mountain caves."[222]

Narayana's text, like the *Arthasastra* and the *Nitisara*, describes the mandala system of international relations.[223] Before resorting to force, conciliatory measures, gifts, and dissension should be tried. Fighting with a more powerful enemy is not advised; instead a weaker king should "contract [himself] like a tortoise" to survive the blows.[224] When a king is attacked by a stronger enemy, "he should try to make peace and so gain some time."[225] Likewise, one should make peace with enemies who are equally matched.[226] Nonetheless, when a king enjoys more power than his enemies, however, he may go to war to gain "land, allies and gold."[227] Kings in the text are frequently encouraged not to be passive, but to seek prosperity and security by acting forcefully.

The *Hitopadesa* has little to say about *in bello* regulations. There is no evident discussion of noncombatant immunity, or the importance of protecting the property of noncombatants. The point is made, however, that envoys should not be killed, because they serve as the "mouthpiece" of the king.[228] They are not responsible for the message, but are merely its bearers. Too little is known about the composition of the *Hitopadesa* to say definitively that the increasing insecurity faced in its region contributed to its perspective on *in bello* concerns. It is intriguing, however, that its apparent concern with discouraging kings from going to war in the first place is not coupled with much encouragement to fight in more restrained ways.

CONCLUSION

Because of the difficulty in ascribing Hindu texts to a particular time and place, it is hard to demonstrate definitively that Hindu ways of thinking about the ethics of war change over time in response to changing geostrategic and political conditions. The tone of the *Hitopadesa* offers some

---

[221] Ibid., 3.135–3.140, 372–373.   [222] Ibid., 3.415, 441.   [223] Ibid., 4.140, 483.
[224] Ibid., 3.160, 375.   [225] Ibid., 4.300, 525.
[226] Ibid., 4.95, 469. See also 4.100, 471.   [227] Ibid., 3.210, 389.
[228] Ibid., 3.200, 387.

suggestion of this, but the more dramatic shift seems to have happened much earlier. The marked difference between the pre-Vedic and post-Vedic period seems to uphold my hypothesis. While the pre-Vedic texts offer little in the way of suggestions for restraining war, the post-Vedic texts – which are written in a context of competition between polities that share many similar cultural and political features – reveal highly developed ways of thinking about both *ad bellum* and *in bello* issues.

More broadly, all the Hindu texts considered here clearly reveal a realist approach to thinking about the international sphere. Not only do the texts share the basic assumptions of realism that we have seen in the Christian and Islamic texts – the belief that war is inevitable, and that power is needed to maintain order – but the advice to kings even bears a passing similarity to structural realism. Imagining the international system as a mandala leads Kautilya, Kamandaka, and Narayana to describe the balance of power in a way that is quite familiar to modern realists.

And yet, the realism expressed by these texts is not an amoral, anything goes kind of realism. By contrast, it is a realism that takes morality seriously. In so doing, it suggests something rather radical: that doing the right thing can have material benefits in the here and now. A wise king is a realistic and restrained statesman. He always pursues justice at home, but when the time is right, he may promote justice abroad as well. But the obligation to seek justice internationally is contingent, applying only when he has enough strength to do so successfully. The moral implication is clear: pursuing a just, but hopeless, cause is no real justice at all. This is the tragedy at the heart of the world's just war traditions: recognizing injustice and being able to effectively combat it are two different things. To fail to recognize our limitations is as morally risky as failing to be concerned about justice in the first place.

PART III

7

What's Old Is New Again

The Future of Just War Thinking

As we've seen in the previous chapters, historical just war thinking and realism are not as far apart as the common wisdom suggests, in any of the religious traditions. Realism, I've argued, is a tradition that privileges order, and so frames the anarchical international system as one in which political communities, out of necessity, struggle to survive. The brokenness of human nature generates conflict, and the distrust that pervades human interactions means that each polity's pursuit of security seems threatening to others. The resulting cycle of fear and armament makes war all but inevitable. Realism also attaches normative value to the survival of political communities, and thus to the maintenance of balance in the international system.

The just war traditions of Christianity, Islam, and Hinduism differ, of course, both in the types of wars they permit and in the limitations they place on the conduct of war. These differences are significant enough to give us pause when we hear talk of universal norms. This is especially true when we think not about broad principles – the importance of a just cause, for example, or humanitarian restraint – but about specific claims of what exactly constitutes a just cause or who exactly counts as a civilian. Nonetheless, thinly universal norms are held in common across all three traditions.

Fundamentally, all three share with each other – and with realism – an underlying concern with order. Because polities serve an important function – maintaining domestic order so that human communities and spirituality can thrive – states are permitted to do what is necessary for their own defense. The fallen nature of earthly life makes defensive war all but inevitable. Read in this light, just war thinking has a strongly realist bent. Yet just war thinking also permits a second type of war fighting that realists are unlikely to advocate. Because order is such an important good, states may fight to restore a *just* order (or establish it, where it had not existed before) abroad. This makes traditional just war thinking in any of the historical traditions more likely to approve of a wider spectrum of wars than those permitted by realists. A constant tension between force as a tool of justice and force as a disrupter of order lies at the very heart of the just war tradition.

Just war thinking entered a period of dormancy in the Western world from the seventeenth century until the twentieth.[1] Meanwhile, its principles and underlying logics were recast in secular legal terms – a process that altered some of them considerably. When just war thinking returned as a subject of academic discourse in the twentieth century, it was not merely reviving the older tradition. It was rereading the old tradition through the lens of international law. The conceptions of just cause, legitimate authority, and *in bello* restrictions invoked by contemporary just war thinkers often reflect the idealist or institutionalist aspects more than the realism of the historical just war tradition.

In this chapter, we will first explore the relationship between the historical just war thinking and the law of war. I argue that the law of war reflects a more optimistic, institutional (or "liberal") approach to international relations.[2] Then we will consider the state of just war argument today, examining the consequences of this interaction between the tradition and the law. Ironically, these new, liberal interpretations of just war thinking push the tradition in opposing directions: one vision toward pacifism and the other toward interventionism. To conclude, I make the case that just war thinking would do well to return to its realist roots.

---

[1] Inis Claude, "Just Wars: Doctrines and Institutions," *Political Science Quarterly* 95(1), Spring 1980, 92; Oliver O'Donovan, *Just War Revisited* (Cambridge: Cambridge University Press, 2003); Johnson, "Just War, As It Was and Is," vii; Johnson, *Sovereignty*, 44; Rengger, *Just War and International Order*, 62, 66. Charles A. Jones dates this rebirth to a half century earlier (1815) in *More than Just War: Narratives of the Just War Tradition and Military Life* (New York: Routledge, 2013), 46.

[2] Political liberalism, like realism, is a tradition with a long history. In invoking liberalism here, I have in mind Mill's understanding of liberalism rooted in the belief that individuals should be freed up to develop themselves because it "the cultivation of individuality" produces "well-developed human beings," who are "nearer to the best thing they can be." John Stuart Mill, *On Liberty and Other Writings* (Cambridge: Cambridge University Press, 1999), 64. While realists are concerned about *groups*, liberals emphasize the significance of *individuals*.

THE LIBERAL TURN TOWARD LAW: CONTEMPORARY JUST WAR THINKING

Contemporary just war thought is far more optimistic that its predecessors about the possibility of a stable, peaceful international society and far more pessimistic about the possibility of war serving as a useful tool for the preservation of order and the restoration of justice. This theoretical sea change reflects two shifts in the underlying logics of just war thinking. First, some just war thinkers have come to believe in a robust, norm-governed international society.[3] In this society war is not a tool, but a destructive force.[4] Thus, Walzer argues that aggression "is the name we give to the crime of war."[5] This perspective limits any possible justification of war to self-defense, which (by definition) turns all other wars into crimes. This has led to a cautious dance around humanitarian interventions – seen as necessary for protecting civilians from their governments – which are treated as something somehow different from war.[6] The emerging *jus ad vim* category incorporates these sorts of violent-but-not-quite-war acts, including not only

---

[3] Renggar critiques this shift in "On the Just War Tradition in the 21st Century," 359. For example, Nicholas Wheeler draws explicitly on an English School–inspired understanding of international society to justify humanitarian intervention in *Saving Strangers: Humanitarian Intervention in International Society* (Oxford: Oxford University Press, 2000); Simon Chesterman argues that appeals to morality should not trump legality lest they undermine the international order in *Just War or Just Peace? Humanitarian Intervention and International Law* (Oxford: Oxford University Press, 2001); Alex Bellamy describes the obligation of international society to limit the punishment inflicted by victors in "The Responsibilities of Victory: 'Jus Post Bellum' and the Just War," *Review of International Studies* 34(4), October 2008, 624.

[4] The language of "destructive force" appears frequently in works claiming that modern war-fighting technology has rendered the old categories of just war thought obsolete. Fiala argues, for example, that "as war has become more destructive, our ideas about justice have become more exacting," making it nearly impossible "for us to believe that modern wars can be just." Andrew G. Fiala, *The Just War Myth – The Moral Illusions of War* (New York: Rowman & Littlefield, 2008), 29.

[5] Walzer, *Just and Unjust Wars*, 51.

[6] Note Michael Walzer's treatment of humanitarian intervention as a separate category than war in "Regime Change and Just War," *Dissent* (Summer 2006), 103–108. See also George Lucas, "The Role of the 'International Community' in Just War Tradition – Confronting the Challenges of Humanitarian Intervention and Preemptive War," *Journal of Military Ethics* 2(2), 2003, 122–144. James Pattison has also explored the difficulty of applying just war thinking to humanitarian intervention from a revisionist point of view. See, for example, "The Ethics of Humanitarian Intervention in Libya," *Ethics and International Affairs* 25(3), 2011, 271–277.

humanitarian interventions but also small-scale uses of force against transnational terrorists and criminal elements.[7]

Second, just war thinking has come to focus on rights and protections for individuals, rather than states. Historically, the just war traditions placed more emphasis on *ad bellum* matters, having relatively less to say about *in bello* concerns. The civilian protections established within any of the historical traditions are far too thin for comfort, particularly in light of the horrors unleashed against civilians in the twentieth century. (The twenty-first century has not started out much better.) Contemporary efforts to expand and clarify the principles protecting civilians are vitally important. And yet this effort can backfire. When any level of civilian deaths becomes unacceptable, fighting justly becomes impossible. Under such circumstances, states will either refuse fight all unnecessary wars (thus failing to carry out their moral obligations to uphold order in the system) or they will simply abandon the rules entirely.

Both the optimistic belief in a robust international society and the new focus on individual human rights emerge from a single source. While contemporary just war theorizing uses categories and terms familiar from the historical tradition, these are mediated through international law.[8] Walzer's work is emblematic of this development. In the opening sections of *Just and Unjust Wars*, Walzer describes his project in deceivingly humble terms. His aim is to capture our intuitions about just war on paper, using a moral language that he claims we already know. But Walzer is not merely rehashing the historical just war tradition, nor even simply translating it into modern terms. Strikingly, there are few references at all to the Christian just war cannon. Neither Augustine nor Aquinas is cited in the body of the text. Vitoria is referred to just four times.

Instead, Walzer argues that "the language with which we argue about war and justice is similar to the language of international law," and it is this language that shapes his arguments.[9] Walzer groups international law together with other "norms, customs, professional codes, legal

---

[7] Walzer, *Just and Unjust Wars*, xv. Daniel Brunstetter and Megan Braun, "From Jus ad bellum to Jus ad Vim: Recalibrating Our Understanding of the Moral Use of Force," *Ethics and International Affairs* 27(1), March 2013, 87–106.

[8] As James Turner Johnson points out, the incorporation of legal language into just war reasoning began when "in the late nineteenth and early twentieth centuries, the Roman church began to come out of its cloisters and meet the world," it came out speaking "the language of international law." Johnson, *Ideology, Reason, and the Limitation of War*, 18.

[9] Walzer, *Just and Unjust Wars*, xviii.

precepts, religious and philosophical principles," as the embodiment of what he calls "the war convention." Although "the terms of our judgments are most explicitly set forth in positive international law," the decentralized nature of international law means that a rich tradition of common law regarding just combat still exists.[10] As a result, the just war thinker's job is to "look to the lawyers for general formulas, but to historical cases and actual debates for those particular judgments that both reflect the war convention and constitute its vital force."[11]

While Walzer is careful to argue that the war convention is not synonymous with the law of war, but rather with the religious, cultural, and political "moral arguments" that accompany it, the parallels between the international law of war and his moral theory are clear.[12] Thus, when Walzer lays out the *ad bellum* principles governing the recourse to war, he begins with a discussion of "law and order in international society," describing the crime of aggression as a violation of the fundamental right of a political community to build its own domestic life.[13] Legal language also permeates his discussion of *in bello* principles, which – in a departure from the historical just war canon – constitute nearly half of the book.

It is not at all surprising that Walzer saw just war thinking and international law as deeply intermeshed. In the West, Christian just war thinking ceased to be a matter of serious academic scholarship within a generation after the deaths of Vitoria and Luther. While the language of just war was periodically invoked politically, just war thinking remained intellectually dormant for some three hundred years. After World War II, which etched images of horrific civilian suffering on a hitherto unimaginable scale in the public mind, the threat of a future nuclear war spurred the reemergence of just war thinking.[14]

FROM JUST WAR THINKING TO INTERNATIONAL LAW AND BACK AGAIN

Although Walzer's version of just war thinking is farther from the historical tradition than many contemporary scholars realize, the legal tradition

---

[10] Ibid., 44.   [11] Ibid.   [12] Ibid., 44–45.   [13] Ibid., 51–53.

[14] Key works from this era include Paul Ramsey, *War and the Christian Conscience* (Durham, NC: Duke University Press, 1961), and G. E. M. Anscombe, "War and Murder," in Walter Stein, ed., *Nuclear Weapons: A Catholic Response* (New York: Sheed and Ward, 1961).

on which he draws is itself closely reflective of that older tradition.[15] In a way, Walzer brought the just war tradition full circle. For just war discourse did not die in the generation after Vitoria. Instead, it took on a new life in the laws of war. The initial transition of just war thinking into international law is worth a closer look, as the three key differences between traditional just war thought and its contemporary equivalent are rooted in this period. First, international law perceives the international system more optimistically, inclining it toward an institutionalist perspective that treats states as members of a society. Second, international law emphasizes *in bello* concerns more than *ad bellum* ones. Third, international law has further developed and expanded the idea of the civilian, including protections for civilian property, while at the same time incorporating a concern for the human rights of combatants.

OPTIMISM AND INSTITUTIONALISM

Early legal scholars were more optimistic about the possibility for a durable peace between states than the Christian just war thinkers who preceded them. Fundamentally, this optimism hinged on the idea that history is the story of nations' progress toward "civilization."[16] Hugo Grotius (1583–1645), a Dutch scholar often called the "father" of international law, imagined that a thin society existed between states.[17] For Grotius, the belief in an international society stems naturally from his

[15] Consider, for example, the brief history of just war thinking provided by Brian Orend in *The Morality of War* (Peterborough, Ontario: Broadview Press, 2006), which treats Grotius's work as one of the "landmark pieces of just war theory" (while admitting that it is also "one of the first productions of the laws of armed conflict), and nonchalantly identifies the legal scholars Pufendorf and Vattel as just war theorists (19, 21). For a discussion of the relationship between the early international legal tradition and just war thinking, see James Turner Johnson's analysis in *Sovereignty*, especially chapter 4, "Grotius and His Impact."

[16] Theodore Christov, "Liberal Internationalism Revisited: Grotius, Vattel, and the International Order of States," *The European Legacy* 10(6), 2005, 561–584, 562.

[17] The distinction of being the founder of secular international law may more properly fall to Alberico Gentili, a Protestant legal scholar to the English court, who – like Grotius – was deeply influenced by the Roman classics. It is also noteworthy that some scholars argue that Grotius's work is better explained as the "summation" of the just war tradition up to his time. See Greg Reichberg, Henrik Syse, and Endre Begby, *The Ethics of War: Classic and Contemporary Readings* (Oxford: Blackwell Publishing, 2006), 386. Johnson's view is subtler. While he acknowledges Grotius's dependence on the historical just war tradition, he argues that Grotius "importantly changes the focus, reshapes the content, and gives new intentionality to the just war idea" in drafting his version of international law. Johnson, *Sovereignty*, 81.

belief – drawn from the Greco-Roman philosophical tradition – in the natural sociability of man.[18] Just as domestic society restrains individuals so that the exercise of their rights does not infringe on the rights of others, this thin international society defined the scope of justice in international affairs.[19] Thus, Grotius suggests that states (at least in Europe) do not inhabit the state of nature. As a result, states are bound by the more restrictive law of nations, and not merely the law of nature.

In support of this society, Grotius laid out a set of norms that served as the basis for more robust institutions developed in subsequent centuries. To do so, Grotius returned to the Roman idea of the *jus gentium*, the law of peoples. This law derives from the common practices and beliefs of states, or at least the "wisest" and the "more civilized" among them.[20] Following Cicero, Grotius insisted that war must be publicly declared, giving the opponent the chance to rectify the injustice at hand (thus adverting war).[21] Furthermore, an "independent and disinterested state" should be called upon to serve as an arbitrator, determining where justice lies.[22] If the justness of the cause is uncertain, both sides should seek peaceful means of resolving their differences.[23] The idea that states would willingly accept such mediation implies that states' actions are not determined only by self-interest, or the imposition of external force. Instead, it suggests that states "share a common worldview" that makes them sensitive to the judgments of others.[24] In an age plagued by wars fanned by religious differences, Grotius emphasized pluralism. Reason could serve as a foundation on which both "pagans and infidels" could construct an international legal system.[25]

If Grotius was cautiously optimistic about the possibility of a peaceful society of nations, his intellectual successor, Samuel Pufendorf

[18] Philippe Raynaud, "Entre droit et politique: des origines romaines de la guerre juste au système international des états," *Raisons Politiques* 1(45), 2012, 19–34, 23.

[19] Hugo Grotius, *Rights of War and Peace*, trans. A. C. Campbell (London: B. Boothroyd, 1814), I.1.7.

[20] Christov, "Liberal Internationalism Revisited," 569.

[21] Grotius, *Rights of War and Peace*, III.3.6. Cicero argues that without a formal declaration of war, through the *fetiales*, a war is inherently unjust. *On the Commonwealth*, II.31, III.20a; *On the Laws*, II.19, in Cicero, *On the Commonwealth and On the Laws*, ed. James E. G. Zetzel (Cambridge: Cambridge University Press, 1999), 42, 66, 137.

[22] Ibid., II.2.18 and II.18.4.   [23] Ibid., II.22.11.

[24] Christov, "Liberal Internationalism Revisited," 569.

[25] Andreas Harald Aure, "Hugo Grotius – Individual Rights as the Core of Natural Law," in Guttorm Fløistad, ed., *Contemporary Philosophy: A New Survey, Vol. 12: Philosophy of Justice* (Dordrecht: Springer, 2015), 75–94. 79.

(1632–1694), was radically so. "It is most agreeable to natural law that men should live in peace," Pufendorf declares, which "itself is a state peculiar to man, insofar as he is distinct from the beasts."[26] Pufendorf was not naïve about the very real potential for war. By the time he wrote *On the Duty of Man and Citizen*, he had already experienced war first hand, as a resident of Copenhagen when the Swedes laid siege to the city. The Danish authorities imprisoned Pufendorf, an employee of the Swedish ambassador and hence an enemy national, for eight months.[27] Nonetheless, Pufendorf imagined that humans' primal need for security drove them toward peace. In the state of nature, human passions – the "insatiable craving for more than he needs, ambition (the most terrible of evils), too-lively remembrance of wrongs, and a burning desire for revenge which constantly grows in force over time" – drive conflict.[28] Yet because no individual can single-handedly guarantee his own security, man is forced to "be sociable," that is, to join a polity that will protect him.[29]

Since we depend upon society for security, we have a responsibility to behave sociably. Consequently, it is an "absolute duty not to harm others," because without such a duty "human social life would be utterly impossible."[30] Seeking security is as much a collective endeavor for Pufendorf as an individual imperative. Just as individuals unite to form states for the sake of security, states can protect themselves by forming collective security arrangements. States may fight not only to right wrongs against themselves, but also on behalf of third parties when the other party has a "just cause."[31] Nonetheless, even when a state has a right to fight, amicable settlement should always be sought first. Here Pufendorf reiterates Grotius's caution: if there "remains some doubt about right or fact," one should avoid turning to arms.[32]

The work of Emer de Vattel (1714–1767) completes the bridge from traditional Christian just war thought to contemporary international law. Vattel, too, is an optimist. But his optimism is subtler. On the one hand, he is unconvinced by Grotius's and Pufendorf's claims that a naturally occurring civil law applies to the society of states. He doubts that this

---

[26] Samuel Pufendorf, *On the Duty of Man and Citizen* (Cambridge: Cambridge University Press, 1991), II.16.1, 168.

[27] His luck was less than ideal. Twenty years later, while serving as professor of international law at the University of Lund (Sweden), the Danes invaded, and Pufendorf had to flee again.

[28] Ibid., II.5.6, 133. See also I.3.4, 34.

[29] Ibid., I.3.7, 35. See also II.5.8, 13 and II.5.4–7, 132–133.   [30] Ibid., I.6.2, 56.

[31] Ibid., II.16.11, 170.   [32] Ibid., II.16.3, 168.

"fiction" can afford "sufficiently solid grounds on which to build the rules of the universal law of nations," since states have no external judges, nor lawmakers, nor police.[33] While he recognizes a "general society between mankind," which leads individual human beings to recognize their interdependence, no similar society exists naturally between states.[34] Instead, he argued, states are equals before the law, and hence "no nation can enforce on the international plane rules based on the voluntary law of nations."[35] Anarchy remains in force.

Yet states can establish binding rules for themselves, including rules permitting them a right of enforcement. Through treaties, states create a "conventional law of nations, peculiar to the contracting powers."[36] Nations may also be bound by "tacit consent," including by customary practice.[37] Customary international law applies, however, only "to those particular nations who have, by long use, given their sanction to its maxims."[38] Ultimately, both conventional and customary laws are binding because of "that maxim of the natural law which makes it the duty of nations to fulfill their engagements, whether express or tacit."[39]

Together, these rules generate a thin international society. Like Grotius and Pufendorf, Vattel requires states to declare war openly. States must articulate the specific wrong they believe they have suffered and outline the steps they expect the other state to take in response. Such demands should be reasonable, and the language of the declaration should reflect "decorum and moderation."[40] After all, expressions of "hatred, animosity, and rage" only further incite the enemy, inflaming the quarrel rather than encouraging reconciliation.[41] Vattel here seems to be embodying the epitome of what Morgenthau describes as the aristocratic mode of handling foreign affairs, in which aristocratic heads of state and their ambassadors were bound by "family ties, a common language (which was French), common cultural values, a common style of life, and common moral conviction as to what a gentleman was and was not allowed to do."[42]

---

[33] Emer de Vattel, *The Law of Nations*, ed. Béla Kapossy (Indianapolis: Liberty Fund, 2014), 25.

[34] Ibid., 25. The same logic is present in Kant's *Perpetual Peace*, which asserts a cosmopolitan right for individuals on the basis of this general society of humankind.

[35] Stéphane Beaulac, "Emer de Vattel and the Externalization of Sovereignty," *Journal of the History of International Law* 5, 2003, 237–292, 272.

[36] Vattel, *The Law of Nations*, 27.   [37] Ibid.   [38] Ibid.   [39] Ibid.   [40] Ibid., 332.

[41] Ibid.

[42] Hans J. Morgenthau, "The Twilight of International Morality," *Ethics* 58(2), 1948, 79–99, 88.

In other words, these "princes competing for power considered themselves to be competitors in a game whose rules were accepted by all the other competitors."[43] These shared norms enabled the diplomatic engagement Vattel recommended.[44]

PRIVILEGING IN BELLO

Furthermore, these early legal scholars shifted the focus from *ad bellum* issues to *in bello* ones. Grotius, Pufendorf, and Vattel all devote far more verbiage to the discussion of just means and tactics than their just war predecessors. One reason for this emphasis, suggested by Vattel himself, is pragmatic: states are unlikely to tie their own hands by accepting legal principles restricting their right to resort to force. The solution is to downplay potentially contentious *ad bellum* issues, focusing instead on *in bello* concerns. After all, if *in bello* restrictions are reciprocally accepted, all states benefit. Thus, while Vattel admits that logically "war cannot be just on both sides," he argues that both parties can be "candid and sincere in their intentions," making it hard to definitively judge the case.[45] As a result, Vattel accords some rights even to states whose cause is objectively unjust.[46]

Effectively bracketing considerations of just cause in this way also serves an important function *in bello*. Vattel recognizes that states are unlikely to accept regulations on means unless wars are "accounted just on both sides."[47] Divorcing *in bello* principles from *ad bellum* ones removes a key disincentive to obeying the laws of war in battle. It permits states to be credited for doing the right thing by fighting moderately, even if the justness of their cause is in doubt. This encourages *in bello* principles to be observed reciprocally. Contemporary international law has largely inherited this point of view.

The "fiction" that both parties to a conflict act legally served an important function.[48] Treating belligerents as if they shared the same moral playing field made it possible to regulate war's conduct, albeit forfeiting the chance to regulate its initiation.[49] After all, "regulation goes

---

[43] Ibid.

[44] Christian Reus-Smit describes the process by which European elites came to share a normative understanding of the international order richly in *The Moral Purpose of the State: Culture, Social Identity, and Institutional Rationality in International Relations* (Princeton: Princeton University Press, 1999). See especially 94–129.

[45] Vattel, *The Law of Nations*, 320.   [46] Ibid.   [47] Ibid., 387.

[48] Claude, "Just Wars," 89.   [49] Ibid., 90.

with permission, not with prohibition."[50] As Hedley Bull later noted, "to the extent that it influences the course of events, the doctrine that war should be fought only for a just cause is injurious to the institutions with which international society had equipped itself for the limitation of war."[51]

IN BELLO *CHANGES*

The early law of war literature is notable not only because it devotes more time to *in bello* issues, but also because its treatment of just conduct gives rise to three important innovations. First, the category of the civilian is expanded. Vitoria had recognized that not all persons residing in enemy territory should be treated as enemies. Women and children were "obviously innocent," as were travelers and visitors who were likely to be innocent because (to use modern parlance) they were not enemy nationals.[52] The only males Vitoria specifically categorized as innocent were clergy and monks.[53] Grotius and Vattel, however, expand the category of the civilian to all those who do not take up arms.[54] This includes men of religion, but also "men of letters," peasant farmers, merchants, artisans, and the old or sick.[55] This definitional change is reflected in contemporary humanitarian law, which treats the civilian as encompassing all those who are not members of the armed forces, and who do not participate in hostilities.

Second, the early law of war literature begins to consider protections for civilian property. Admittedly, Vitoria had raised the issue, but only to suggest that destroying fields and storehouses could be a legitimate tactic.[56] Similarly, Grotius admits that custom permits widespread damage, such as the burning of fields, homes, and cities, and made no "exemption in favour of things deemed sacred."[57] While he makes no mention of protections for homes and farms, he does assert that charity

---

[50] Ibid.

[51] Hedley Bull, "The Grotian Conception of International Society," in *Diplomatic Investigations*, ed. Herbert Butterfield and Martin Wight (Cambridge, MA: Harvard University Press, 1966), 70–71, cited in Inis Claude, Jr., "Just Wars: Doctrines and Institutions," 91.

[52] Vitoria, *Political Writings*, 315.   [53] Ibid.

[54] Grotius, *Laws of War and Peace*, III.11.12.

[55] Ibid., III.11.10–11, and Vattel, *The Law of Nations*, III.8.145–147. Interestingly, Grotius draws his inspiration from the Hindus, whom he admiringly describes as forbearing from "destroying or even hurting those employed in husbandry."

[56] Vitoria, *Political Writings*, 1.2, 317.

[57] Grotius, *Laws of War and Peace*, III.51 and III.12.6.

requires a "rule of moderation" be applied to holy places, gravesites, monuments, and works of art.[58] Contemporary humanitarian law specifically forbids attacks against cultural property, ever since the first codification of the Hague Regulations in 1899.

Likewise, Vattel argues that "we ought to spare those edifices which do honour to human society, and do not contribute to increase the enemy's strength – such as temples, tombs, public buildings, and all works of remarkable beauty." Destroying such buildings yields no military advantage. Reducing our shared human cultural heritage to rubble makes one "an enemy to mankind."[59] Vattel also takes a few steps in the direction of broader protections for civilian homes and farms. On the one hand, Vattel argues that it is permissible to lay waste to the countryside and to destroy provisions, because such tactocs "promote the main object of the war."[60] Yet he declares that those who burn villages are "savage barbarians," who needlessly "desolate a country beyond what their own safety requires."[61] Reflecting earlier Christian just war thinkers' concerns with internal motivations, Vattel decries the fact that such "conduct is not dictated by prudence, but by hatred and fury."[62] In short, although Vattel accepts the destruction of easily replaceable, movable goods, he forbids the destruction of civilian property that is permanent or hard to replace. Likewise, although he treats food supplies as dual use goods, necessary for both civilians and soldiers, he refuses to categorize either the peasants (who provide necessary labor) or their homes in such a way. His protections for civilian property are far short of contemporary humanitarian law, but already quite distant from the just war tradition.[63]

Third, early international legal scholars became increasingly interested in protections for combatants. This is a marked shift from the earlier Christian just war tradition, which was more concerned with protecting civilians from combatants.[64] New combatant protections include protections for prisoners of war and bans on certain weapons and tactics deemed to be cruel. For example, both Grotius and Vattel argue that

---

[58] Ibid., III.12.6.   [59] Vattel, *The Law of Nations*, 374.   [60] Ibid., 373.   [61] Ibid.
[62] Ibid.
[63] Vitoria, after all, would have permitted the destruction of civilians' property, and to plunder their goods, so long as doing so was necessary to the war effort.
[64] Recall that the Islamic tradition laid out protections for prisoners of war early on, and that the Hindu tradition included rules for sparing the lives of soldiers who were not ready or able to be engaged in the fight. In the West, such rules pertained to the chivalric tradition. See David Whetham, *Just Wars and Moral Victories: Surprise, Deception, and the Normative Framework of European War in the Later Middle Ages* (Amsterdam: Brill, 2009).

in bello, armies should only use necessary force in order to win. As Grotius remarks, once they have surrendered "there is no danger to be apprehended from the prisoners," and thus "nothing to justify the further effusion of blood."[65] Consequently, while the law of nations permits killing prisoners, "more civilized manners" have "abolished the barbarous practice of putting prisoners to death."[66] Likewise, Vattel asserts that the practice of executing prisoners of war should be understood as "a dreadful error of antiquity."[67] Prisoners may be confined, but they should not "be treated harshly, unless personally guilty of some crime."[68] If there are insufficient resources to keep them imprisoned, they should not be put to death, but rather released on parole.[69]

Laying the ground for the late nineteenth-century war conventions, Vattel also considers specific weapons and tactics. Poisoned weapons are not treacherous, "but the practice is nevertheless prohibited by the law of nature, which does not allow us to multiply the evils of war beyond all bounds."[70] Once a soldier has been disabled, his death becomes unnecessary. An injured soldier no longer poses a threat. Only necessity justifies war, and thus nations at war "ought universally to abstain from every thing that has a tendency to render it more destructive: it is even a duty incumbent on them, to oppose such practices."[71] Furthermore, Vattel states pragmatically that once one side initiates this practice, the other will follow. It is thus in states' self-interest to moderate their own behavior.

The first formal legal conventions governing war were drafted just one hundred years after Vattel's death. In keeping with the radical transformations introduced by Grotius, Pufendorf, and Vattel, the conventional law of war focused not on *ad bellum* concerns, but on *in bello* ones. What's more, states seem to have been motivated to sign such instruments primarily out of concern for their own soldiers (rather than care for civilians). Indeed, the brief ten articles of the original 1864 Geneva Convention emphasize the care of wounded and sick soldiers, although they also include protections for those civilians who care for them.[72] The 1868 Declaration of Saint Petersburg, likewise, outlaws military technologies considered inhumane, including exploding bullets.[73]

---

[65] Grotius, *Laws of War and Peace*, III.12.19.   [66] Ibid., III.11.13–14.
[67] Vattel, *The Law of Nations*, 363.   [68] Ibid.   [69] Ibid.   [70] Ibid., 368.   [71] Ibid.
[72] Geoffrey Best, *Humanity in Warfare* (New York: Columbia University Press, 1980), 242.
[73] Dieter Fleck, ed., *The Handbook of Humanitarian Law in Armed Conflicts* (Oxford: Oxford University Press, 1995), 119. This ban was repeated in the Hague Conventions. Hague II, Annex, II.1.23. 1899.

The 1899 Hague Declarations (and the subsequent 1907 Hague Conventions) continued in the same vein, banning asphyxiating gases and projectiles launched from balloons.[74] It further establishes civilian protections reminiscent of those described by Grotius, Pufendorf, and Vattel. The "attack or bombardment of towns, villages, habitations or buildings which are not defended, is prohibited."[75] Commanders should attempt to warn the leaders of a town before bombarding it, presumably so that civilians can flee, so long as it is militarily feasible to do so.[76] Likewise, "in sieges and bombardments all necessary steps should be taken to spare as far as possible edifices devoted to religion, art, science and charity, hospitals, and places where the sick and wounded are collected," so long as those locations are not also used for military purposes.[77] For the first time, the pillaging of villages is also prohibited.[78]

Rules are also established for military control over hostile territory, providing protections for civilians.[79] Civilians are not to be pressured to take oaths of loyalty to the occupying power or to serve in its military.[80] Private property is to be respected, as well as "religious convictions and liberty."[81] Seizure and destruction of religious, charitable and educational institutions, historical monuments, and works of art or science is prohibited.[82] Limitations on the taxation of such areas, along with the requisition of goods from the occupied region, are also established.[83] In essence, the occupying power should not use economic means to devastate the region, instead taking only what is necessary to defray the costs of administration and to provide for the occupying armies' necessities. Altogether, the rules worked out at The Hague and later in Geneva were designed to reflect military realities. Academics, lawyers, and diplomats were involved, of course, but so were military authorities.[84] Creating an "insider vocabulary common to humanitarian and military professionals was intended to place the new rules on a firm footing in the military plausible."[85]

---

[74] Hague IV, Declaration I and Declaration II, 1899, www.avalon.law.yale.edu/20th_century/hague04.asp.

[75] Hague II, Annex, II.1.25, 1899.   [76] Ibid., II.1.26, 1899.   [77] Ibid., II.1.27, 1899.

[78] Ibid., II.1.28, 1899. See also II.3.47.

[79] It is interesting to note that such rules had long since existed in the Hindu tradition, although such principles do not seem to have consciously influenced the Hague drafters.

[80] Hague II, Annex, II.3.44–45.   [81] Ibid., II.3.46.   [82] Ibid., II.3.56.

[83] Ibid., II.3.50–53.

[84] David Kennedy, *Of War and Law* (Princeton: Princeton University Press, 2009), 84.

[85] Ibid., 85, 166.

As for *ad bellum* concerns, the Hague agreements steered clear of any effort to adjudicate the content of just cause.[86] They did, however, refer to the idea of a robust international community. In their own words, the conventions were aimed to recognize "the solidarity which unites the members of the society of civilized nations," and to extend "the empire of law," "while 'strengthening the appreciation of international justice'".[87] War was to be relegated to a last resort.

A new idea was added here – states ought to seek "the good offices or mediation of one or more friendly Powers" before appealing to arms.[88] To this end, a permanent court of arbitration was established at The Hague. This development sought to institutionalize the principle that states should seek other forms of remedy first. It thus reinforced the idea – already nascent in early legal texts – of the existence of a society of states. If states would accept an external court, they would effectively exit the state of nature.

BACK TO THE FUTURE?

What made this transformation from a realist leaning just war tradition to a more liberal conception of international law possible? The short answer is a series of fundamental changes in the way political authority was understood in Europe led to a period of devastating conflict, which in the end gave way to a remarkably stable balance of power system. The Renaissance and the Protestant Reformation weakened the Catholic Church's control of society and politics, making it possible to imagine fully sovereign states.[89] Questions about the Church's authority over various religious and social practices inextricably generated tough questions about the complex political and economic ties between the Church and various states, which were called upon to finance or carry out the Church's endeavors. Thus, the theological reforms suggested by the first Reformers sparked intense political tensions across the continent.[90]

---

[86] Best, *Humanity in Warfare*, 5.

[87] Hague I: Pacific Settlement of International Disputes, July 29, 1899, Prologue, Yale Law School Lillian Goldman Law Library: The Avalon Project, www.avalon.law.yale.edu/19th_century/hague01.asp. See also Hague I, October 18, 1907, www.avalon.law.yale.edu/20th_century/pacific.asp.

[88] Hague I, 1899, and I.2, 1907.

[89] J. Samuel Barkin and Bruce Cronin, "The State and the Nation: Changing Norms and the Rules of Sovereignty in International Relations," *International Organization* 48(1), 1994, 107–130, 111.

[90] Despite the struggle being described then – as now – in religious terms, "there was remarkably little sectarian violence." Peter H. Wilson, "Meaningless Conflict? The

These tensions drove the extraordinarily bloody Thirty Years War, which spiraled across Europe, leaving a wide swath of destruction. This cataclysm inspired Grotius to pen the *Law of War and Peace*:

Fully convinced ... that there is a common law among nations, which is valid alike for war and in war, I have had many and weighty reasons for undertaking to write upon this subject. Throughout the Christian world I observed a lack of restraint in relation to war, such as even barbarous races should be ashamed of; I observed that men rush to arms for slight causes, or no cause at all, and that when arms have once been taken up there is no longer any respect for law, divine or human; it is as if, in accordance with a general decree, frenzy had openly been let loose for the committing of all crimes.[91]

And yet the same Europe that was tearing itself apart was also simultaneously coming to understand itself as an *idea*. New communications technologies – namely the printing press – made it possible for the Reformation to spread like wildfire, but also created a pan-European community of readers and intellectuals. This sense of a common culture was encouraged by Europeans' exploration of Asia, Africa, and the Americas. The discovery of new lands and peoples created an "other" against which European identity could be defined. Europeans saw themselves as respecters of the rule of law, in contrast to the barbaric despotism they claimed to find everywhere else.[92] In the end, a secular, territorial concept of "Europe" came to replace the older idea of Christendom.[93] Vattel himself gave voice to this new conception, describing Europe as "a political system in which the Nations ... are bound together by their relations and various interests into a single body ... whose members – *each independent, but all bound together by a common interest* – unite for the maintenance of order and the preservation of liberty."[94]

This understanding of Europe as an entity gave rise to what Vattel recognized as the balance of power principle, "an arrangement of affairs

---

Character of the Thirty Years War," in Frederick C. Schneid, ed., *The Projection and Limitations of Imperial Powers, 1618–1850* (Leiden: Brill, 2012), 16.

[91] Hugo Grotius, *Prolegomena to the Laws of War and Peace*, trans. Francis W. Kelsay (Loang Institute, 2005), https://lonang.com/library/reference/grotius-law-war-and-peace/gro-100/, para. 28.

[92] Anthony Pagden, "Europe: Conceptualizing a Continent," in Anthony Pagden, ed., *The Idea of Europe: From Antiquity to the European Union* (Washington, DC: Woodraw Wilson Center Press, 2002), 37–38.

[93] John Hale, *The Civilization of Europe in the Renaissance* (New York: Simon and Schuster, 1995), 3, 5.

[94] Vattel, *Le Droit des gens*, book II, chapter 7, cited in Christov, "Liberal Internationalism Revisited," 573–574.

so that no State shall be in a position to have absolute mastery and dominate over others."[95] Fundamentally, this requires that states must respect each others' sovereignty, even when this means ignoring the others' perceived injustices, "to the extent that this is necessary to ward off the greater evil of the breakdown of international society."[96] While we sometimes imagine the balance of power as purely a strategy of *realpolitik*, for seventeenth- and eighteenth-century thinkers it also served as a principle on which international society could be based.[97] After all, equilibrium *through deterrence* could guarantee pan-European peace.

At the same time as war was being relegated to the realm of disorder, the practice of war fighting itself was becoming ever more orderly. (Or, at least, the *ideal* of strategy had come to be fixated on order even battle.) War during the age of battles – roughly from the final years of the Thirty Years War through to Waterloo in 1815 – involved massive, preset battles, in conditions where the battlefields were generally clearly separate from civilian areas. Changes in military financing meant that these huge armies no longer needed to pillage to fund their forays into enemy territory (or their passage through friendlier fields, for that matter).[98] What's more, kings and generals feared that such "indiscipline would undercut all the professionalizing reforms that were making the new armies increasingly useful tools to serve the ambitions of the state"; soldiers allowed to run amok as they sacked a city or explored the countryside foraging for food might prove difficult for officers to control in battle.[99] Only a highly disciplined fighting force could effectively execute the complex firing formations of the time.[100] Maintaining discipline at all times – both on and off the battlefield – was understood to be necessary for developing a successful professional military.

---

[95] Ibid.

[96] Ian Hunter, "Kant and Vattel in Context: Cosmopolitan Philosophy and Diplomatic Casuistry," *History of European Ideas* 39(4), 2013, 477–502, 495.

[97] Randall Lesaffer, "Paix et guerre dans les grand traités du dix-huitième siècle," *Journal of the History of International Law* 7, 2005, 25–41, 39.

[98] Tuba Inal, *Looting and Rape in Wartime: Law and Change in International Relations* (Philadelphia: University of Pennsylvania Press, 2013). See also Christon I. Archer, John R. Ferris, Holger H. Herwig, and Timothy E. H. Travers, *World History of Warfare* (London: Cassell, 2003), 322.

[99] Russell F. Weigley, *The Age of Battles: The Quest for Decisive Warfare from Breitenfeld to Waterloo* (Bloomington: Indiana University Press, 2004), 70. See also Larry H. Addington, *The Patterns of War since the Eighteenth Century* (Bloomington: Indiana University Press, 1994), 7. See also Archer et al., *World History of Warfare*, 357.

[100] Philip Bobbit, *The Sword of Achilles: War, Peace, and the Course of History* (New York: Anchor Books, 2002), 100.

During this era, international law came into its own. Warfare was seen as relatively restrained, and the principle of noncombatant immunity had come to protect the lives and property of noncombatants.[101] But we should be cautious of presuming that during this era of limited warfare attitudes to war had become more humanitarian.[102] Instead, "practical constraints" – economic costs and technological limits – discouraged unnecessary battles.[103] Clausewitz put it bluntly:

the invention of gunpowder and the constant improvement of firearms are enough in themselves to show that the advance of civilization has done nothing practical to alter or deflect the impulse to destroy the enemy ... [so if] civilized nations do not put their prisoners to death or devastate cities and countries, it is because intelligence plays a larger part in their methods of warfare and has taught them more effective ways of using force than the crude expression of instinct.[104]

Contrary to idealists' expectations, necessity – and not moral development – fostered restraint.

The multiplication of international laws and institutions over the past century and a half has encouraged many international relations scholars to describe the modern international system as a society of states. Neo-liberal institutionalists believe that the institutions that hold this society together are growing deeper and richer over time. As a result, the pernicious effects of anarchy – states' overwhelming insecurity and fixation on survival – are increasingly mitigated. In this new system, states can manage their disagreements through law, courts, and international organizations, rather than resorting to war. Even great powers such as the United States have "come to accept their value," albeit grudgingly: after all, it "would be unable to achieve its foals through the bilateral exercise of influence" alone, as the costs would simply be too high.[105] Indeed, some contemporary policy priorities – like encouraging the spread of democracy, protecting human rights through humanitarian interventions, and countering terrorism – can sometimes be better managed through institutions and cooperation.[106]

---

[101] Weigley, *The Age of Battles*, xv.

[102] Archer et al., *World History of Warfare*, 323, 328, 356.

[103] Hew Strachan, *European Armies and the Conduct of War* (London: Routledge, 2001), 15.

[104] Carl von Clausewitz, *On War*, ed. and trans. Michael Howard and Peter Paret (Princeton: Princeton University Press, 1984), I.1.3, 76.

[105] Robert Keohane, "International Institutions: Can Interdependence Work?" *Foreign Policy* 110, 1998, 82–96, 83.

[106] Nye, "Public Diplomacy and Soft Power," 107.

Contemporary realists, like Clausewitz two centuries ago, remain unconvinced. Great powers invoke the law when it suits their interests – especially to govern the behavior of small states – but flagrantly break it when it impedes their pursuits. For realists, institutions "mirror the distribution of power," rather than shaping it.[107] Rogue powers know that the emperor has no clothes and are simply unafraid of pronouncements and threats from international organizations, including the United Nations. War – and the threat of war – is still the only real enforcement mechanism in the system.

While our sensitivity to the anarchical nature of the system may be heightened due to recent insecurity – the events of September 11th, the still ongoing War on Terror, the emergence of ISIS from the rubble of the failed Syrian and Iraqi states – it is useful to remember that just war thinking itself emerged in similar contexts. Unlike international law, which developed during an era of relative balance, just war thinking across the three traditions developed in insecure international environments. For example, in the Christian tradition, Augustine responded to the rising tide of disorder faced by the collapsing Roman Empire. The authors of the Islamic tradition faced internal rebellions and outside incursions from both Europe and Central Asia. And the mandala imagined by Kautilya and Kamandaka imagined individual kings motivated by self-interest, not the guiding hand of an international institution. Put simply, the various just war traditions have historically developed within conditions characterized by insecurity and imperfect institutions.

Contemporary just war thinking, however, has grown away from its realist roots. Instead, it has come to reflect the innovations introduced by early law of war scholars.[108] Walzer, as we have seen, frames his discussion of just war in the language of international law. Analysis and interpretation of Walzer himself – evidence of an emerging Walzerian tradition – has become a rich source of contributions to just war conversations.[109] Other scholars rely primarily on early law of war scholars

---

[107] Mearsheimer, "False Promise of International Institutions," 13.

[108] Jeff McMahan, "The Morality of War and the Law of War," in David Rodin and Henry Shue, eds., *Just and Unjust Warriors: The Moral and Legal Status of Soldiers* (Oxford: Oxford University Press, 2010), 20. See also George Lucas, "Defense or Offense? The Two Streams of Just War Theory," in Peter A. French and Jason A. Short, eds., *War and Border Crossings: Ethics When Cultures Clash* (Lanham, MD: Rowman & Littlefield, 2005), 50. And also Rengger, "On the Just War Tradition in the Twenty-first Century," 360.

[109] See Terry Nardin, "From Right to Intervene to Duty to PROTECT: Michael Walzer on Humanitarian Intervention," *European Journal of International Law* 24(1), 2013, 67–82;

(such as Grotius, Vattel, and Pufendorf) to develop arguments that they classify as just war thought.[110] Yet another productive vein of contemporary just war work combines a close reading of Walzer with reference to black letter international law to make claims about what just war thinking does and does not permit.[111] The arguments advanced by thinkers operating within this legalist paradigm incorporate the early legal scholars' optimism, internationalism, and deep-seated concern with *in bello* issues.

This is also true of those thinkers classified as "revisionists." Their critical responses to Walzer cannot help but incorporate aspects of his legalism.[112] At times, the links to the international legal tradition are conscious. David Rodin argues, for example, that the origins of the just war tradition are doubly linked with the law of war.[113] Although he acknowledges that just war thinking includes theological writings, Rodin favors the legalistic approaches of Grotius and his contemporaries as well as Michael Walzer.[114] The legalist approach favored by the analytic philosophers further diverges from the tradition by eschewing case-based reasoning in favor of developing logically consistent, ideal rules, and principles.[115] These rules and principles, unsurprisingly, bear a greater similarity to the underlying logics of the international law of war than to the pre-Grotian just war tradition.

Ronan O'Callaghan, *Walzer, Just War and Iraq – Ethics as Response* (New York: Routledge, 2016); Brian Orend, *Michael Walzer on War and Justice* (Montreal: McGill-Queen's University Press, 2000), and *The Morality of War* (Peterborough, Ontario: Broadview Press, 2006); Igor Primoratz, "Michael Walzer's Just War Theory: Some Issues of Responsibility," *Ethical Theory and Moral Practice* 5(2), 2002, 221–243.

[110]   Consider, for example, David Boucher, "The Just War Tradition and Its Modern Legacy: *Jus ad bellum* and *jus in bello*," *European Journal of Political Theory* 11(2), 2011, 92–111; Whitley Kaufman, "What's Wrong with Preventive War? The Moral and Legal Basis for Preventive Use of Force," *Ethics and International Affairs* 19(3), 2005, 23–38; and Larry May, *War Crimes and Just War* (Cambridge: Cambridge University Press, 2007).

[111]   David Luban, "Preventive War," *Philosophy and Public Affairs* 32(3), Summer 2004, 207–248; Mary Ellen O'Connell, "The Just War Tradition and International Law against War: The Myth of Discordant Doctrines," *Journal of the Society of Christian Ethics* 35(2), Fall/Winter 2015, 33–51.

[112]   Jeff McMahan discusses the intimate relationship between his work and Walzer's in "The Sources and Status of Just War Principles," *Journal of Military Ethics* 6(2), 2007, 91–106.

[113]   David Rodin, *War and Self-Defense* (Oxford: Oxford University Press, 2005), 6, 103.

[114]   Ibid., 103.

[115]   Mathias Thaler, "On Time in Just War Theory: From *Chronos* to *Kairos*," *Polity* 46, 2014, 520–546.

OPTIMISM, INSTITUTIONS, AND HUMAN RIGHTS
IN CONTEMPORARY JUST WAR THOUGHT

First, as this brief introduction to the legal tradition illustrates, the legal approach is more optimistic about the nature of the international system than realism. Likewise, many contemporary just war thinkers imagine the international system as a society of states. This was particularly evident in the debate about preemption provoked by the 2003 Iraq War. Critics relied heavily on the assumption that "there is a robust and meaningful notion of 'the international community' toward which ... appeals for the justifiable use of military force should be addressed, and from whom prior approval should be sought."[116] As a result, contemporary just war thinking tends to privilege supranational politics – and the role of the United Nations in particular – over national politics.[117] For example, Buchanan and Keohane have argued that in morally complex circumstances – namely, preventive war and humanitarian intervention – states should have to make their case before the UN Security Council, or some similarly diverse set of states.[118] McMahan goes the farthest in this respect. In sketching out a vision that he "[hopes] is not altogether utopian," he suggests that a "neutral, impartial, international court" should be created to adjudicate whether particular wars (and their conduct) can be considered just.[119] Even scholars who deny the moral necessity of United Nations approval nonetheless argue that in "contested cases," such as humanitarian intervention and preemptive war, "the desirability of international authorization increases very considerably."[120]

Another significant difference between contemporary just war thinking and its predecessors is an increased focus on the rights of individuals. Indeed, it was Grotius who took the language of rights once applied uniquely to states and transformed it into a language for describing individuals and their rights.[121] Contemporary international law

---

[116] Lucas, "The Role of the 'International Community' in Just War Tradition," 126.

[117] Eric Patterson, *Just War Thinking* (Lanham, MD: Lexington Books, 2009), 25.

[118] Allen Buchanan and Robert O. Keohane, "The Preventive Use of Force: A Cosmopolitan Institutional Proposal," *Ethics and International Affairs*, 18(1), 2004, 1–22. See also Allen Buchanan, "Institutionalizing the Just War," *Philosophy and Public Affairs* 34(1), Winter 2006, 2–38. It's telling that Keohane is a liberal institutionalist.

[119] McMahan, "The Morality of War and the Law of War," 41, 42.

[120] Orend, *Morality of War*. 59.

[121] Richard Tuck, *Rights of War and Peace* (Oxford: Oxford University Press, 2001), 84. See also Peter Pavel Remec, *The Position of the Individual in International Law*

specifically confers certain rights on both combatants and civilians as individuals.[122] This includes the humanitarian protections of the Geneva Conventions, individual liability for war crimes, and the broader framework of human rights. Over time, humanitarian legal principles have been revised to incorporate the growing influence of human rights norms.[123] The centrality of individual human rights is particularly obvious in the work of revisionist scholars, whose analysis depends on a careful determination of an individual's liability to harm based on his or her responsibility for posing a direct and unjustified threat.[124] McMahan, for example, argues that "people can become morally *liable* to be killed or maimed only by virtue of action ... that wrongs or threatens to wrong others."[125] Nonetheless, the rights of individuals are also foundational for Walzerians.[126] As Walzer puts it, "individual rights (to life and liberty) underlie the most important judgments that we can make about war."[127]

DEFAULTING TO PACIFISM

One effect of combining an internationalist bent with a deep concern for human rights is a decided trend toward pacifism within contemporary just war thought.[128] Just war thinking can arrive at functional pacifism in two different ways. It can begin with a presumption against war, a belief that if only institutions worked better and states tried harder at diplomacy, war would be unnecessary.[129] Alternately, pacifism can be the logical consequence of an emphasis on human rights, and a presumption against killing.

According to Grotius and Vattel (New York: Springer Science and Buisness Media, 2012), 105.

[122] Quincy Wright, "The Outlawry of War and the Law of War," *American Journal of International Law* 47(3), July 1953, 365–376, 373.

[123] René Provost, *International Human Rights and Humanitarian Law* (Cambridge: Cambridge University Press, 2002), 200, 345.

[124] Janina Dill, *Legitimate Targets? Social Construction, International Law, and US Bombing* (Cambridge: Cambridge University Press, 2014), 276.

[125] Jeff McMahan, "Just Cause for War," *Ethics and International Affairs* 19(3), 2005, 1–21, 18. See claims abound in the revisionist literature. See Christopher J. Finlay, "Fairness and Liability in the Just War: Combatants, Non-combatants, and Lawful Irregulars," *Political Studies* 61(1), 2013, 142–160, 143; Pattison, "When Is It Right to Fight?," 36.

[126] McMahan, "The Sources and Status of Just War Principles," 94. See also Kai Draper, *War and Individual Rights: The Foundations of Just War Theory* (Oxford: Oxford University Press, 2016), 6.

[127] Walzer, *Just and Unjust Wars*, 51.   [128] Patterson, *Just War Thinking*, 28.

[129] Ibid., 25.

INSTITUTIONAL PACIFISM

Just war thinking becomes pacifistic when it values order more than justice, for example, by presuming that war is always worse than peace. After Augustine, the just war tradition did not treated war as something that is "inherently suspect morally," but much of today's just war reasoning begins with a presumption against war.[130] Johnson, who argues that recent just war thinking overemphasizes "instrumentalities," in other words, particular institutions and practices, has also critiqued this tendency toward a pacifism inspired by a faith in institutions.[131] The danger is that "when particular historical means are assimilated to ideal goals, the result is a form of utopianism in politics," which rules out the possibility of necessary, but imperfect, action.[132] Specifically, many contemporary just war thinkers tend to be committed to two ideal stances. First, they see aggression as the *only* crime justifying war. Second, they suggest legitimate authority ought to lie with the United Nations – or at least, that multilateralism is an important good.

Limiting just cause to self-defense and privileging multilateralism reflects our modern, secular treatment of the here and now as the be all and end all of politics.[133] Traditional just war thinking was deeply conscious of the inherent tragedy of political action, especially in war. Even wars fought for just causes disrupt order and threaten the lives and livelihoods of innocent people. At the same time, traditional just war thinkers also realized that not all orders could be called just, and not all peaces are worthy of the name. War for the sake of justice was a trade-off between an imperfect order now and the hope of a better order in the future. The inevitable sacrifice of human lives was justified in eternal terms. Human life in the theological just war traditions is certainly a good, but a belief in the hereafter means that life is not the *only* good worth preserving. The secularization of modern politics (and modern discourse on ethics) makes human life the only relevant good. Consequently, modern just war thinking has lost its conviction in "an ultimate non-temporal resolution of the problem of historical action and sacrifice."[134] Treating the earthly city as though it is all that exists places

---

[130] George Weigel, "The Development of Just War Thinking in the Post-Cold War World: An American Perspective," in Charles Reed and David Ryall, eds., *The Price of Peace: Just War in the Twenty-First Century* (New York: Cambridge University Press, 2007), 24.
[131] Johnson, Morality and Contemporary Warfare, 15.   [132] Ibid.
[133] Ramsey, The Just War, 17.   [134] Ibid.

order above justice. This, in turn, results in the presumption that peace is always to be preferred. The current emphasis on self-defense also reflects a fundamental change in our understanding of what justifies war. While historically, just war thinkers across the traditions justified the use of force in terms of the ruler's moral responsibility to provide order, since Grotius Western thinkers have reasoned in the reverse – locating the polity's right to use force in the individual's right to self-defense.[135]

The roots of the internationalist approach to legitimate authority can be found in eighteenth-century conceptions of the "perpetual peace" and the nineteenth-century development of positive international law.[136] The rapid growth of the UN system led some just war theorists to imagine that "national sovereignty in its post-Westphalian form would gradually wither away," transferring sovereign authority to a "universal public authority."[137] This made it possible to imagine a "world order that rises above the selfish interest of states and thus eliminates conflict among them."[138] Some theorists even claim that legitimate authority today may lie neither in the sovereign state nor in the United Nations, but in "some notion of international public opinion."[139] The difficulty with the internationalist approach is that it serves as a better brake than a motor. While consensus sounds desirable, the fact that any one state (in the case of the Security Council) can veto action that is morally correct, yet contrary to its own interests, should give us pause.[140]

Beginning in the interwar period, just war thinkers started to treat "the purely defensive war as the uniquely just war."[141] The other just causes identified by the historical tradition, including righting wrongs and punishing evil, were displaced, leaving defense as "the primary, even sole, meaning of just cause."[142] The emphasis on defense as the only legitimate

---

[135] For a discussion of this shift in Grotius and Pufendorf in particular, see Johnson, *Sovereignty*, 84, 96.
[136] James Turner Johnson, "The Right to Use Armed Force: Sovereignty, Responsibility, and the Common Good," in Anthony F. Lang, Jr., Cian O'Driscoll, and John Williams, eds., *Just War: Authority, Tradition, and Practice* (Washington, DC: Georgetown University Press, 2013), 22.
[137] Weigel, "The Development of Just War Thinking in the Post-Cold War World: An American Perspective," 21.
[138] Johnson, "The Right to Use Armed Force," 22.
[139] Brown, "Just War and Political Judgment," 41.
[140] Biggar, "National Flourishing as the Normative Ground of Just War," 55.
[141] O'Donogan, *Just War Revisited*, 54.
[142] Weigel, "The Development of Just War Thinking in the Post-Cold War World: An American Perspective," 27.

form of war became pronounced during the Cold War, reflecting fears that any direct confrontation between the superpowers might lead to a nuclear apocalypse. For example, by the 1980s, American Catholic bishops had ruled out "offensive war of any kind" as ever potentially justifiable morally.[143] This move was followed by several mainstream Protestant denominations.[144]

HUMAN RIGHTS PACIFISM

Contemporary just war pacifism is not always derived from an overriding faith in institutional solutions. It can also emerge out of an increased emphasis on individual human rights and, hence, a presumption against *killing*. Childress, for example, argues that "the traditional just-war criteria can be reconstructed, explicated, and defended in relation to a prima facie duty of nonmaleficence – the duty not to harm or kill others."[145] This way of conceiving just war thinking is radically different from the historical approach, which saw just war as being motivated by a desire to help and protect others – using force if necessary.

Revisionist just war thinking shares this presumption against killing, arguing that "our moral understanding of war must respect and take seriously people's rights, including the right to not be killed unjustly, just as those rights demand respect in any context other than war."[146] Revisionists argue that the traditional combatant/noncombatant distinction is insufficient. Instead of focusing broadly on individuals' status, revisionists assert that individual determinations of their liability to be harmed must be made. Only individuals posing an active and unjust threat to the other are liable; all others must be spared. The result is that a few noncombatants are indeed partially liable (because they participate directly in war-related efforts, such as government work or armament manufacturing). Simultaneously, many combatants end up not being liable – including all combatants fighting for a just cause, and even some

---

[143] Johnson, *Morality and Contemporary Warfare*, 11–12.

[144] For a discussion of the evolution of Protestant just war thinking into just peace thought, see Valerie Morkevičius, "Changing the Rules of the Game: A Just Peace Critique of Just War Thought," *Nova et Vetera* 10(4), 2002, 1115.

[145] James F. Childress, *Moral Responsibility in Conflicts* (Baton Rouge: Louisiana State University Press, 1982), 64.

[146] Bradley Jay Strawser, "Revisionist Just War Theory and the Real World," in Fritz Allhoff, Nicholas G. Evans, and Adam Henscke, eds., *Routledge Handbook of Ethics and War* (Oxford: Routledge, 2013), 76.

combatants fighting for an unjust cause, if the latter have been coerced into fighting, or play minor roles only indirectly related to the war effort (such as cooks and drivers).[147]

Drawing such fine lines makes even self-defense "a morally risky activity," in which "we run a substantial risk of wrongdoing."[148] Adherents of this approach to just war thinking argue that "we have indeed historically been overpermissive of the unintended killing of civilians in war. The prohibition on collateral killing should be much closer to the prohibition on intentional killing than current norms recognize."[149] Specifically, the restrictions on unintentional killing – that is to say, double effect – should be tightened "so as to bring them more into line with domestic self-defense and rescue norms."[150]

The idea that the norms governing killing in war should reflect peacetime policing relies on a deeper assumption about the nature of the international community. As Maguire puts it, "state-sponsored violence can only be justified in a community context with legal and internationally enforceable restrictions comparable to the restraints we put upon our police."[151] Domestically, we expect police to exercise due care – to accept risks to their own lives – to protect innocents from harm. This makes sense, as the police, the innocent bystanders, and even the criminals are all members of one political community, with mutual obligations to each other. It is hard to see, however, the same level of community existing across national boundaries at this point in history. How do we reconcile such a high standard of due care with a polity's responsibility not to waste the lives of its citizen-soldiers?

Unfortunately, the idea of a war that does not endanger civilians at all (nor target nonliable combatants) is pure fiction. Requiring adherence to impossible standards forecloses the possibility of using force in humanitarian interventions or to support rebels with a just cause. When coupled with the presumption that *only* defense is truly a legitimate cause, this approach to just war thinking leads to paralysis in the face of humanitarian crises and the need to preempt terrorist attacks.

---

[147] See, for example, McMahan, *Killing in War*.
[148] David Rodin, "Justifying Harm," *Ethics* 122(1), October 2011, 74–110, 106.
[149] Ibid., 108.   [150] Ibid., 109.
[151] Daniel Maguire, *The Horrors We Bless: Rethinking the Just-War Legacy* (Minneapolis: Fortress Press, 2007), 3.

LIBERAL CRUSADING

Not all contemporary just war scholars are moving in the direction of effective pacifism, however. Others have reinvigorated the tradition's earlier concern with justice, supporting the emerging responsibility to protect norm.[152] The responsibility to protect is a legal concept tying a state's right to sovereignty to its duty to protect its people's human rights. It simultaneously places a duty to protect basic human rights on individual states and the international community, whose responsibility it is to intervene when a particular state fails to uphold its end of the bargain. Supporting the idea of humanitarian intervention was not such a stretch for just war thinkers as it was for legal scholars, whose concern with the traditional Westphalian concept of sovereignty made accepting interventions in the name of human rights a rather large leap. After all, as Elshtain argued, just war thinkers do not evaluate "liberal internationalism with its justifications of intervention in the name of sustaining, supporting, or building a universal culture of Kantian republics" as harshly, even if they are concerned about the possibility of overreach.[153]

The shift toward interventionism (and away from the defensive pacifism described above) began in the 1990s.[154] The tragedies of Bosnia and Rwanda led many just war thinkers – and their counterparts in international law and policy circles – to reconsider their presumption against the use of force. Genocide and massive ethnic cleansing constitute "supreme humanitarian [emergencies]," which can best be curtailed by responding with force.[155] Thinking about such crises through a lens of human rights theory expanded "the acceptable causes for going to war" within just war discourse.[156]

---

[152] James Turner Johnson, "The Idea of Defense in Historical and Contemporary Thinking about Just War," *Journal of Religious Ethics* 36(4), 2008, 543–556, 555.

[153] Jean Bethke Elshtain, "The Third Annual Grotius Lecture: Just War and Humanitarian Intervention," *American University International Law Review* 17(1), 2001, 1–25, 4–5.

[154] The idea that it might be justified to fight to defend basic human rights had been reintroduced to contemporary just war thinking earlier, but due to the political exigencies of the Cold War, it could not make the leap from theory to practice. See David Luban, "Just War and Human Rights," *Philosophy and Public Affairs* 9(2), Winter 1980, 160–181.

[155] Alex J. Bellamy, "Humanitarian Responsibilities and Interventionist Claims in International Society," *Review of International Studies* 29(3), July 2003, 321–340, 333.

[156] David Rodin, "The Ethics of War: State of the Art," *Journal of Applied Philosophy* 23 (3), 2006, 241–246, 244.

The danger, of course, is that reading just war theories in this way turns them into "mere variants on liberal institutionalism," which "quickly degenerate into internationalist sentimentalism."[157] Further-more, this approach makes just war thinking easy fodder for government leaders seeking to justify their national security policies to audiences both at home and abroad. Thus, "military intervention by the United States and Great Britain in Afghanistan (ostensibly to seek out and punish terrorists and destroy their paramilitary organizations) swiftly came to be represented to the world as a humanitarian intervention."[158] Likewise, the Bush administration invoked the language of just war theory and humanitarian intervention to justify its invasion of Iraq in 2003.[159] In this way, the liberal version of just war theory fell victim to the same illness that plagues liberalism more generally: "international 'imprudence.'"[160]

BRINGING REALISM BACK: A THEORETICAL DEFENSE

The liberalism that contemporary just war thinking has imported from the legal tradition certainly appeals to our commonsense intuitions in many ways. We live in insecure times. Nation states have had a rather disappointing record of maintaining peaceful relations among themselves, not to mention fostering domestic human rights for all their citizens – including ethnic and religious minorities. While interstate war may be in a period of decline, intrastate conflict has proven to be equally (if not even more) bloody.[161] When states break down into civil war, civilians

---

[157] Elshtain, "Just War and Humanitarian Intervention," 10–11.

[158] George R. Lucas, Jr., "From *Jus ad bellum* to *Jus ad Pacem*: Re-Thinking Just War Criteria for the Use of Military Force for Humanitarian Ends," in Larry May, ed., *The Morality of War: Classical and Contemporary Readings* (New York: Pearson Education, 2006), 370.

[159] See Andrew Fiala, "The Bush Doctrine, Democratization, and Humanitarian Interven-tion: A Just War Critique," *Theoria* 114, December 2007, 28–47. The politicized use of this rhetoric sharply undermined the partial consensus that had been emerging in the 1990s regarding the justifiability of humanitarian intervention. See Alex J. Bellamy, "Responsibility to Protect or Trojan Horse? The Crisis in Darfur and Humanitarian Intervention after Iraq," *Ethics and International Affairs* 19(2), 2005, 31–53, and James Turner Johnson, "Humanitarian Intervention after Iraq: Just War and International Law Perspectives," *Journal of Military Ethics* 5(2), 2006, 114–127.

[160] Michael Doyle, "Liberalism and World Politics," *American Political Science Review* 80(4), 1986, 1151–1169, 1156.

[161] John Mueller, "War Has Almost Ceased to Exist: An Assessment," *Political Science Quarterly* 124(2), (2009), 297–321.

disproportionately bear the burden.[162] And failed states threaten the international community as well, providing fertile ground for terrorist organizations, whose agendas are not limited to a national or even regional scale.[163] In the face of this strategic insecurity, the idea of a robust international governance structure is appealing. In the face of this human insecurity, the need for strong *in bello* protections is especially acute.

In theory, the idea of shifting the nexus of right authority upward to a supranational institution such as the UN Security Council (or, somewhat more plausibly, the European Union), is appealing on many levels. After all, it is not easy to be honest in just war thinking.[164] The flexibility allowed by each of the principles, especially the consequentialist ones, makes it all too tempting to massage the logic in one's own favor. And history is studded with politicians and publics who have willfully used just war principles purely rhetorically, to further their wrong ends. In principle, if the decision to go to war had to be agreed upon by multiple states, the risk of going to war for self-serving ends should be decreased.

However, as Ramsey pointed out, it isn't possible to shift the right and duty of intervention to an institution if that institution does not yet have the necessary strength to act independently and efficiently.[165] And as Walzer quipped, recognizing the inefficiency of waiting for decisions to be made via political committee, waiting for the United Nations is like waiting for the Messiah.[166] If international institutions were more robust, then it would be quite sensible to consider shifting legitimate authority upwards, out of the hands of self-interested states. But currently existing institutions lack the capacity to effectively make and enforce decisions about the use of force. (And, especially in the case of the Security Council, contemporary institutions are subject to the will of powerful states, who use them for their own interests.)[167] Given the role power necessarily plays in the formation of such institutions, there isn't

---

[162] Kristine Eck and Lisa Hultman, "One-Sided Violence against Civilians in War," *Journal of Peace Research* 44(2), 2007, 232–246.

[163] James A. Piazza, "Incubators of Terror: Do Failed and Failing States Promote Transnational Terrorism," *International Studies Quarterly* 52(3), 2008, 469–488.

[164] John Paul Yoder, *When War Is Unjust: Being Honest in Just War Thinking* (Maryknoll, NY: Orbis Books, 1996).

[165] Paul Ramsey, "The Ethics of Intervention," *Review of Politics* 27(3), July 1965, 287–310, 293.

[166] Walzer, *Just and Unjust Wars*.

[167] Martha Finnemore, "Fights about Rules: The Role of Efficacy and Power in Changing Multilaterlaism," *Review of International Studies* 31, 2005, 187–206, 196, 198–199.

much reason for confidence that any reorganized future version of such bodies will be functional.[168]

Nonetheless, international law serves a vital function. Creating institutions that offer alternatives to war fighting as a way of solving problems between (and within) states is important work. But when just war thinking replicates the work done by international law, something important is lost. The discourse of international law and human rights is essential to everyday politics. But (thankfully) war is not an everyday activity. It is not ordinary politics. War is the politics of the unideal – the politics of crisis. We know, from sad experience, that despite an increasingly thick network of laws and institutions, states continue to behave asocially in the international arena. Although interstate warfare is on the decline, states still go to war with each other. Intrastate violence spills over national borders. Weak political actors use terrorism to force the powerful to consider accommodating their demands. And great powers struggle with each other – and with small powers and terrorist organizations – to dominate the global order.

The problem with liberalizing just war thinking in such a world is that it either gives up too little or sacrifices too much. A heaping dose of optimism and confidence in the possibility of creating a liberal peace through remaking troubled states leads to well-meaning liberal imperialism. The aims are well intentioned – the desire for justice and human rights is one that traditional just war theorists can understand – but also impossible to achieve through force. Violence can be used to check violence. Violence can be used to deny others the ability to control territory. But violence cannot change the way others think about politics, or alter the values they hold – even if the threat of hurt may alter their behavior for a season.[169]

On the other hand, a heaping dose of optimism and confidence in the existence of a robust international society can lead to the development of just war principles that are impracticable. States will fight, even if the *in bello* rules are impossible to obey. Rules that curtail states' abilities to win wars (or to win them with politically acceptable losses) will simply be ignored whenever victory is on the line. Wars between and within states will devolve into total war. The results for humanitarian interventions

---

[168] Johnson, "Humanitarian Intervention after Iraq," 125.

[169] Robert J. Art, "To What Ends Military Power," *International Security* 4(3), 1980, 3–35. See also Thomas C. Schelling, *Arms and Influence* (New Haven: Yale University Press, 1967), 1–34.

will be equally dire: we may still "follow the impulse to intervene, but . . . do so with such restraint and caution that we merely add damage to an already bad situation, with no reasonable hope of success in solving the underlying cause of the intervention."[170]

But it is at exactly this point where a more realistic approach to just war thinking can be the most effective. Although we may wish states held themselves to a higher standard, historically the just war traditions have asked only that states restrain themselves from the worst of crimes. The bar has traditionally been set quite low. This serves a useful function. When the rules are pragmatic – when they reflect the ways wars are fought and won – they are more likely to be obeyed. At the very least, a common excuse for overriding the rules has been eliminated.

In other words, if international law sets the aspirational bar – the standard of careful and responsible behavior we hope states will train their armies to uphold – just war thinking can demarcate the minimum acceptable standard. It is vitally important to think carefully about where the bar should be set on both ends. A state that fails to uphold the higher standard expressed in international law (and in contemporary just war thinking shaped by the legal tradition) violates the law and, in moral terms, fails to live up to an ideal standard. But if it has not violated the minimal standards of justice as expressed in the historical just war tradition, it has avoided committing the worst of crimes, and that in itself is noteworthy. Such a state may not be an ideal moral actor, but it has not completely dispatched with moral reasoning. Effort matters.

In the process, it has likely made a series of arguments justifying its choices, explaining why it felt unable to abide by the higher standard. Whether or not these arguments are morally satisfactory must be judged not only by the state's own citizens, but also by the world community. In keeping with the history of the just war traditions, such judgments will necessarily be contingent. They will reflect not only what we believe to be morally right, but also what we believe to be morally feasible. As technology and tactics change, our evaluations of what it means to observe civilian immunity will also evolve. Even our understandings of *ad bellum* considerations, such as just cause and legitimate authority, are subject to alteration if the nature of the state system itself changes.

---

[170] Martin Cook, "'Immaculate War': Constraints on Humanitarian Intervention," *Ethics and International Affairs* 14(1), 2000, 55–65, 65.

BRINGING REALISM BACK: A PRACTICAL PROPOSAL

I've argued that value can be added to our just war discourse by reaching back to our realist roots. But how exactly are we meant to do this? First, being realist in just war thinking requires a realistic appraisal of ground realities. To determine whether one side or another has a just cause, or whether last resort has effectively been reached, requires the application of facts. Just war thinking is a question "not just of bringing the principles to bear upon the facts, but of bringing the relevant facts to bear upon the principles."[171] As theorists, we are often drawn toward "more theoretical elaboration," as we try to relate just war thinking to the contemporary world.[172] But even more importantly, we must attend to a "vigorous cultivation of politico-moral science," in other words the "politico-moral analysis of the divergent and particular conflict situations that have arisen or are likely to arise in the international scene."[173]

Second, realistic just war thinking must pay careful attention to new developments in tactics, technologies, and organizational strategies. In so doing, just war thinkers must avoid pitfalls on both sides of the path. We must not allow our understanding of just war to be dependent on a *particular* version of what war looks like. In other words, we must think realistically about our own historically contingent position in a tradition that began long before our time, and which will likely extend beyond us into the distant future. Surveying more than two millenia of just war thinking across three just war traditions, it is clear that one of just war thinking's strengths is its ability to see commonalities in the moral dilemmas faced by human beings across time and space. Overemphasizing the uniqueness of contemporary practice can lead us to reify current modes of warfare and to harden our understanding of ethical principles in ways may make the tradition less flexible in the future. We must remain skeptical about our ability to speak meaningfully about idealized visions of War and Justice, while remaining critically engaged in critiquing actual wars and injustices in real time.

At the same time, however, we must also not allow ourselves to be either so historically focused or so theoretically minded as to fail to appreciate the very real challenges new developments in warfare pose to our traditional principles. One way to remain engaged is to pay close attention to the dilemmas of warfare as understood by practitioners.

---

[171] A. J. Coates, *The Ethics of War* (Manchester: Manchester University Press, 1997), 100.
[172] Murray, "The Uses of a Doctrine," 246.   [173] Ibid.

Engagement between scholars of the just war tradition and practitioners occurs today at military academies, but it should not be quarantined to service institutions. Furthermore, just war thinking as a scholarly community must open the doors not only to scholars of religion and philosophy, but also to social scientists. If just war thinking seems poised to "become primarily an unfruitful exercise in theoretical ethics," it is largely "due to its abandonment by social scientists."[174] For this reason, developing a sustained conversation between just war thinkers and realists is worthwhile. Prominent realists have been considering many of the same ethical conundrums as we have for the past several years – *ad bellum* issues such as the invasion of Iraq and humanitarian interventions in Libya, as well as *in bello* concerns such as fighting counter-insurgency wars, using torture, and developing drone technology.[175] Enabling this conversation requires reading more broadly – taking the work of international relations theorists and especially scholars engaged in empirical analysis – into consideration.

If we are to evaluate the ethics of wars *ad bellum*, we must be prepared in advance by thinking about the kinds of threats our states are likely to face, the steps our governments have been taking to ameliorate or eliminate such threats, and the military, diplomatic, and economic tools available in our arsenal to address such threats. Put frankly, we cannot wait until a specific war is on the horizon to start paying attention to a crisis. Doing so invariably puts us behind the ball in terms of evaluating whether last resort has really been met, and even challenges our ability to think carefully about whether there is a just cause. One symptom of this practice of responding in real time without having a broader understanding of the political and security environment could be the willingness of prominent just war thinkers to accept that the 2003 Iraq War might have had a just cause.[176] As the conflict wore on, and more facts about the original decision to go to war became available, these thinkers changed their position. But arguably, they were caught unawares in a way that prominent realists – who opposed the war from the beginning – were not.[177]

[174] Patterson, *Just War Thinking*, 27.

[175] Mearsheimer and Walt, "An Unnecessary War"; Robert A. Pape, "When Duty Calls: A Pragmatic Standard of Humanitarian Intervention," *International Security* 37(1), 2012, 41–80.

[176] Elshtain, "A Just War"; Johnson, "Just War, As It Was and Is"; Walzer, "Drums of War, Calls for Peace" and "The Crime of Aggressive War."

[177] Mearsheimer and Walt, "An Unnecessary War."

Bibliography

Abou El Fadl, Khaled. "The Rules of Killing at War: An Inquiry into Classical Sources." *Muslim World* 89(2), 1999, 144–157.

Rebellion and Violence in Islamic Law. Cambridge: Cambridge University Press, 2003.

Abulafia, David. *Frederick II: A Medieval Emperor*. Oxford: Oxford University Press, 1992.

AbuSulayman, 'AbdulHamid A. *Towards an Islamic Theory of International Relations: New Directions for Methodology and Thought*. Herndon, VA: International Institute of Islamic Thought, 1993.

Addington, Larry H. *The Patterns of War since the Eighteenth Century*. Bloomington: Indiana University Press, 1994.

Afsaruddin, Asma. *Striving in the Path of God: Jihad and Martyrdom in Islamic Thought*. Oxford: Oxford University Press, 2013.

"The Siyar Laws of Aggression: Juridical Re-interpretations of Qur'anic Jihad and Their Contemporary Implications for International Law." In Maria-Luisa Frick and Andreas Th. Müller, eds., *Islam and International Law: Engaging Self-Centrism from a Plurality of Perspectives*, 45–63. Amsterdam: Brill, 2013.

Ahrensdorf, Peter J. "Thucydides' Realistic Critique of Realism." *Polity* 30(2), 1997, 231–265.

Ali, Kecia. *Imam Shafi'i: Scholar and Saint*. Oxford: Oneworld Publications, 2011.

Al-Jamil, Tariq. "Ibn Taymiyya and Ibn al-Mutahhar al-Hilli: Shi'i Polemics and the Struggle for Religious Authority in Medieval Islam." In Yossef Rapoport and Shahab Ahmed, eds., *Ibn Taymiyya and His Times*, 229–246. Oxford: Oxford University Press, 2010.

Al-Mawardi. *Adab al-dunya wa al-din*. Mustafa al-Saqqa, ed. Cairo, Egypt: Mustafa Babi al-Halabi and Sons, 1955.

"Sufis and Shamans: Some Remarks on the Islamization of Mongols in the Ilkhanate." *Journal of the Economic and Social History of the Orient* 42(1), 1999, 27–46.

Amitai-Preiss, Reuven. "The Logistics of the Mongol-Mamluk War, with Special Reference to the Battle of Wadi 'l-Khaznadar, 1299 C.E." In John H. Pryor, ed., *Logistics of Warfare in the Age of the Crusades*. Aldershot, UK: Ashcroft, 2006.

Anscombe, G. E. M. "War and Murder." In Walter Stein, ed., *Nuclear Weapons: A Catholic Response*. New York: Sheed and Ward, 1961.

Appiah, Kwame. *Ethics of Identity*. Princeton: Princeton University Press, 2005.

Aquinas, Thomas. *Aquinas: Political Writings*. R. W. Dyson, ed. Cambridge: Cambridge University Press, 2002.

On Evil. Richard J. Regan and Brian Davies, eds. Oxford: Oxford University Press, 2003.

Arbesmann, Rudolph, Sister Emily Joseph Daly, and Edwin A. Quain, trans. *Tertullian: Disciplinary, Moral and Ascetical Works*. New York: Fathers of the Church, 1955.

Archer, Christon, John R. Ferris, Holger H. Herwig, and Timothy E. H. Travers. *World History of Warfare*. London: Cassell, 2003.

Arjomand, Said Amir. "Religion, Political Action and Legitimate Domination in Shi'ite Iran: Fourteenth to Eighteenth Centuries AD." *European Journal of Sociology* 20(1), 1979, 59–109.

Arkin, Ronald C. *Governing Lethal Behavior in Autonomous Robots*. New York: Taylor and Francis, 2009.

Art, Robert J. "To What Ends Military Power." *International Security* 4(3), 1980, 3–35.

Ashley, Richard K. "Political Realism and Human Interests." *International Studies Quarterly* 25(2), 1981, 204–236.

Augustine of Hippo. *City of God*. London: Penguin Books, 1984.

Aure, Andreas Harald. "Hugo Grotius – Individual Rights as the Core of Natural Law." In Guttorm Fløistad, ed., *Contemporary Philosophy: A New Survey, Vol. 12: Philosophy of Justice*, 75–94. Dordrecht: Springer, 2015.

Avant, Deborah. "From Mercenary to Citizen Armies: Explaining Change in the Practice of War." *International Organization* 54(1), 2000, 41–72.

Axelrod, Robert. "An Evolutionary Approach to Norms." *American Political Science Review* 80(4), 1986, 1095–1111.

Baer, Helmut David, and Joseph E. Capizza. "Just War Theories Reconsidered: Problems with Prima Facie Duties and the Need for a Political Ethic." *Journal of Religious Ethics* 33(1), 2005, 119–137.

Bainton, Roland. *Christian Attitudes toward War and Peace: A Historical Survey and Critical Re-Evaluation*. New York: Abingdon Press, 1960.

Here I Stand: A Life of Martin Luther. Nashville: Abingdon Press, 2013.

Barkin, J. Samuel, and Bruce Cronin. "The State and the Nation: Changing Norms and the Rules of Sovereignty in International Relations." *International Organization* 48(1), 1994, 107–130.

Baron, Salo Wittmayer. *A Social and Religious History of the Jews: Late Middle Ages and the Era of European Expansion, 1200–1650*. New York: Columbia University Press, 1970.

Beaulac, Stéphane. "Emer de Vattel and the Externalization of Sovereignty." *Journal of the History of International Law* 5, 2003, 237–292.

Begby, Endre, Gregory M. Reichberg, and Henrik Syse. "The Ethics of War. Part II: Contemporary Authors and Issues." *Philosophy Compass* 7(5), 2012, 328–347.

Bellamy, Alex J. "Humanitarian Responsibilities and Interventionist Claims in International Society." *Review of International Studies* 29(3), 2003, 321–340.

"Responsibility to Protect or Trojan Horse? The Crisis in Darfur and Humanitarian Intervention after Iraq." *Ethics and International Affairs* 19(2), 2005, 31–53.

"The Responsibilities of Victory: 'Jus Post Bellum' and the Just War." *Review of International Studies* 34(4), 2008, 601–625.

Berkman, John, and Michael Cartwright, eds. *The Hauerwas Reader*. Raleigh, NC: Duke University Press, 2001.

Berman, Harold J. "The Influence of Christianity upon the Development of Law." *Oklahoma Law Review* 12, 1959, 86–101.

Best, Geoffrey. *Humanity in Warfare*. New York: Columbia University Press, 1980.

Bew, John. *Realpolitik: A History*. Oxford: Oxford University Press, 2016.

Beza, Thomas. *The Life of John Calvin*. Lindenhurst, NY: Great Christian Books, 2012.

Bhakari, S. K. *Indian Warfare: An Appraisal of Strategy and Tactics of War in Early Medieval Period*. New Delhi: Munshiram Manoharlal Publishers, 1980.

Bhatia, H. S., ed. *International Law and Practice in Ancient India*. New Delhi: Deep & Deep Publications, 1977.

Bhattacharya, K. K. *Public International Law*. Allahabad, India: Central Law Agency, 1982.

Biggar, Nigel. "Natural Flourishing as the Normative Ground of Just War." In Anthony Lang and Cian O'Driscoll, eds., *Just War: Authority, Tradition and Practice*, 49–62. Washington, DC: Georgetown University Press, 2013.

In Defense of War. Oxford: Oxford University Press, 2013.

Black, Anthony. *The History of Islamic Political Thought: From the Prophet to the Present*. New York: Routledge, 2001.

Bligh-Abramski, Irit. "Evolution versus Revolution: Umayyad Elements in the 'Abbasid Regime 133/750–320/932." In Fred M. Donner, ed., *The Articulation of Early Islamic State Structures*, 389–406. Burlington, VT: Ashgate, 2012.

Bobbit, Philip. *The Sword of Achilles: War, Peace, and the Course of History*. New York: Anchor Books, 2002.

Boesche, Roger. "Kautilya's 'Arthasastra' on War and Diplomacy in Ancient India." *Journal of Military History* 67(1), 2003, 9–37.

Boisard, Marcel A. "On the Probable Influence of Islam on Western Public and International Law." *International Journal of Middle East Studies* 11(4), 1980, 429–450.

Bonner, Michael. *Jihad in Islamic History: Doctrines and Practice*. Princeton: Princeton University Press, 2006.

Boucher, David. "The Just War Tradition and Its Modern Legacy: *Jus ad bellum* and *jus in bello*." *European Journal of Political Theory* 11(2), 2011, 92–111.

Brekke, Torkel. "Wielding the Rod of Punishment – War and Violence in the Political Science of Kautilya." *Journal of Military Ethics* 3(1), 2004, 40–52.

"The Ethics of War and the Concept of War in India and Europe." *Numen* 52 (1), 2005, 59–86.

Brent, Allen. *A Political History of Early Christianity*. London: T&T Clark International/Continuum, 2009.

Brewer, Kimberly Gross, Sean Aday, and Lars Willnat. "International Trust and Public Opinion about World Affairs." *American Journal of Political Science* 48(1), 2004, 93–109.

Brilmayer, Lea. "Realism Revisited: The Moral Priority of Means and Ends in Anarchy." *Nomos* 41, 1999, 192–215.

Brown, Chris. "Just War and Political Judgment." In Anthony Lang and Cian O'Driscoll, eds., *Just War: Authority, Tradition and Practice*, 35–48. Washington, DC: Georgetown University Press, 2013.

Brunstetter, Daniel, and Megan Braun. "From *Jus ad Bellum* to *Jus ad Vim*: Recalibrating Our Understanding of the Moral Use of Force." *Ethics and International Affairs* 27(1), 2013, 87–106.

Buch, Maganlal A. *The Principles of Hindu Ethics*. Baroda, India: "Arya Sudharak" Printing Press, 1921.

Buchanan, Allen. "Institutionalizing the Just War." *Philosophy and Public Affairs* 34(1), 2006, 2–38.

Buchanan, Allen, and Robert O. Keohane. "The Preventive Use of Force: A Cosmopolitan Institutional Proposal." *Ethics and International Affairs* 18(1), 2004, 1–22.

Bull, Hedley. "The Grotian Conception of International Society." In Herbert Butterfield and Martin Wight, eds., *Diplomatic Investigations*, 70–71. Cambridge, MA: Harvard University Press, 1966.

The Anarchical Society: A Study of Order in World Politics. New York: Columbia University Press, 1977.

Burke, Anthony. "Just War or Ethical Peace? Moral Discourses of Strategic Violence after 9/11." *International Affairs* 80(2), 2004, 329–353.

Butterfield, Herbert. "The Scientific versus the Moralistic Approach in International Affairs." *International Affairs* 27(3), 1951, 411–422.

Buzan, Barry. "The Timeless Wisdom of Realism?" In Steve Smith, Ken Booth, and Marysia Zalewski, eds., *International Theory: Positivism and Beyond*, 47–65. Cambridge: Cambridge University Press, 1996.

Cadoux, Cecil John. *The Early Christian Attitude to War*. New York: Seabury Press, 1982.

Cahill, Lisa Sowle. *Love Your Enemies: Discipleship, Pacifism, and Just War Theory*. Minneapolis: Augsburg Fortress, 1994.

Calhoun, Laurie. "Regarding War Realism." *International Journal on World Peace* 18(4), 2001, 37–61.

Calvin, John. *Institutes of the Christian Religion*, trans. Henry Baeveridge. Grand Rapids, MI: Eerdmans, 2001.

Carr, E. H. *What Is History?* Harmondsworth, UK: Penguin Books, 1987.

The Twenty Years Crisis: 1919–1939. New York: Perennial, 2001.

Chambour, Raafat. *Les Institutions sociales, politiques et juridiques de l'Islam.* Lausanne: Éditions Méditerranéennes, 1978.

Charles, J. Daryl, and Timothy J. Demy. *War, Peace, and Christianity.* Wheaton, IL: Crossway, 2010.

Chatterjee, R. K. *The Gita and Its Culture.* New Delhi: Sterling Publishers, 1987.

Checkel, Jeffery T. "Norms, Institutions and National Identity in Contemporary Europe." *International Studies Quarterly* 43(1), 1999, 84–114.

Chesterman, Simon. *Just War or Just Peace? – Humanitarian Intervention and International Law.* Oxford: Oxford University Press, 2001.

Childress, James F. "Just War Theories: The Bases, Interrelations, Priorities, and Functions of Their Criteria." *Theological Studies* 39, 1978, 427–445.

Moral Responsibility in Conflicts. Baton Rouge: Louisiana State University Press, 1982.

Christiansen, Eric. *The Northern Crusades.* London: Penguin Books, 1998.

Christov, Theodore. "Liberal Internationalism Revisited: Grotius, Vattel, and the International Order of States." *The European Legacy* 10(6), 2005, 561–584.

Cicero. *On the Commonwealth and on the Laws.* James E. G. Zetzel, ed. Cambridge: Cambridge University Press, 1999.

Claude, Inis. "Just Wars: Doctrines and Institutions." *Political Science Quarterly* 95(1), 1980.

von Clausewitz, Carl. *On War.* Michael Howard and Peter Paret, eds. and trans. Princeton: Princeton University Press, 1984.

Coady, C. A. J. "The Moral Reality in Realism." *Journal of Applied Philosophy* 22(2), 2005, 121–136.

Coates, A. J. *The Ethics of War.* Manchester: Manchester University Press, 1997.

Collingsworth, R. G. *The Idea of History.* Oxford: Clarendon Press, 1964.

Cook, Martin. "'Immaculate War': Constraints on Humanitarian Intervention." *Ethics and International Affairs* 14(1), 2000, 55–65.

Lessons in Military Ethics. Albany: State University of New York Press, 2013.

Cox, Robert W. "Multilateralism and World Order." *Review of International Studies* 18(2), 1992, 161–180.

Cozette, Murielle. "Reclaiming the Critical Dimension of Realism: Hans J. Morgenthau on the Ethics of Scholarship." *Review of International Studies* 34(1), 2008, 5–27.

Crawford, Neta C. "Just War Theory and the U.S. Counterterror War." *Perspectives on Politics* 1(10), 2003, 5–25.

Crépon, Pierre. *Les religions et la guerre.* Paris: Éditions Albin Michel, 1991.

Crone, Patricia, and Martin Hinds. *God's Caliph: Religious Authority in the First Centuries of Islam.* Cambridge: Cambridge University Press, 2003.

Crouzel, Henri. *Origen.* San Francisco: Harper & Row, 1989.

Davies, Brian. *Thomas Aquinas on Good and Evil.* Oxford: Oxford University Press, 2011.

Davis, G. Scott. *Believing and Acting: The Pragmatic Turn in Comparative Religion and Ethics.* Oxford: Oxford University Press, 2012.

Decosimo, David. *Ethics as a Work of Charity: Thomas Aquinas and Pagan Virtue.* Stanford, CA: Stanford University Press, 2014.

Desch, Michael C. "It Is Kind to Be Cruel: The Humanity of American Realism." *Review of International Studies* 29(3), 2003, 415–426.

Digeser, Elizabeth DePalma. *A Threat to Public Piety: Christians, Platonists, and the Great Persecution*. Ithaca: Cornell University Press, 2012.

Dikshitar, V. R. *Ramachandra. War in Ancient India*. Delhi: Motilal Banarsidass, 1987.

Dill, Janina. *Legitimate Targets? Social Construction, International Law, and US Bombing*. Cambridge: Cambridge University Press, 2014.

Dill, Janina, and Henry Shue. "Limiting Killing in War: Military Necessity and the St. Petersburg Assumption." *Ethics and International Affairs* 26(3), 2012, 311–333.

Doniger, Wendy. *The Hindus: An Alternative History*. New York: Penguin Books, 2009.

Donnelly, Jack. *Themes in International Relations: Realism and International Relations*. Cambridge: Cambridge University Press, 2002.

"The Ethics of Realism." In Christian Reus-Smit and Duncan Snidal, eds., *The Oxford Handbook of International Relations*, 150–162. Oxford: Oxford University Press, 2010.

Donner, Fred M., ed. *The Articulation of Early Islamic State Structures*. Burlington, VT: Ashgate, 2012.

Doyle, Michael. "Liberalism and World Politics." *American Political Science Review* 80(4), 1986, 1151–1169.

"Thucydidean Realism." *Review of International Studies* 16(3), 1990, 223–237.

Draper, Kai. *War and Individual Rights: The Foundations of Just War Theory*. Oxford: Oxford University Press, 2016.

Drekmeier, Charles. *Kingship and Community in Early India*. Stanford, CA: Stanford University Press, 1962.

Drezner, Daniel. "The Realist Tradition in American Public Opinion." *Perspectives on Politics* 6(1), 2008, 51–70.

Eck, Kristine, and Lisa Hultman. "One-Sided Violence against Civilians in War." *Journal of Peace Research* 44(2), 2007, 232–246.

Eickelmann, Allan, Eric Nelson, and Tom Lansford, eds. *Justice and Violence: Political Violence, Pacifism and Cultural Transformation*. Burlington, VT: Ashgate, 2005

Elshtain, Jean Bethke. "Reflections on War and Political Discourse: Realism, Just War, and Feminism in a Nuclear Age." *Political Theory* 13(1), 1985, 39–57.

"Just War as Politics: What the Gulf War Told Us about Contemporary American Life." In David E. Decosse, ed., *But Was It Just? Reflections on the Morality of the Persian Gulf War*, 43–60. New York: Doubleday, 1992.

"Just War and Humanitarian Intervention." *Proceedings of the Annual Meeting, American Society of International Law* 95, 2001, 1–12.

"A Just War." *Boston Globe*, October 6, 2002. www.boston.com/news/pack ages/iraq/globe_stories/100602_justwar.htm.

Just War against Terror. New York: Basic Books, 2003.

"Politics and Persons." *Journal of Religion* 86(3), 2006, 402–411.

Elshtain, Jean Bethke, ed. *Just War Theory*. New York: New York University Press, 1992.

Esposito, John. *The Oxford History of Islam*. Oxford: Oxford University Press, 2000.

al-Farabi, Abu Nasr, *Alfarabi: The Political Writings; "Selected Aphorisms" and Other Texts*. Charles E. Butterworth, trans. Ithaca: Cornell University Press, 2004.

Fay, Thomas A., "Thomas Aquinas on the Justification of Revolution." *History of European Ideas* 16, 1993, 4–6.

Feinstein, Lee, James M. Lindsay, and Max Boot. "On Foreign Policy, Red and Blue Voters Are Worlds Apart." Council on Foreign Relations, August 2004.

Fiala, Andrew. "The Bush Doctrine, Democratization, and Humanitarian Intervention: A Just War Critique." *Theoria: A Journal of Social and Political Theory* 54(114), 2007, 28–47.

The Just War Myth – The Moral Illusions of War. New York: Rowman & Littlefield, 2008.

Field, Lester L. *Liberty, Dominion, and the Two Swords: On the Origins of Western Political Theology*. South Bend, IN: University of Notre Dame Press, 1998.

Finlay, Christopher J. "Fairness and Liability in the Just War: Combatants, Non-combatants, and Lawful Irregulars." *Political Studies* 61(1), 2013, 142–160.

Finnemore, Martha. "Fights about Rules: The Role of Efficacy and Power in Changing Multilateralism." *Review of International Studies* 31, 2005, 187–206.

Firestone, Reuven. *Holy War in Judaism*. Oxford: Oxford University Press, 2012.

Fleck, Dieter, ed. *The Handbook of Humanitarian Law in Armed Conflicts*. Oxford: Oxford University Press, 1995.

Flori, Jean. *Guerre sainte, jihad, croisade: violence et religion dans le christianisme et l'islam*. Paris: Éditions du Seuil, 2002.

Foot, Rosemary. "Introduction." In Rosemary Foot, John Lewis Gaddis, and Andrew Hurrell, eds., *Order and Justice in International Relations*, 1–23. Oxford: Oxford University Press, 2003.

Forde, Steven. "International Realism and the Science of Politics: Thucydides, Machiavelli, and Neorealism." *International Studies Quarterly* 39(2), 1995, 141–160.

Fortin, Ernest L., Roland Gunn, and Douglas Kries, eds. *Augustine: Political Writings*. Indianapolis: Hackett, 1994.

Foucault, Michel. "Nietzsche, Genealogy, History." In Paul Rabinow, ed., *The Foucault Reader*, 76–100. New York: Pantheon Books, 1984.

Discipline and Punish. New York: Vintage Books, 1995.

Frankel, Benjamin. "Restating the Realist Case: An Introduction." In Benjamin Frankel, ed., *Realism: Restatements and Renewal*, ix–xx. London: Frank Cass, 1996.

Frei, Daniel. "The Regulation of Warfare: A Paradigm for the Legal Approach to the Control of International Conflict." *Journal of Conflict Resolution* 18(4), 1974, 620–633.

Freund, Norman C. "The Just War: Viable Theory or Moral Anachronism?" *American Journal of Theology and Philosophy* 3(3), 1982, 71–79.

Freund, Robert A. *Understanding Jewish Ethics*. San Francisco: Edwin Mellen Press, 1990.

Frost, William J. *A History of Christian, Jewish, Hindu, Buddhist and Muslim Perspectives on War and Peace, vol. 1: The Bible to 1914*. Lampeter, Wales: Edwin Mellen Press, 2004.

Gaddis, John Lewis. *The Landscape of History: How Historians Map the Past*. Oxford: Oxford University Press, 2002.

Geerz, Clifford. *The Interpretation of Cultures*. New York: Basic Books, 1973.

Ghosh, Jagat J. *Indian Thesis on War and Peace*. Raniganj, India: Mahima Ranjan Sarkar (Rajashree Press), 1972.

Gilpin, Robert. *War and Change in World Politics*. Cambridge: Cambridge University Press, 1981.

"The Richness of the Tradition of Political Realism." *International Organization* 38(2), 1984, 287–304.

Glaser, Charles L. "Structural Realism in a More Complex World." *Review of International Studies* 29(3), 2003, 403–414.

Gordis, Robert. *Judaic Ethics for a Lawless World*. New York: Jewish Theological Seminary of America, 1986.

Gordon, Bruce. *Calvin*. New Haven: Yale University Press, 2009.

John Calvin's Institutes of the Christian Religion: A Biography. Princeton: Princeton University Press, 2016.

Gottlieb, Stuart. "Judaism, Israel and Conscientious Objection." *Christian Century*, September 3, 1969, 1136–1137.

Gowen, Herbert H. "'The Indian Machiavelli' or Political Theory in India Two Thousand Years Ago." *Political Science Quarterly* 44(2), 1929, 173–192.

Greenslade, S. L., trans. and ed. *Early Latin Theology: Selections from Tertullian, Cyprian, Ambrose and Jerome, vol. 5*. Philadelphia: Westminster Press, 1956.

Gross, Michael L. *The Ethics of Insurgency: A Critical Guide to Just Guerilla Warfare*. Cambridge: Cambridge University Press, 2015.

Grotius, Hugo. *Prolegomena to the Laws of War and Peace*. Francis W. Kelsay, trans. Loang Institute, 2005. https://lonang.com/library/reference/grotius-law-war-and-peace/gro-100/

Rights of War and Peace. A. C. Campbell, trans. London: B. Boothroyd, 1814.

Guraya, Muhammad Yusuf. "Historical Background of the Compilation of the Muwatta' of Malik b. Anas." *Islamic Studies* 7(4), 1968, 379–392.

Haines, Keith. "Attitudes and Impediments to Pacifism in Medieval Europe." *Journal of Medieval History* 7, 1981, 369–388.

Hale, John. *The Civilization of Europe in the Renaissance*. New York: Simon and Schuster, 1995.

Hallaq, Wael B. "Was al-Shafi'i the Master Architect of Islamic Jurisprudence?" *International Journal of Middle East Studies* 25(4), 1993, 587–605.

Hamidullah, Muhammad. *Muslim Conduct of State*. Lahore, India: Sh. Muhammad Ashraf, 1945.

Hariman, Robert, and Francis A. Beer. "What Would Be Prudent? Forms of Reasoning in World Politics." *Rhetoric and Public Affairs* 1(3), 1998, 299–330.

Hartigan, Richard Shelly. "Francesco de Vitoria and Civilian Immunity." *Political Theory* 1(1), 1973, 79–91.

The Forgotten Victim: A History of the Civilian. Chicago: Precedent Publishing, 1982.

Hashmi, Sohail H., and Stephen P. Lee, eds. *Ethics and Weapons of Mass Destruction: Religious and Secular Perspectives*. Cambridge: Cambridge University Press, 2004.

Hassan, Mona. "Modern Interpretations and Misinterpretations of a Medieval Scholar: Apprehending the Political Thought of Ibn Taymiyya." In Yossef Rapoport and Shahab Ahmed, eds., *Ibn Taymiyya and His Times*, 338–366. Oxford: Oxford University Press, 2010.

Hastell, Guy. *Barbarian Migrations and the Roman West, 376–568*. Cambridge: Cambridge University Press, 2007.

Hegel, G. W. F. *Elements of the Philosophy of the Right*. Allen B. Wood, ed., H. B. Nisbet, trans. Cambridge: Cambridge University Press, 1991.

Helgeland, John. "Christians and the Roman Army AD 173–337." *Church History* 43(2), 1974, 149–200.

Hensel, Howard, ed. *The Prism of Just War*. Burlington, VT: Ashgate, 2010.

Hitti, Philip K. *History of the Arabs*. New York: Palgrave Macmillan, 2002.

Hobbes, Thomas. *Leviathan*. Richard Tuck, ed. Cambridge: Cambridge University Press, 1996.

Hodgson, Marshall G. S. *The Venture of Islam: Conscience and History in a World Civilization, Vol. 1: The Classical Age of Islam*. Chicago: University of Chicago Press, 1988.

The Venture of Islam: Conscience and History in a World Civilization, Vol. 2: The Expansion of Islam in the Middle Periods. Chicago: University of Chicago Press, 1974.

Hoffman, Stanley. "An American Social Science: International Relations." *Daedalus* 106(3), 1977, 41–60.

Duties beyond Borders. Syracuse: Syracuse University Press, 1981.

Holmes, Robert L. *On War and Morality*. Princeton: Princeton University Press, 1989.

Holsti, Kalevi. *The Dividing Discipline: Hegemony and Diversity in International Theory*. London: Allen & Unwin, 1985.

Höpfl, Harro, ed. *Luther and Calvin on Secular Authority*. Cambridge: Cambridge University Press, 2010.

Hourani, Albert. "From Jabal 'Amil to Persia." *Bulletin of the School of Oriental and African Studies* 49(1), 1986, 133–140.

A History of the Arab Peoples. New York: Warner Books, 1991.

Howard, Michael. *War in European History*. Oxford: Oxford University Press, 1977.

Hunter, Ian. "Kant and Vattel in Context: Cosmopolitan Philosophy and Diplomatic Casuistry." *History of European Ideas* 39(4), 2013, 477–502.

Hurd, Ian. "Legitimacy and Authority in International Politics." *International Organization* 53(2), 1999, 379–408.

ibn 'Abd al-Barr. *Jami'bayan al-'ilm*. Abu al-Ashbal al-Zuhayri, ed. 2 vols. Dammam: Dar Ibn al-Jawzi, 1994.

ibn al-Matroudi, Abdul Hakim. *The Hanbali School of Law and Ibn Taymiyyah*. New York: Routledge, 2006.

ibn Anas, Malik. *Al-Mudawwanna al-Kubra li al-Imam Malik ibn Anas al-Ashabhi* (Beirut, Lebanon: Dar al-Kutub al-'Ilmiya, 1994), trans. Aziz el Kaissouni in Nesrine Badawi, "Sunni Islam, Part I: Classical Sources," in Greg Reichberg, Henrik Syse, and Nicole Hartwell, eds., *Religion, War and Ethics: A Sourcebook of Textual Traditions*, 301–369. Cambridge: Cambridge University Press, 2014.

Muwatta Imam Malik. Muhammad Rahimuddin, trans. Lahore: Sh. Muhammad Ashraf, 1980.

Al-Muwatta of Imam Malik ibn Anas. Aisha Abdurrahman Bewley, trans. and ed. New York: Routledge, Chapman and Hall, 1989.

ibn Khaldûn, 'Abd-ar-Rahman Abu Zayd ibn Muhammad ibn Muhammad. *The Muqaddimah: An Introduction to History*. Franz Rosenthal, trans. Princeton: Princeton University Press, 1967.

ibn Kudamah, Muwaffak al-Din. *Le Précis de droit d'Ibn Qodama*. Henri Laoust, trans. Beirut: Institut Français de Damas, 1950.

ibn Taimiya, Ahmad ibn 'Abd al-Halim. *Le Traité de droit public d'Ibn Taimiya: Traduction annoté de la Siyasa sariya*. Henri Laoust, trans. Beirut: Institut Français de Damas, 1948.

Public Duties in Islam: The Institution of the Hisba. Muhatar Holland, trans. Leicester: Islamic Foundation, 1985.

Lettre à un roi croisé. Jean R. Michot, trans. Lyon: Tawhid, 1995.

A Muslim Theologian's Response to Christianity: Ibn Taymiyya's Al-Jawab Al-Sahih. Thomas F. Michel, S.J., trans. Delmar, NY: Caravan Books, 1984.

Al-'Ubudiyyah: Being a True Slave of Allah. Nasiruddin al-Khattab, trans. London: Ta-Ha Publishers, 1999.

Ikenberry, G. John, and Charles A. Kupchan. "Socialization and Hegemonic Power." *International Organization* 44(3), 1990, 283–315.

"Liberal Realism: The Foundations of a Democratic Foreign Policy." *The National Interest*, Fall 2004, 38–49.

Inal, Tuba. *Looting and Rape in Wartime: Law and Change in International Relations*. Philadelphia: University of Pennsylvania Press, 2013.

Jackson, Peter. "The Crisis in the Holy Land in 1260." *English Historical Review* 95, 1980, 481–513.

Jervis, Robert. *Perception and Misperception in International Politics*. Princeton: Princeton University Press, 1976.

"Cooperation under the Security Dilemma." *World Politics* 30(2), 1978, 167–214.

"Realism in the Study of World Politics." *International Organization* 52(4), 1998, 971–991.

"Realism, Neoliberalism, and Cooperation: Understanding the Debate." *International Security* 24(1), 1999, 42–63.

Johnson, James Turner. *Ideology, Reason, and the Limitation of War: Religious and Secular Concepts, 1200–1740*. Princeton: Princeton University Press, 1975.

Can Modern War Be Just? New Haven: Yale University Press, 1984.

Morality and Contemporary Warfare. New Haven: Yale University Press, 1999.

"Paul Ramsey and the Recovery of the Just War Idea." *Journal of Military Ethics* 1(2), 2002, 136–144.

The War to Oust Saddam Hussein: Just War and the New Face of Conflict. Lanham, MD: Rowman and Littlefield, 2005.

"Just War, As It Was and Is." *First Things*, January 2005.

"Humanitarian Intervention after Iraq: Just War and International Law Perspectives." *Journal of Military Ethics* 5(2), 2006, 114–127.

"The Idea of Defense in Historical and Contemporary Thinking about Just War." *Journal of Religious Ethics* 36(4), 2008, 543–556.

"Thinking Historically about Just War." *Journal of Military Ethics* 8(3), 2009, 246–259.

Ethics and the Use of Force: Just War in Historical Perspective. Burlington, VT: Ashgate, 2011.

"Contemporary Just War Thinking: Which Is Worse, to Have Friends or Critics." *Ethics and International Affairs* 27(1), 2013, 25–45.

"The Right to Use Armed Force: Sovereignty, Responsibility, and the Common Good." In Anthony F. Lang, Jr., Cian O'Driscoll, and John Williams, eds., *Just War: Authority, Tradition, and Practice*, 19–34. Washington, DC: Georgetown University Press, 2013.

Sovereignty: Moral and Historical Perspectives. Washington, DC: Georgetown University Press, 2014.

Jones, Charles A. *More than Just War: Narratives of the Just War Tradition and Military Life.* New York: Routledge, 2013.

Kamandaki. *The Nitisara or The Elements of Polity.* Sisr Kumar Mitra, trans., Rajendralala Mitra, ed. Kolkata: Asiatic Society, 2008.

Kamandakiya Nitisara: or, The Elements of Polity. Manmatha Nath Dutt, trans. Varanasi, India: Chowkhamba Sanskrit Series Office, 1979.

Kaufman, Whitley. "What's Wrong with Preventive War? The Moral and Legal Basis for Preventive Use of Force." *Ethics and International Affairs* 19(3), 2005, 23–38.

Kautilya. *The Arthashastra.* L. N. Rangarajan, ed. and trans. New York: Penguin Books, 1992.

Keith, Arthur Berriedale, trans. *Rigveda Brhamanas: The Aitareya and Kausitaki Brhamanas of the Rigveda.* Cambridge, MA: Harvard University Press, 1920.

Kelsay, John. *Islam and War: A Study in Comparative Ethics.* Louisville: Westminster/John Knox Press, 1993.

Arguing the Just War in Islam. Cambridge, MA: Harvard University Press, 2007.

"The Triumph of Just War Theory and Imperial Overstretch." In Anthony F. Lang, Cian O'Driscoll, and John Williams, eds., *Just War: Authority, Tradition and Practice*, 267–282. Washington, DC: Georgetown University Press, 2013.

Kennedy, David. *Of War and Law.* Princeton: Princeton University Press, 2009.

Keohane, Robert. "International Institutions: Can Interdependence Work?" *Foreign Policy* 110, 1998, 82–96.

Kertzer, Joshua D., and Kathleen M. McGraw. "Folk Realism: Testing the Microfoundations of Realism in Ordinary Citizens." *International Studies Quarterly* 56, 2012, 245–258.

Khadduri, Majid. *War and Peace in the Law of Islam*. Baltimore: Johns Hopkins Press, 1955.

 The Islamic Conception of Justice. Baltimore: Johns Hopkins University Press, 1984.

 The Islamic Law of Nations: Shaybani's Siyar. Baltimore: Johns Hopkins University Press, 2001.

Khan, Qumar-ud-Din. *Al-Mawardi's Theory of the State*. Lahore: Islamic Book Foundation, 1983.

King, Mark D. "Just War as Compromise: Rethinking Walzer's Position on Realism." *Soundings* 95(12), 2012, 1–23.

Kinsella, Helen. *The Image before the Weapon: A Critical History of the Distinction between Combatant and Civilian*. Ithaca: Cornell University Press, 2011.

Kissinger, Henry. *World Order*. New York: Penguin Press, 2014.

Kohlberg, Etan. "The Development of the Imam Shi'i Doctrine of *jihad*." *Zeitschrift der Deutschen Morgenländsichen Gesellschaft* 126(1), 1976, 64–86.

Lang, Anthony F., Cian O'Driscoll, and John Williams, eds. *Just War: Authority, Tradition and Practice*. Washington, DC: Georgetown University Press, 2013.

The Law Code of Manu. Patrick Olivelle, trans. Oxford: Oxford University Press, 2004.

The Laws of Manu. Wendy Doniger, trans. London: Penguin Books, 1991.

Layne, Christopher. "From Preponderance to Offshore Balancing: America's Future Grand Strategy." In Michael E. Brown, Owen R. Coté, Jr., Sean M. Lynn-Jones, and Steven E. Miller, eds., *America's Strategic Choices*, 99–140. Cambridge, MA: MIT Press, 2000.

Lesaffer, Randall. "Paix et guerre dans les grand traités du dix-huitième siècle." *Journal of the History of International Law* 7, 2005, 25–41.

Levy, Jack S. "Too Important to Leave to the Other: History and Political Science in the Study of International Relations." *International Security* 22(1), 1997, 22–33.

Lipson, Charles. *Reliable Partners: How Democracies Have Made a Separate Peace*. Princeton: Princeton University Press, 2005.

Little, David, and Sumner B. Twiss. *Comparative Religious Ethics*. San Francisco: Harper and Row, 1978.

Lopez, David A. *Separatist Christianity: Spirit and Matter in the Early Church Fathers*. Baltimore: Johns Hopkins University Press, 2004.

Luban, David. "Just War and Human Rights." *Philosophy and Public Affairs* 9 (2), 1980, 160–181.

 "Preventive War." *Philosophy and Public Affairs* 32(3), 2004, 207–248.

Lucas, George. "The Role of the 'International Community' in Just War Tradition – Confronting the Challenges of Humanitarian Intervention and Preemptive War." *Journal of Military Ethics* 2(2), 2003, 122–144.

 "Defense or Offense? The Two Streams of Just War Theory." In Peter A. French and Jason A. Short, eds., *War and Border Crossings: Ethics When Cultures Clash*. Lanham, MD: Rowman & Littlefield, 2005.

Lucas, George R., Jr. "From *Jus ad Bellum* to *Jus ad Pacem*: Re-Thinking Just War Criteria for the Use of Military Force for Humanitarian Ends."

In Larry May, ed., *The Morality of War: Classical and Contemporary Readings*, 369–380. New York: Pearson Education, 2006.

Ludlow, Morwenna. *The Early Church*. New York: Palgrave Macmillan, 2009.

Luther, Martin. *Luther: Selected Political Writings*. J. M. Porter, ed. Philadelphia: Fortress Press, 1974.

Lynn-Jones, Sean, and Steven E. Miller, eds. *Offensive, Defense, and War*. Cambridge, MA: MIT Press, 2004.

Machiavelli, Niccolò. *The Prince*. Quentin Skinner and Russell Price, eds. Cambridge: Cambridge University Press, 1988.

Maguire, Daniel. *The Horrors We Bless: Rethinking the Just-War Legacy*. Minneapolis: Fortress Press, 2007.

Mahabharata, Book Five, Preparations for War, Part I. Kathleen Garbutt, trans. New York: New York University Press, 2008.

Mahabharata, Book Five, Preparations for War, Part II. Kathleen Garbutt, trans. New York: New York University Press, 2008.

Mahabharata, Book Six, Bhisma, Volume One. Alex Cherniak, trans. New York: New York University Press, 2008.

Mahabharata, Book Six, Bhisma, Volume Two. Alex Cherniak, trans. New York: New York University Press, 2009.

Mahbharata, Book Ten, Dead of Night and Book Eleven, The Women. Kate Crosby, trans. New York: New York University Press, 2009.

The Mahabharata, Volume 1: The Book of the Beginning, J. A. B. van Buitenen, trans. Chicago: University of Chicago Press, 1973.

The Mahabharata, Volume 2. A. B. van Buitenen, trans. Chicago: University of Chicago Press, 1975.

Markus, Robert A. *Saeculum: History and Society in the Theology of St. Augustine*. Cambridge: Cambridge University Press, 1988.

Mastanduno, Michael. "A Realist View: Three Images of the Coming International Order." In T. V. Paul and John A. Hall, eds., *International Order and the Future of World Politics*, 19–40. Cambridge: Cambridge University Press, 1999.

May, Larry. *War Crimes and Just War*. Cambridge: Cambridge University Press, 2007.

McGinn, Bernard. *Thomas Aquinas' Summa Theologiae: A Biography*. Princeton: Princeton University Press, 2014.

McMahan, Jeff. "Just Cause for War." *Ethics and International Affairs* 19(3), 2005, 1–21.

"The Sources and Status of Just War Principles." *Journal of Military Ethics* 6 (2), 2007, 91–106.

Killing in War. Oxford: Oxford University Press, 2009.

"The Morality of War and the Law of War." In David Rodin and Henry Shue, eds., *Just and Unjust Warriors: The Moral and Legal Status of Soldiers*. Oxford: Oxford University Press, 2010.

Meagher, Robert Emmet. *Killing from the Inside Out: Moral Injury and Just War* Eugene, OR: Cascade Books, 2014.

Mearsheimer, John. "The False Promise of International Institutions." *International Security* 19(3), 1994–1995, 5–49.

The Tragedy of Great Power Politics. New York: W. W. Norton, 2001.

"Through the Realist Lens: The United States and Realism." Interview with Harry Kreisler, April 8, 2002, http://globetrotter.berkeley.edu/people2/Mear sheimer/mearsheimer-cono.html.

"Hans Morgenthau and the Iraq War: Realism versus Neo-conservatism." Online at *Democracy News Analysis* (opendemocracy.net), created May 18, 2005.

Why Leaders Lie. Oxford: Oxford University Press, 2011.

Mearsheimer, John J., and Stephen M. Walt. "An Unnecessary War." *Foreign Policy,* 134, 2003, 51–59.

Megivern, James J. "Early Christianity and Military Service." *Perspectives in Religious Studies,* 12(3), 1985.

Memon, Muhammad Umar. *Ibn Taymiyya's Struggle against Popular Religion, with an Annotated Translation of His Kitab iqtida' as-sirat al-mustaqim mukhalafat ashab al-jahim.* The Hague: Mouton & Co., 1976.

Meyerowitz, Arthur. *Social Ethics of the Jews.* New York: Bloch Publishing Company, 1935.

Mikhail, Hanna. *Politics and Revelation: Mawardi and After.* Edinburgh: Edinburgh University Press, 1995.

Mill, John Stuart. *On Liberty and Other Writings.* Cambridge: Cambridge University Press, 1999.

Miller, Richard B. "Aquinas and the Presumption against Killing and War." *Journal of Religion* 82(2), 2002, 173–204.

Miller, Barbara Stoler, trans. *The Bhagavad Gita: Krishna's Council in Time of War.* New York: Bantam Books, 1986.

al-Misri, Ahmad ibn Naqib. *Reliance of the Traveler: A Classic Manual of Islamic Sacred Law.* Nuh Hah Mim Keller, trans. Beltsville, MD: Amana Publications, 1994.

Montgomery, Evan Braden. "Breaking Out of the Security Dilemma." *International Security* 31(2), 2006, 151–185.

More, S. S. *The Gita: A Theory of Human Action.* Delhi: Sri Satguru Publications, 1990.

Morgenthau, Hans J. "The Twilight of International Morality." *Ethics* 58(2), 1948, 79–99.

In Defense of the National Interest: A Critical Examination of American Foreign Policy. New York: Alfred A. Kopf, 1951.

Scientific Man versus Power Politics. Chicago: University of Chicago Press, 1952.

Dilemmas of Politics. Chicago: University of Chicago Press, 1958.

Politics among Nations, 7th ed. New York: McGraw Hill, 2006.

"Positivism, Functionalism, and International Law." *American Journal of International Law* 34(2), 1940, 260–284.

Morkevičius, Valerie. "Just War: An Ethic of Restraint or the Defense of Order?" In Allan Eickelmann, Eric Nelson, and Tom Lansford, eds., *Justice and Violence: Political Violence, Pacifism and Cultural Transformation,* 3–20. Burlington, VT: Ashgate Press, 2005.

"Changing the Rules of the Game: A Just Peace Critique of Just War Thought." *Nova et Vetera* 10(4), 2012, 1115–1140.

"Protestant Christianity." In Gregory M. Reichberg, Henry Syse, and Nicole M. Hartwell, eds., *Religion War and Ethics: A Sourcebook of Textual Traditions*. Cambridge: Cambridge University Press, 2014.

"Power and Order: The Shared Logics of Realism and Just War Theory." *International Studies Quarterly* 59(1), 2015, 11–22.

Morrison, Karl Frederick. "Rome and the City of God: An Essay on the Constitutional Relationships of Empire and Church in the Fourth Century." *Transactions of the American Philosophical Society* 54(1), 1964.

Mueller, John. "War Has Almost Ceased to Exist: An Assessment." *Political Science Quarterly* 124(2), 2009, 297–321.

al-Muhaqqiq al-Hilli, Ja'far ibn al-Hasan. *Droit Musulman: Recueil de Lois concernant les Musulmans Schyites*. Amédée Querry, trans. Paris: L'Imprimérie Nationale, 1871.

Mukherjee, Bharati. *Kautilya's Concept of Diplomacy: A New Interpretation*. Calcutta: Minerva Associated Publications, 1976.

Muldoon, James. "Francisco de Vitoria and Humanitarian Intervention." *Journal of Military Ethics* 5(2), 2006, 128–143.

Murray, John Courtney. "The Uses of a Doctrine on the Uses of Force as a Moral Problem." In *We Hold These Truths: Catholic Reflections on the American Proposition*, 227–248. New York: Rowman and Littlefield, 2005.

an-Na'im, Abdullahi. *Toward an Islamic Reformation: Civil Liberties, Human Rights, and International Law*. Syracuse: Syracuse University Press, 1990.

Nardin, Terry. "From Right to Intervent to Duty to PROTECT: Michael Walzer on Humanitarian Intervention." *European Journal of International Law* 24 (1), 67–82.

Niebuhr, Reinhold. *Moral Man and Immoral Society: A Study in Ethics and Politics*. Louisville: Westminster John Knox Press, 1932.

Christian Realism and Political Problems. New York: Charles Scribner's Sons, 1953.

The Structure of Nations and Empires. New York: Charles Scribner's Sons, 1958.

Nye, Joseph S., Jr. "Soft Power." *Foreign Policy* 80, Autumn 1990, 153–171.

"Public Diplomacy and Soft Power." *Annals of the American Academy of Political and Social Science* 616, 2008, 94–109.

"Toward a Liberal Realist Foreign Policy: A Memo for the Next President." *Harvard Magazine* 110(4), 2008, 36–38.

O'Callaghan, Ronan. *Walzer, Just War and Iraq – Ethics as Response*. New York: Routledge, 2016.

O'Connell, Mary Ellen. "The Just War Tradition and International Law against War: The Myth of Discordant Doctrines." *Journal of the Society of Christian Ethics* 35(2), 2015, 33–51.

O'Donovan, Oliver. *Just War Revisited*. Cambridge: Cambridge University Press, 2003.

O'Driscoll, Cian. *Renegotiation of the Just War Tradition and the Right to War in the Twenty-First Century*. New York: Palgrave Macmillan, 2008.

"Talking about Just War: Obama in Oslo, Bush at War." *Politics* 31(2), 2011, 82–90.

"Divisions within the Ranks? The Just War Tradition and the Use and Abuse of History." *Ethics and International Affairs* 27(1), 2013, 47–65.

Olivelle, Patrick, ed. and trans. *Dharmasutras: The Law Codes of Apastamba, Gautama, Baudhyana and Vasistha.* Oxford: Oxford University Press, 1999.

Orend, Brian. *Michael Walzer on War and Justice.* Montréal: McGill-Queen's University Press, 2000.

The Morality of War. Peterborough, Ontario: Broadview Press, 2006.

Origen. *Contra Celsum*, Henry Chadwick, trans. Cambridge: Cambridge University Press, 1953.

Osborn, Ronald E. "Obama's Niebuhrian Moment (Part I)." *First Things* 11, January 2010.

O'Shea, Stephen. *Sea of Faith: Islam and Christianity in the Medieval Mediterranean World.* New York: Walker Publishing Company, 2009.

Pagden, Anthony, "Europe: Conceptualizing a Continent." In Pagden, ed., *The Idea of Europe: From Antiquity to the European Union*, 33–54. Washington, DC: Woodrow Wilson Center Press, 2002.

Pape, Robert A. "The World Pushes Back." *Boston Globe*, March 23, 2003, H1.

"When Duty Calls: A Pragmatic Standard of Humanitarian Intervention." *International Security* 37(1), 2012, 41–80.

Pattison, James. "The Ethics of Humanitarian Intervention in Libya." *Ethics and International Affairs* 25(3), 2011, 271–277.

"When Is It Right to Fight? Just War Theory and the Individual-Centric Approach." *Ethical Theory and Moral Practice* 16, 2013, 35–54.

Patterson, Eric. *Just War Thinking.* Lanham, MD: Lexington Books, 2009.

Pearce, Kimber Charles, and Dean Fadley. "George Bush's 'Just War' Rhetoric: Paradigm of Universal Morality." *Journal of Communication and Religion* 16(2), 1993, 139–152.

Pelikan, Jaroslav, and Helmut T. Lehmann, eds. *Luther's Works.* St. Louis: Concordia, 1955–1986.

Peters, Rudolph. *Jihad in Classical and Modern Islam.* Princeton: Markus Wiener Publishers, 1996.

Piazza, James A. "Incubators of Terror: Do Failed and Failing States Promote Transnational Terrorism." *International Studies Quarterly* 52(3), 2008, 469–488.

Pocock, J. G. A. *Political Thought and History.* Cambridge: Cambridge University Press, 2009.

Popovski, Vesselin, Gregory Reichberg, and Nicholas Turner, eds. *World Religions and Norms of War.* New York: United Nations University Press, 2009.

Posen, Barry R. "Military Responses to Refugee Disasters." *International Security* 21(1), 1996, 72–111.

Priest, James E. *Governmental and Judicial Ethics in the Bible and Rabbinic Literature.* Malibu, CA: Pepperdine University Press, 1980.

Primoratz, Igor. "Michael Walzer's Just War Theory: Some Issues of Responsibility." *Ethical Theory and Moral Practice* 5(2), 2002, 221–243.

Provost, René. *International Human Rights and Humanitarian Law.* Cambridge: Cambridge University Press, 2002.

Pryor, John H., ed. *Logistics of Warfare in the Age of the Crusades.* Aldershot: Ashcroft, 2006.

Pufendorf, Samuel. *On the Duty of Man and Citizen.* Cambridge: Cambridge University Press, 1991.

al-Qadi, Wadad. "The Religious Foundation of Late Umayyad Ideology and Practice." In Fred M. Donner, ed., *The Articulation of Early Islamic State Structures*, 37–79. Burlington, VT: Ashgate, 2012.

The Qur'an. M. A. S. Abdel Haleem, trans. Oxford: Oxford University Press, 2005.

Rahman, Fazlur. *Major Themes of the Qur'an.* Minneapolis: Bibliotheca Islamica, 1994.

Ramayan of Valmiki. Ralph T. H. Griffith, trans. London: Trübner and Co., 1870.

The Ramayana of Valmiki, Volume VI: Yuddhakanda. Robert P. Goldman, Sally J. Sutherland Goldman, and Barend A. van Nooten, trans. Princeton: Princeton University Press, 2009.

Ramsey, Paul. *War and the Christian Conscience.* Durham, NC: Duke University Press, 1961.

"The Ethics of Intervention." *Review of Politics* 27(3), 1965, 287–310.

The Just War: Force and Political Responsibility. Lanham, MD: Rowman & Littlefield, 2002.

Rapoport, Yossef, and Shahab Ahmed, eds. *Ibn Taymiyya and His Times.* Oxford: Oxford University Press, 2010.

Raynaud, Philippe. "Entre droit et politique: des origines romaines de la guerre juste au système international des états." *Raisons Politiques* 1(45), 2012, 19–34.

Rébullard, Éric. *Christians and Their Many Identities in Late Antiquity, North Africa, 200–450 CE.* Ithaca: Cornell University Press, 2012.

Reichberg, Gregory, Henrik Syse, and Endre Begby. *The Ethics of War: Classic and Contemporary Readings.* Oxford: Blackwell Publishing, 2006.

Reichberg, Gregory, Henrik Syse, and Nicole, Hartwell, eds. *Religion, War and Ethics: A Sourcebook of Textual Traditions.* Cambridge: Cambridge University Press, 2014.

Remec, Peter Pavel. *The Position of the Individual in International Law According to Grotius and Vattel.* New York: Springer Science and Business Media, 2012.

Rengger, Nicholas. "On the Just War Tradition in the Twenty-first Century." *International Affairs* 78(2), 2002, 353–363.

Just War and International Order: The Uncivil Condition in World Politics. Cambridge: Cambridge University Press, 2013.

"The Wager Lost by Winning: On the 'Triumph' of the Just War Tradition." In Anthony F. Lang, Cian O'Driscoll, and John Williams, eds., *Just War: Authority, Tradition and Practice*, 283–298. Washington, DC: Georgetown University Press, 2013.

Reus-Smit, Christian. *The Moral Purpose of the State: Culture, Social Identity, and Institutional Rationality in International Relations.* Princeton: Princeton University Press, 1999.

The Rig Veda. Wendy Doniger, trans. London: Penguin Books, 1981.

Rodin, David. *War and Self-Defense.* Oxford: Oxford University Press, 2005.

"The Ethics of War: State of the Art." *Journal of Applied Philosophy* 23(3), 2006, 241–246.

"Justifying Harm." *Ethics* 122(1), 2011, 74–110.

Rodin, David, and Henry Shue. *Just and Unjust Warriors: The Moral and Legal Status of Soldiers*. Oxford: Oxford University Press, 2010.

Rose, Gideon. "Neoclassical Realism and Theories of Foreign Policy." *World Politics* 51(1), 1998, 144–172.

Rosenstock, Bruce. "Against the Pagans: Alonso de Cartagena, Francisco de Vitoria, and *Converso* Political Theology." In Amy Aronson-Friedman and Gregory Kaplan, eds., *Marginal Voices: Studies in Converso Literature of Medieval and Golden Age Spain*, 117–140. Boston: Brill, 2012.

Roy, Kaushik. *From Hydaspes to Kargil: A History of Warfare in India from 326 BCE to CE 1999*. New Delhi: Manohar, 2004.

"Hinduism." In Gregory Reichberg, Henrik Syse, and Nicole M. Hartwell, eds., *Religion, War, and Ethics*, 471–543. Cambridge: Cambridge University Press, 2014.

Hinduism and the Ethics of Warfare in South Asia. Cambridge: Cambridge University Press, 2012.

Russell, Frederick H. *The Just War in the Middle Ages*. Cambridge: Cambridge University Press, 1975.

Sahlins, Marshall *Historical Metaphors and Mythical Realities: Structure of the Early History in the Sandwich Islands Kingdom*. Ann Arbor: University of Michigan Press, 2000.

Sandhu, Gurcharn Singh. *A Military History of Ancient India*. New Delhi: Vision Books, 2000.

Sarkar, Jagadish Narayan. *The Art of War in Medieval India*. Delhi: Munshiram Manoharlal Publishers, 1984.

Sawant, Ankush R. *Manu-Smriti and Republic of Plato: A Comparative and Critical Study*. Bombay: Himalaya Publishing House, 1996.

Schelling, Thomas C. *Arms and Influence*. New Haven: Yale University Press, 1967.

Schneid, Frederick C. *The Projection and Limitations of Imperial Powers, 1618–1850*. Leiden: Brill, 2012.

Schroeder, Paul W. "Not Even for the Seventeenth and Eighteenth Centuries: Power and Order in the Early Modern Era." In Ernest R. May, Richard Rosecrance, and Zara Teiner, eds., *History and Neorealism*, 78–102. Cambridge: Cambridge University Press, 2010.

Schweller, Randall L. and Xiaoyu Pu. "After Unipolarity: China's Visions of International Order in an Era of U.S. Decline." *International Security* 36 (1), 2011, 41–72.

Scott, James Brown. *The Spanish Origin of International Law: Francisco de Vitoria and His Law of Nations*. Oxford: Clarendon, Press, 1934.

al-Shafi'i, Muhammad ibn Idris. *al-Shafi'i's Risala: Treatise on the Foundations of Islamic Jurisprudence*. Majid Khadduri, trans. Cambridge: Islamic Texts Society, 1997.

El Shamsy, Ahmed. *The Canonization of Islamic Law*. Cambridge: Cambridge University Press, 2013.

Sharma, Ram Sharan. *Aspects of Political Ideas and Institutions in Ancient India*, 4th ed. Delhi: Motilal Banarsidass Publishers, 1996.

al-Shaybani, Muhammad ibn al-Hasan. *The Islamic Law of Nations: Shaybani's Siyar*. Majid Khadduri, trans. Baltimore: Johns Hopkins University Press, 1966.

ash-Shaybani, Muhammad ibn al-Hasan. *The Muwatta' of Imam Muhammad*. Mohammed Abdurrahman and Abdassamad Clark, trans. London: Turath Publishing, 2004.

Sidgwick, Henry. "The Morality of Strife." *International Journal of Ethics* 1(1), 1890, 330–354.

Sil, Narsingha Prosad. "Political Morality vs. Political Necessity: Kautilya and Machiavelli Revisited." *Journal of Asian History* 19(2), 1985, 101–142.

Singh, Upinder. *A History of Ancient and Early Medieval India*. Chennai: Pearson, 2016.

Sinha, Manoj Jumar. "Hinduism and International Humanitarian Law." *International Review of the Red Cross* 87(858), 2005, 285–294.

Skinner, Quentin. *The Foundations of Modern Political Thought, Volume I*. Cambridge: Cambridge University Press, 1978.

Visions of Politics, Volume I: Regarding Method. Cambridge: Cambridge University Press, 2002.

Smith, Michael Joseph. *Realist Thought from Weber to Kissinger*. Baton Rouge: Louisiana State University Press, 1986.

Smith, Steve. "The United States and the Discipline of International Relations: 'Hegemonic Country, Hegemonic Discipline.'" *International Studies Review* 4(2), 2002, 67–85

Smock, David R. *Religious Perspectives on War*. Washington, DC: United States Institute of Peace, 2002.

Snyder, Jack. *Myths of Empire: Domestic Politics and International Ambition*. Ithaca: Cornell University Press, 1991.

Strachan, Hew. *European Armies and the Conduct of War*. London: Routledge, 2001.

Strawser, Bradley Jay. "Revisionist Just War Theory and the Real World." In Fritz Allhoff, Nicholas G. Evans, and Adam Henscke, eds., *Routledge Handbook of Ethics and War*, 76–90. Oxford: Routledge, 2013.

Strayer, Joseph R. *On the Medieval Origins of the Modern State*. Princeton: Princeton University Press, 2005.

Taliaferro, Jeffrey W. "Security Seeking under Anarchy: Defensive Realism Revisited." *International Security* 25(3), 2000–2001, 128–161.

Terrill, Robert E. "An Uneasy Peace: Barack Obama's Nobel Prize Peace Lecture." *Rhetoric and Public Affairs* 14(4), 2011, 761–779.

Thaler, Mathias. "On Time in Just War Theory: From *Chronos* to *Kairos*." *Polity* 46, 2014, 520–546.

Thapar, Romila. *The Past before Us: Historical Traditions of Early North India*. Cambridge, MA: Harvard University Press, 2013.

Tierney, Brian. *The Crisis of Church and State 1050–1300*. Toronto: University of Toronto Press, 1988.

Toft, Monica Duffy. "Getting Religion? The Puzzling Case of Islam in Civil War." *International Security* 31(4), 2007, 97–131.

Torrell, Jean-Pierre. *Saint Thomas Aquinas, Volume I: The Person and His Work.* Robert Royal, trans. Washington, DC: Catholic University of America, 2005.

Törzsök, Judit, trans. *"Friendly Advice" by Narayana and King Vikrama's Adventures.* New York: New York University Press, 2007.

Tuck, Richard. *Rights of War and Peace.* Oxford: Oxford University Press, 2001.

Tucker, Robert W. *The Just War.* Baltimore: Johns Hopkins University Press, 1960.

Tully, James. "The Pen Is a Mighty Sword: Quentin Skinner's Analysis of Politics." in James Tully, ed., *Meaning and Context: Quentin Skinner and His Critics,* 7–28. Princeton: Princeton University Press, 1988.

Turner, Denys. *Thomas Aquinas: A Portrait.* New Haven: Yale University Press, 2013.

Upanishads. Patrick Olivelle, trans., Oxford: Oxford University Press, 1996.

Vasquez, John A. *The Power of Power Politics: From Classical Realism to Neotraditionalism.* Cambridge: Cambridge University Press, 1998.

de Vattel, Emer. *The Law of Nations.* Béla Kapossy, ed. Indianapolis: Liberty Fund, 2014.

Vikør, Knut S. *Between God and Sultan.* Oxford: Oxford University Press, 2006.

Vitoria, Francisco. *Vitoria: Political Writings.* Anthony Padgen and Jeremy Lawrance, eds. Cambridge: Cambridge University Press, 2003.

Walasky, Paul W. *'And So We Come to Rome' – The Political Perspective of St. Luke.* Cambridge: Cambridge University Press, 2005.

Walt, Stephen M. "Was Obama's Nobel Peace Prize Speech Really Realist." *Foreign Policy,* December 18, 2009.

"Is IR Still 'an American Social Science'?" *Foreign Policy,* June 6, 2011.

"International Affairs and the 'Public Sphere,'" *Foreign Policy,* July 22, 2011, http://foreignpolicy.com/2011/07/22/international-affairs-and-the-public-sphere.

"Theory and Policy in International Relations: Some Personal Reflections." *Yale Journal of International Affairs* 7, 2012, 33–43.

Waltz, Kenneth N. "The Politics of Peace." *International Studies Quarterly* 11(3), 1967, 199–211.

Theory of International Politics. New York: McGraw-Hill, 1979.

Walzer, Michael. "The Idea of Holy War in Ancient Israel." *Journal of Religious Ethics* 20(2), 1992, 229–234.

Thick and Thin: Moral Argument at Home and Abroad. South Bend, IN: Notre Dame University Press, 1994.

Just and Unjust Wars. New York: Basic Books, 2000.

"The Triumph of Just War Theory (and the Dangers of Success)." *Social Research* 69(4), 2002, 925–944.

"Drums of War, Calls for Peace: How Should the Left Respond to a U.S. War Against Iraq?" *Dissent* 50(1), 2003, 5–17.

Arguing about War. New Haven: Yale University Press, 2004.

"Regime Change and Just War," *Dissent,* Summer 2006, 103–108.

"The Crime of Aggressive War." *Washington University Global Studies Law Review* 6(3), 2007, 635–643.

Warnock, G. J. *The Object of Morality.* London: Methuen, 1971.

Contemporary Moral Philosophy. London: Macmillan, 1967.

Wasserstrom, Richard. "On the Morality of War: A Preliminary Inquiry." *Stanford Law Review* 21(6), 1969, 1627–1656.

Weigel, George. "The Churches and War in the Gulf." *First Things* 11, March 1991, www.firstthings.com/article/1991/03/the-churches-war-in-the-gulf.

"The Development of Just War Thinking in the Post-Cold War World: An American Perspective." In Charles Reed and David Ryall, eds., *The Price of Peace: Just War in the Twenty-first Century*, 19–36. New York: Cambridge University Press, 2007.

Weigley, Russel F. *The Age of Battles: The Quest for Decisive Warfare from Breitenfeld to Waterloo*. Bloomington: Indiana University Press, 2004.

Wheeler, Nicholas. *Saving Strangers: Humanitarian Intervention in International Society*. Oxford: Oxford University Press, 2000.

Whetham, David. *Just Wars and Moral Victories: Surprise, Deception, and the Normative Framework of European War in the Later Middle Ages*. Amsterdam: Brill, 2009.

White, Stephen K. *Political Theory and Postmodernism*. Cambridge: Cambridge University Press, 1991.

Whitford, David M. "*Cura Religionis* or Two Kingdoms: The Late Luther on Religion and the State in the Lectures on Genesis." *Church History* 73(1), 2004, 41–62.

Williams, Michael C. "Why Ideas Matter in International Relations: Hans Morgenthau, Classical Realism, and the Moral Construction of Power Politics." *International Organization* 58(4), 2004, 633–665.

The Realist Tradition and the Limits of International Relations. Cambridge: Cambridge University Press, 2005.

Wilson, Peter H. "Meaningless Conflict? The Character of the Thirty Years War." In Frederick C. Schneid, ed., *The Projection and Limitations of Imperial Powers, 1618–1850*, 12–32. Leiden: Brill, 2012.

Wright, Quincy. "The Outlawry of War and the Law of War." *American Journal of International Law* 47(3), 1953, 365–376.

Wynn, Philip. *Augustine on War and Military Service*. Minneapolis: Fortress Press, 2013.

Yoder, John Howard. *When War Is Unjust: Being Honest in Just-War Thinking*. Maryknoll, NY: Orbis Books, 1996.

"Just War Tradition: Is It Credible?" *Christian Century*, 108, March 13, 1991, 295–298.

When War Is Unjust: Being Honest in Just War Thinking. Maryknoll, NY: Orbis Books, 1996.

Young, Katherine K. "Hinduism and the Ethics of Weapons of Mass Destruction." In Sohail H. Hashmi and Stephen Lee, eds., *Ethics and Weapons of Mass Destruction: Religious and Secular Perspectives*, 277–307. Cambridge: Cambridge University Press, 2004.

Index